CAMBRIDGE LIBRARY COLLECTION

Books of enduring scholarly value

Spiritualism and Esoteric Knowledge

Magic, superstition, the occult sciences and esoteric knowledge appear regularly in the history of ideas alongside more established academic disciplines such as philosophy, natural history and theology. Particularly fascinating are periods of rapid scientific advances such as the Renaissance or the nineteenth century which also see a burgeoning of interest in the paranormal among the educated elite. This series provides primary texts and secondary sources for social historians and cultural anthropologists working in these areas, and all who wish for a wider understanding of the diverse intellectual and spiritual movements that formed a backdrop to the academic and political achievements of their day. It ranges from works on Babylonian and Jewish magic in the ancient world, through studies of sixteenth-century topics such as Cornelius Agrippa and the rapid spread of Rosicrucianism, to nineteenth-century publications by Sir Walter Scott and Sir Arthur Conan Doyle. Subjects include astrology, mesmerism, spiritualism, theosophy, clairvoyance, and ghost-seeing, as described both by their adherents and by sceptics.

Mesmerism and Christian Science

For most of his life a clerk in the post office, Frank Podmore (1856–1910) was a prolific author on psychical research. As an undergraduate Podmore became interested in spiritualism, and he joined the British National Association of Spiritualists. Eventually disillusioned by that society, Podmore co-founded several organisations: the Progressive Association (in 1882); the Fellowship of the New Life (1883); and, spurred by his desire to see political change, the Fabian Society (1884). Podmore's membership in the Society for Psychical Research influenced his activities and interests, and he spent the next twenty years investigating and writing on psychical phenomena. Podmore's two-volume *Modern Spiritualism* (also reissued in this series) is a source for this 1909 work, which 'constituted the most scholarly history of mesmerism and its offshoots to that date', according to one reviewer. This work will interest historians of science and medicine, and scholars of Victorian religious movements.

Cambridge University Press has long been a pioneer in the reissuing of out-of-print titles from its own backlist, producing digital reprints of books that are still sought after by scholars and students but could not be reprinted economically using traditional technology. The Cambridge Library Collection extends this activity to a wider range of books which are still of importance to researchers and professionals, either for the source material they contain, or as landmarks in the history of their academic discipline.

Drawing from the world-renowned collections in the Cambridge University Library, and guided by the advice of experts in each subject area, Cambridge University Press is using state-of-the-art scanning machines in its own Printing House to capture the content of each book selected for inclusion. The files are processed to give a consistently clear, crisp image, and the books finished to the high quality standard for which the Press is recognised around the world. The latest print-on-demand technology ensures that the books will remain available indefinitely, and that orders for single or multiple copies can quickly be supplied.

The Cambridge Library Collection will bring back to life books of enduring scholarly value (including out-of-copyright works originally issued by other publishers) across a wide range of disciplines in the humanities and social sciences and in science and technology.

Mesmerism and Christian Science

A Short History of Mental Healing

FRANK PODMORE

CAMBRIDGE
UNIVERSITY PRESS

CAMBRIDGE UNIVERSITY PRESS

Cambridge, New York, Melbourne, Madrid, Cape Town, Singapore,
São Paolo, Delhi, Dubai, Tokyo, Mexico City

Published in the United States of America by Cambridge University Press, New York

www.cambridge.org
Information on this title: www.cambridge.org/9781108072465

© in this compilation Cambridge University Press 2011

This edition first published 1909
This digitally printed version 2011

ISBN 978-1-108-07246-5 Paperback

MESMERISM AND CHRISTIAN SCIENCE

MESMERISM AND CHRISTIAN SCIENCE

A SHORT HISTORY OF MENTAL HEALING

BY

FRANK PODMORE

AUTHOR OF "MODERN SPIRITUALISM"

METHUEN & CO.

36 ESSEX STREET W.C.

LONDON

First Published in 1909

PREFACE

THE 11th of August should be observed as a day of humiliation by every learned Society in the civilised world, for on that date in 1784 a Commission, consisting of the most distinguished representatives of Science in the most enlightened capital in Europe, pronounced the rejection of a pregnant scientific discovery—a discovery possibly rivalling in permanent significance all the contributions to the physical Sciences made by the two most famous members of the Commission—Lavoisier and Benjamin Franklin. Not that the report on Animal Magnetism presented by Bailly and his colleagues did serious injustice to Mesmer himself, or to his vaunted science. The magnetic fluid was a chimæra, and Mesmer, it may be admitted, was perhaps three parts a charlatan. He had no pretensions to be a thinker: he stole his philosophy ready-made from a few belated alchemists; and his entire system of healing was based on a delusion. His extraordinary success was due to the lucky accident of the times.

Mesmer's first claim to our remembrance lies in this—that he wrested the privilege of healing from the Churches, and gave it to mankind as a universal possession. In rejecting the gift for themselves and their successors to the third and fourth generation Bailly and his colleagues rejected more than they knew. Now, more than a hundred years later, physicians and laymen alike are coming to realise the benefits of healing by Suggestion. That those benefits should, through carelessness and prejudice, have been withheld from us, *mortalibus ægris*, for so long is, no doubt, a serious loss. But the real significance of the facts brought to light by Mesmer lies deeper. The crisis, the magnetic thrills, the cures themselves, are only as nuggets that lie on the surface : the mother-lode has yet to be worked.

The aim of the present work is briefly to describe the various phases of the movement initiated by Mesmer, and to trace the successive attempts made by those who came after him to get below the surface to the underlying reality. The universal indifferent fluid of the famous Propositions was discredited in the eyes of the scientific world by Bailly's report. By Mesmer's followers, even in his lifetime, it was weighed and found wanting. It would not explain the facts. For gradually, as the pioneers pushed their exploration further into the new territory thrown open to them by the Viennese doctor, the landmarks of terrestrial geography began to fail them. They found, or seemed to themselves to find, that the facts with which they had to deal belonged less to the body than to the soul or *psyche*—to use that term, without prejudice, in its conventional meaning. When this discovery was once made, Animal Magnetism became the fertile matrix from which sprang all the shadowy brood of latter-day mysticisms—Spiritualism, Theosophy, the New Thought, culminating in the Christian Science of Mrs. Mary Baker Eddy, in which we find that the wheel has at last turned full circle, and the practice of healing has once again become inseparably connected with the practice of religion. The art which Mesmer taught his followers to look upon as wholly material—a question simply of radiant fluids and the " coction " of humours—is explained by the Christian Scientists as a wholly spiritual process, in which matter counts for less than nothing.

The Spiritualists may claim the doubtful honour of being

the first in the field: the Church of Christ, Scientist, represents the last word of mysticism. But these are not the only explorers of the wide province. Modern psychology is being forced more and more to take into account the manifestations of the subconscious life; the Society for Psychical Research is exhaustively mapping out one corner of the field ; and the student of religious phenomena finds here data essential to the solution of his special problems.

To all these the present work will, it is hoped, be found useful as offering a brief account of the first steps taken in an exploration which will, it may be anticipated, ultimately furnish the answer to some momentous questions.

I have to thank Mr. A. G. Tolputt, M.R.C.S., L.R.C.P., for his kindness in reading the earlier chapters of the book in the typescript, and in giving me the advantage of his medical knowledge.

March, 1909   F. P.

CONTENTS

MESMERISM AND CHRISTIAN SCIENCE

CHAPTER I

HEALING BY FLUID

Early life of Mesmer—He comes to Paris at the psychological moment : his acquaintance with Deslon : his immediate success—Description of the Baquet and the Magnetic treatment generally—Accounts of typical cures extracted from a contemporary work, the *Supplément aux Deux Rapports*—Discussion of the observed symptoms, and of the nature and significance of the cures.

IN February, 1778, there came to Paris a Viennese physician, Friedrich Anton Mesmer, the originator of the art of Mesmerism, and, incidentally, of many other things. Mesmer was at this time over forty years of age ; the date and the place of his birth are alike uncertain, but he was probably born in 1733 or 1734, somewhere on the borders of Lake Constance ; according to one account at Meersburg, in Suabia.[1] It is known, however, that he had taken his doctor's degree at Vienna twelve years before, in 1766, with an inaugural thesis bearing the title *De planetarum influxu*, or, as he himself translated it later, " On the Influence of the Planets on the Human Body." In 1773 he first came into public notice. In that year he employed in the treatment of some of his patients certain magnetic plates, of a particular form, the invention of the Jesuit Father Hell, a professor of

[1] *Biographie universelle*, art. " Mesmer."

astronomy at Vienna. Father Hell claimed the credit of the resultant cures, as due to the use of his plates. Mesmer retorted that the plates were but a subsidiary part of the treatment, which consisted essentially in a novel method of applying magnetic forces to the human body. The controversy between the two men seems to have been carried on with considerable bitterness. Father Hell found a champion and ally in Dr. Ingenhouze, a member of the Royal Society of London.

Starting from this controversy, and probably as a direct consequence of it, Mesmer proceeded, in the course of the next few years, to define his theory with more precision. Thenceforward his claim is to have discovered a new fluid, having analogies with mineral magnetism, but independent of it, which could be made to act upon the human body. After 1776, he tells us in his *Précis historique*, he ceased altogether to make use of magnets or electricity in his treatment.[1]   His views at this period were set forth in "A letter to a foreign physician," dated January 5, 1775, which was published in the *Nouveau Mercure Savant* of Altona. It will be more convenient to defer the detailed consideration of the theory to the next chapter, and proceed at this point to give some account of Mesmer's career and of the success of his treatment. With the view of making his discoveries better known, as he tells us, he travelled between the years 1773 and 1778 in various parts of the Continent, chiefly in Switzerland, Suabia, and Bavaria. He also sent an account of his new system to the principal learned bodies of Europe, including the Royal Society of London, the Academy of Sciences at Paris, and the Academy at Berlin. The last alone deigned to reply to his communication: the reply was to the effect that the discovery was an illusion.

[1] *Précis historique des Faits relatifs au Magnétisme animal* (London, 1781), p. 12.   Mesmer's original idea would seem to have been that his "new force" was simply a modification of ordinary magnetism, and that it could be reinforced by the use of magnets (see Burdin and Dubois, *Hist. académique*, p. 234).   The construction of the Baquet (see below) shows that he had not entirely disabused himself of this idea even so late as 1778.

In the meantime a good many cures appear to have been effected under Mesmer's treatment. One case, in particular, gave him considerable notoriety and was ultimately the cause of his leaving Vienna. Mdlle. de Paradis was a girl of eighteen, who had been completely blind from the age of four. Mesmer diagnosed the malady, in the medical terminology of the day, as a "complete gutta serena,"[1] and tells us that the eyes were projecting almost out of the sockets ; and that the patient was suffering further from congested liver and spleen, with many disagreeable and painful consequences. The girl, who was in receipt, on account of her blindness, of a pension from the Empress, to whom she was known personally, had been for many years treated, without appreciable relief, by Dr. Störck, President of the Faculty, and by others of the leading physicians in Vienna. Mesmer in 1777 treated the patient by his method, and claimed to have restored her sight. The fame of the cure was blazoned all over Europe. But its reality was immediately contested by some of the faculty, who asserted that the girl on a trial had proved herself unable even to distinguish colours. The girl's father was persuaded to take his daughter out of Mesmer's hands. Mesmer resisted, and retained the charge of the case for a month longer. Considerable scandal was caused ; Mesmer was forced to give the girl up to her relatives, and shortly afterwards found it convenient to leave Vienna.

It is perhaps hardly necessary to say that Mesmer's own account of the Paradis incident differs materially from that of his opponents. It is of course impossible now to disentangle the truth. But it may be pointed out that, from the description given, the disease of the eye may have been functional only ; and the statements of both sides are consistent with the supposition that a considerable improvement in the patient's powers of vision had been effected temporarily under Mesmer's treatment, followed soon afterwards by a relapse

---

[1] Under this term the physicians of that day included all cases of blindness in which no sign of disease could be discovered in the eye itself.

to her former state. Ironical chance brought it to pass that
Mdlle. Paradis appeared as a public singer at Paris in 1784,
Mesmer's fatal year, and she was, according to contemporary
evidence, blind at that date.[1]   It is noteworthy that among
the cures claimed later under Mesmer's treatment there are
several cases of disease of the eye.

   Such, briefly, were the antecedents and such the reputation
of the man who came to Paris at the beginning of 1778, furnished, as he tells us, with an introduction from the Austrian
Minister of Foreign Affairs to the Austrian ambassador in
Paris.   He took lodgings near the Place Vendôme, and
started in a sufficiently humble way, with a single servant
and a second-hand carriage. But he had all the qualities and
conditions that command success.   The cures which he
had already effected, or claimed to have effected, spoke
eloquently for him. The mysterious new principle of life,
of which he vaunted himself the discoverer, appealed to
the imagination of the merely curious, and to the hopes
of all who suffered and could find no relief.   He was a
man of magnificent self-confidence, and spoke with authority.
To judge by his writings he was possessed of a ready wit
and sufficient intellectual resources to back up his pretensions.   Further, we are told that he was an admirable
musician, that he played well on the piano and entranc-
ingly on the harmonica, then an almost unknown instrument.[2]   Add that, according to the testimony of Deleuze,
who conversed with many of those who had been his
patients or pupils, Mesmer was a man of great tenderness
and kindness of heart, devoted to the cause of the sick and
suffering ; that he opened his doors alike to the rich and
poor, and gave to the latter without payment all that he gave
to the rich in return for substantial fees.[3] No doubt such a
course of action was good policy, and Mesmer himself, no
doubt, recognised that fact.   But it is certain that he suc-

---

[1] *Biographie universelle.*
[2] Burdin and Dubois, *Histoire académique du Magnétisme animal*
(1841), p. 5.
[3] *Histoire critique*, vol. ii. p. 11.

ceeded in inspiring lively gratitude in his patients, and invincible enthusiasm in his disciples.

Moreover, Mesmer arrived at the psychological moment. Paris has always been ready to see or hear some new thing. But the years preceding the French Revolution were years of peculiar intellectual ferment. We see the result in the scientific discoveries of Lavoisier and Laplace ; in the new social, political, and philosophic conceptions of Rousseau, Diderot, and the Encyclopædists. But the same causes produced a general licence of speculation and gave birth to innumerable false and extravagant systems. No belief was too preposterous to find a following among the idle rich. The Paris which a generation previously had half believed the monstrous fables of the Count St. Germain, which a few years later was to listen indulgently to another "Count"—Cagliostro—was not likely to be unduly critical in its acceptance of one who not only gave them a new sensation, but promised substantial benefits therewith.

With all these things in his favour Mesmer and his treatment soon became famous. In the autumn of 1778 he made the acquaintance of Charles Deslon, Doctor Regent of the Faculty of Paris, and physician to the Count d'Artois. Deslon happened to meet Mesmer at the bedside of a patient, was much impressed with his conversation and his medical knowledge, and shortly became an enthusiastic advocate of the treatment. At this time Mesmer was devoting himself to writing an account of his discovery. He was very meanly lodged, " un salon que le moindre bourgeois de Paris trouveroit trop petit pour sa compagnie,"[1] and he was treating only a few patients. He was forced, however, as Deslon tells us, by persistent solicitations to enlarge the circle. At the time when Deslon's book was written he had seventy persons actually under treatment ; six hundred places were promised ; and several thousand applications had been received. To enable him to husband his powers in the treatment of a large number of patients, he devised a method, in

---

[1] Deslon, *Observations sur le Magnétisme animal* (London, 1780), p. 29.

accordance with his theory of Animal Magnetism, for treating them *en masse*. This was the Baquet.

The Baquet was a large oaken tub, four or five feet in diameter and a foot or more in depth, closed by a wooden cover. Inside the tub were placed bottles full of water disposed in rows radiating from the centre, the necks in some of the rows pointing towards the centre, in others away from it. All these bottles had been previously "magnetised" by Mesmer. Sometimes there were several rows of bottles, one above the other; the machine was then said to be at high pressure. The bottles rested on layers of powdered glass and iron filings. The tub itself was filled with water. The whole machine, it will be seen, was a kind of travesty of the galvanic cell. To carry out the resemblance, the cover of the tub was pierced with holes, through which passed slender iron rods of varying lengths, which were jointed and movable, so that they could be readily applied to any part of the patient's body. Round this battery the patients were seated in a circle, each with his iron rod. Further, a cord, attached at one end to the tub, was passed round the body of each of the sitters, so as to bind them all into a chain. Outside the first a second circle would frequently be formed, who would connect themselves together by holding hands. Mesmer, in a lilac robe, and his assistant operators—vigorous and handsome young men selected for the purpose—walked about the room, pointing their fingers or an iron rod held in their hands at the diseased parts.

The progress of the cures was generally furthered by the application of the operator's hand to various parts of the body, and especially by the pressure of the fingers on the abdomen. And this pressure was often maintained for a considerable time—sometimes even for several hours.[1] The proceedings were enlivened throughout by excellent music from a piano or other instrument.

The effect produced by this procedure varied naturally according to the temperament of the patient and the nature of his ailment. A frequent and characteristic phase, especi-

[1] According to Bailly's Report.

ally with women, was the occurrence of the "crisis." The
following description of the crisis, as observed amongst
Deslon's patients in 1784, is taken from the Report of the
Commission appointed by the King from the Royal
Academy of Science and the Faculty of Medicine :—[1]

"The tableau presented by the patients is one of extreme diversity.
Some are calm, composed, and feel nothing ; others cough, spit, have
slight pains, feel a glow locally or all over the body, accompanied by
perspiration ; others are shaken and tormented by convulsions. These
convulsions are remarkable in their frequency, their duration, and their
intensity. As soon as one attack begins others make their appearance.
The Commission has seen them last for more than three hours ; they
are accompanied by expectorations of a viscous matter, torn from the
chest by the violence of the attack. Sometimes there are traces of
blood in the expectoration. The convulsions are characterised by
involuntary spasmodic movements of the limbs and of the whole body,
by contractions of the throat, by spasms of the hypochondriac and
epigastric regions ; the eyes are wandering and distracted ; there are
piercing cries, tears, hiccoughs, and extravagant laughter. The convulsions are preceded and followed by a state of languor and reverie,
by exhaustion and drowsiness. Any sudden noise causes the patients
to start, and even a change in the music played on the piano has an
effect—a lively tune agitates them afresh and renews the convulsions."

A special room—the Salle des Crises—carefully padded,
was set aside for the reception of the more violent patients.

Such was the nature of the treatment practised by Mesmer
and his disciples. Of its effect in curing or alleviating
suffering we can judge by the claims put forward by his
disciples ; by the admissions made by his adversaries ; and,
above all, by the great and continually greater crowds which
thronged his reception-rooms. In the one year—1784—Mesmer and Deslon are said to have treated about eight thousand
persons.[2] Mesmer's clients were drawn in great part from
the upper ranks of society, and included, as will be shown

[1] Deslon was, as said, a pupil of Mesmer's, and had adopted his
methods, including the Baquet, so that the following description, which
has the advantage of being drawn up by a committee of medical men
and scientific experts, would apply equally to the treatment of the
patients in Mesmer's own practice.

[2] Regnier, *Hypnotisme et Croyances anciennes* (1891), p. 123.

later, many officials, landed proprietors, officers of the army, priests, and even physicians. It is incredible that the fame of his treatment could have persisted and continually increased unless many of these persons had derived substantial benefit from it. We are not left, however, without more precise and circumstantial evidence of Mesmer's success.

In 1780 Deslon published the book already cited, *Observations sur le Magnétisme animal*, giving details of eighteen cases treated by Mesmer, in which of his own observation he could testify to substantial relief or a complete cure. Of these eighteen patients, ten were males, including Deslon himself, and eight women. Amongst the women were two or three cases of swellings diagnosed as schirri or "cancer occulte." For the rest, the ailments treated included three cases of blindness, complete or partial; two of deafness, paralysis, marasmus, hepatic flux, epilepsy, obstructed spleen, &c. The history of these cases is not given very fully, and the details furnished are probably not sufficient in most cases to enable a modern physician to determine exactly the nature of the ailment. The book is valuable chiefly as indicating the impression created by Mesmer's treatment on a contemporary observer who was himself a physician of some standing in his profession.

In August, 1784, appeared the Report of Bailly's Commission, from which a passage has been already quoted. This Report, whilst severely condemning the practice of Animal Magnetism, deliberately ignored its therapeutic effects, for reasons which will be considered later on. Some one, possibly Deslon himself, proceeded to supply this extraordinary omission by collecting reports of cases actually treated, chiefly by Deslon. The results were published in an anonymous pamphlet before the end of the year. There was not, of course, time to hunt up older cases; and as a matter of fact nearly all the records relate to the years 1782–1784. But, apart from the fact that the "crisis" seems to have been a less prominent feature than earlier accounts would have led us to suppose, there is no reason to think that the treatment and the results in these later years differed materially from what had gone before. These records were at any rate admirably fitted to the particular purpose in view, since the Commissioners did not begin their investigations until 1784, and all this material for forming a judgment on the curative effects of the treatment was actually ready to their hands. Some account of these cures is introduced here, that the reader may see what grounds there were for the extraordinary vogue attained by Mesmer and his disciples, and, it may be added, for the extreme embitterment of the profession.

The records published in 1784, under the title *Supplément aux Deux Rapports de MM. les Commissaires*, &c., deal with 115 cases.[1] They are for the most part written by the patients themselves ; the physicians were, no doubt for professional reasons, reluctant to let themselves appear as in any way concerned with a treatment which had just been authoritatively denounced as a gross and dangerous imposture. But it is clear that the diagnosis—where the nature of the disease permitted the science of that date to furnish any diagnosis—was derived in many instances from the physicians who had previously treated the case without success. And, it may be added, the few reports furnished by medical men which are included are scarcely more illuminating, from the standpoint of modern medicine, than those written by laymen. It should be noted, further, that in several cases the physicians, confessedly at the end of their resources, themselves advised recourse to Animal Magnetism.

No doubt the records were to some extent selected, though in one passage the editor implies that they were not. But, in view of the pressure of time, the collectors probably took every fairly good case which they could get. A large number of those included, indeed, refer to cures still proceeding, and the patients can in such cases, therefore, record only

---

[1] The summary at the end of the book speaks of 111 persons. But the number is not correct. The book, as will appear from the date, was compiled under great pressure ; there are many mistakes in proper names, and the compiler has omitted to take notice that some of the reports deal with more than one patient.

partial alleviation of their symptoms. If the reports were not deliberately selected with that view, it is certainly note-worthy that the men are more numerous than the women. Of 103 adults 56 are men and 47 women. A notable proportion of the men are persons of distinction, or at least of good social position—marquises, counts, high officials and men of affairs, doctors, abbés, &c. There are also many titled ladies. For the rest, the list includes a few domestic servants, artisans, and working men and women.

As already indicated, the reports are cited not so much for their medical interest—which must be left for the profession to determine—as for the evidence they afford of the effect produced on Mesmer's patients and on the public. Whatever explanation we may choose to give of the facts, it is certain that a large number of persons believed themselves to be seriously ill for months or years before they went to Mesmer or Deslon for treatment, and believed themselves after that treatment to be relieved of their worst symptoms, or even to be completely restored to health. Some of them, perhaps were not really ill when they went, and some others may not have been really cured when they left. But it is impossible after reading these reports to doubt that, in a large number of cases, obstinate and long-standing ailments, which had resisted all the ordinary remedies, were cured or substantially alleviated. Whether these results were produced by a subtle fluid, by the imagination of the patient, by the curative processes of Nature when no longer embarrassed by drugs, the cupping-glass, and the moxa, or by any other cause, seems at this distance of time a question which even the Royal Commission might not have found beneath the dignity of their science to examine. Bailly and his brother Commissioners had excused themselves from pursuing their inquiries into the curative effects of Magnetism partly on the ground that they feared to annoy by their questions the distinguished patients who sat round the Baquet. It is worth noting that many of these distinguished patients came forward to give their testimony in this volume. For persons of education and refinement it can scarcely have been a congenial task to enter into intimate and frequently repulsive details of their maladies and cure. It is evident, in fact, that in many cases nothing short of a conviction of the unfairness of the Report, and a strong sense of gratitude to Deslon and his colleagues, would have induced them to come forward.[1] The circumstance should certainly be taken into account in considering the value of their testimony.

In the brief summary which follows of some of the most interesting of the cases the words of the original records have been followed as closely as possible. The medical reader will, no doubt, in many cases be able to form his own conclusions as to the nature of the malady. It has not been thought necessary to give in detail an account of the effects produced. Apart from the subjective sensations of warmth, tickling, and pain referred to later, the chief effect of the treatment, at any rate in its initial stages, was to cause copious purging, vomiting, expectoration, and sweating. These results, or some of them, followed practically in every case; and no doubt the beneficial effects of the treatment were largely due to this circumstance. For the richer classes, at any rate, in that day seem generally to have been of a plethoric habit, and the treatment usually adopted consisted in purges, emetics, and the cupping-glass. It should be added that both Mesmer and Deslon frequently made use of cream of tartar in their treatment; but whereas cream of tartar without "Magnetism" had in the cases recorded proved ineffectual, there were many cases in which Magnetism brought about the desired result without cream of tartar.

With a view to meeting the objection that the cures were due to the imagination of the patients, the editors placed at the head of their list twelve cases in which the subjects were children, sometimes of very tender years. We need not, of

---

[1] See, for instance, the letter from Commandant de la Vaultière (p. 47) : " Il en coûte infiniment, Monsieur, a ma façon de penser . . . puisque ma reponse court les risques de la publicité. Cependant je me rends par respect . . . que j'ai pour la vérité, autant encore par reconnoissance pour MM. Deslon et Bienaymé, aux soins desquels j'avais cru jusqu'ici devoir mon existence et ma santé."

SUMMARY OF TWELVE CASES OF DISEASE IN CHILDREN UNDER TWELVE YEARS OF AGE.

	Sex.	Age in Years.	Previous Duration of Malady.	Duration of Treatment by Animal Magnetism.	Diagnosis and Description of Symptoms.	Effect Produced.
1	M.	11	6 weeks.	10 weeks.	Chorea; grew worse under medical treatment; convulsions were succeeded by partial paralysis. The boy could not use his right arm and leg, and his tongue was affected.	Cured. The disease returned in a milder form 15 months later, and was again cured by Magnetism.
2	F.	5	A year.	9 months.	*Humeur de gourme;* violent pains in side, unable to walk. Accident to spine feared.	Cured. Profuse and long-continued expectoration. After some months the humour discharged by the ear.
3	M.	10	6 weeks.	2 months.	Eruption (*dartre*) on chin. Cough, and general debility.	Completely cured. (? Herpes.)
4	M.	1 $\frac{8}{12}$	Not stated.	10 days. *Treatment proceeding.*	Convulsions four or five times a day.	Reduced to two or three times daily. Calm sleep under treatment.
5	F.	11	Some years.	3 months. *Treatment proceeding.*	"Oppression tending to asthma." Severe cough recurring monthly. Marked elevation of chest.	Much improved in health; has grown at least two inches in the 3 months. (? Whooping cough.)

6	M.	10	Not stated.	3 months. *Treatment proceeding.*	Glands under chin and armpits.	Reduced.
7	M.	$\frac{6}{12}$	Not stated.	7 days (?)	Eyes inverted (*tournés*), breathing spasmodic; skin livid.	Eyes resumed their natural position, and breathing became easier after treatment by Animal Magnetism for 1¼ hours. After further treatment there was a discharge from nose. Cured. (? Symptoms due to retropharyngeal abscess.)
8	M.	2	One day.	9 days.	Arm burnt to elbow and skin entirely destroyed.	Cured without any drug or ointment. No mark left.
9	F.	$\frac{6}{12}$	Not stated.	12 days.	Severe diarrhœa, with passing of blood. Much pain.	Completely cured.
10	F.	$1\frac{3}{12}$	Not stated.	8 days.	Fever and convulsions. Doctor recommended bleeding and blisters.	Complete cure; abscess discharged after 2 days' treatment.
11	M.	6 weeks.	Not stated.	8 days.	Violent colic; thrush on tongue, palate, and throat; unable to take the breast.	Could suck 6 hours after treatment. Cured in 8 days.
12	F.	Not stated.	2 days.	4 days.	Fever and blood-spitting; *un point de côté.*	Calmed and had a good night after one treatment. Completely cured. (?Pneumonia.)

course, endorse the editors' reasoning; for in some of the cases cited the children were quite old enough to be amenable, as in the modern treatment of hypnotism, to psychological influences. In other cases the improvement observed may reasonably be attributed to Nature and freedom from drugs and bleeding. As the symptoms, however, are fairly well defined, and the cases admit therefore of being summarised, a table is appended showing the results. The report is furnished by the parents of the little patients, except in case 8, where the child belonged apparently to poor persons. The facts in this case are attested by three persons— M. Perruchot, Viscountess d'Allard, and Commandant de la Vaultière.

There are ten reports from doctors or other persons—a student of surgery and a member of the College of Pharmacy — who may be credited with some medical knowledge. A brief summary of these cases is given.

Cases recorded by Doctors

M. Patillon, doctor of the faculty of Besançon, gives particulars of three cases in his own practice treated by Animal Magnetism.

The first case (p. 30) was that of a domestic servant who had been suffering for five weeks from severe pains in the head. The malady, of which the cause could not be discovered, resisted all the usual remedies. As a last resource Patillon counselled a trial of Magnetism, and the patient after some hesitation consented. From the commencement of the treatment the pulse became softer and more frequent. After ten minutes the pain in the head was transferred to the muscles of the neck; thence successively to the shoulder, the elbow, and the wrist. The pain was so intense that the patient fainted. She was placed on her bed and the treatment continued. On waking she complained of the severe pain in her wrist, and Patillon implored her to endure for a few minutes longer, in order that the cure might be complete. In effect, she soon went to sleep again under the magnetic finger, and awoke completely freed from pain after fifty minutes' treatment.

The second case (p. 31) was that of a lady of the Faubourg St. Germain, who had suffered from severe sciatica following on child-birth. The whole lumbar region was affected so that she could not move without pain. Many doctors were consulted in vain. The patient was unable to leave the house, the general health gave way, and the digestion was impaired. Finally, after five years of suffering, she applied to Patillon for treatment by Magnetism, with the result that after forty days all pain left her, her general health was completely restored, and she was able to go into the world again (*elle vaque sans peine à ses affaires*).

The third case (p. 32) was that of a young girl of eleven, suffering from a congenital skin disease (*gale*) "which might be termed leprous." All the ordinary remedies had proved useless. After fifteen days' treatment by Animal Magnetism the skin had changed from leaden colour to white and the scabs had begun to fall off, leaving a healthy skin behind. The treatment was still proceeding, and Patillon was confident of a complete cure.

Dr. Hourry (p. 33) furnishes a diagnosis of his own case. He suffered from a congested spleen (*une obstruction à la rate d'un volume considérable*); he was thin, the skin yellow, had dyspepsia and attacks of slow fever. After four months' treatment he found his powers of digestion completely restored, the spleen greatly reduced in bulk and much less inflamed. Treatment still proceeding.

Dr. Thomas Magnines (p. 33) had also suffered for about four years from congestion of the spleen. In the winter of 1783 he became much worse, and the spleen was enormously enlarged. After three months' treatment he finds that his appetite is good and that he can digest well; the yellowness of the skin is almost gone, and the congestion of the spleen is lessened. A notable point is that Magnetism first made him conscious of pain in the spleen. Treatment proceeding.

Dr. Pinorel (p. 55) had suffered for some months from quartan fever, colic, dysentery, and finally " angine catarrale." After being very near death, he began to recover, and then fell a victim to a new fever (*erratique*), and suffered excruciating pains from head to foot. After some weeks' treatment by M. Deslon he finds himself almost well again, his only remaining symptom a slight congestion of the spleen (apparently first revealed to him by Animal Magnetism).

M. Durand (p. 56), oculist and surgeon to the Duke of Orleans, reports that he had suffered for ten years from convulsive asthma and severe rheumatism in the legs and feet. Further, he had had during the last two years three attacks of blood-spitting, for which he had been bled fifteen times. After a few months' treatment by Animal Magnetism he finds his health so much improved that he can now discharge his duties without difficulty. Treatment apparently still proceeding.

M. Joyau (p. 62), pupil in surgery, was suffering from attacks of fever, congestion, and pain in spleen. After some weeks of treatment he finds his health completely restored. The yellow tint of the skin has disappeared ; he has no more pain, and no pain or congestion of the spleen.

M. Michaud (p. 65), surgeon, sent a full description of his ailments, which the editors apparently found too long to print. But it appears from his account that his attacks have under magnetic treatment diminished in frequency, but proportionally increased in duration and intensity. He has recovered his sleep, and is putting on flesh a little. Treatment, which had been in operation for a month, is still proceeding.

M. Quinquet (p. 66), member of the College of Pharmacy, had suffered for a month from severe sciatica, which robbed him of sleep at night, and compelled him to make use of a crutch. Other distressing symptoms made their appearance. His physician recommended the application of a moxa   He preferred to try Magnetism before consenting to so severe a remedy. He received immediate relief, and after some weeks' treatment he left completely cured, and able to walk without a crutch.

To these reports we may add the record (p. 68) of a case in which we have a description of the patient's symptoms both from herself and from her physician, M. de la Fisse, doctor of the Faculty of Paris. The Countess de la Blache had been ill for eight years; for the last fourteen months she had been bedridden, and unable even to rest at ease in bed. Her physician, writing on the 12th of August, 1782, to a near relative, describes the state of the patient as leading him to fear the worst. She has almost lost hearing, power of speech or movement. She breathes with great difficulty, and that solely by the use of the abdominal muscles, the chest remaining quite motionless. Frequent bleedings and the whole resources of the pharmacopœia have failed to give appreciable relief. The patient is reduced to the last extremity. Immediately after this report Deslon was called in. Madame de la Blache could not bear to be touched, and it was found necessary therefore to magnetise her from a distance. After two years' treatment she finds herself, not indeed completely cured, but better than she had been for eight years previously: no longer bedridden, but able to move about, and with the full use of her voice and senses. Her general health is improved; and three tumours (*squirres*) have disappeared under the treatment.

The modern physician can probably do no more than conjecture the nature of some of the diseases diagnosed by his predecessors of 1784. When we turn to the descriptions given by the patients themselves, inspired though these probably were in most cases by the attendant physician, the difficulty is certainly not diminished. Congested spleen, retention of milk, "depôts" of stagnant, viscous, milky, or vicious humours, vaguely localised "obstructions," "gutta serena," agitation of nerves, &c., play a considerable part in these reports. But there are many in which the ailment is clearly defined and the relief afforded

c

incontrovertible. "Animal Magnetism" appears to have been specially efficacious in the treatment of gouty and rheumatic affections.

Cases recorded by Laymen

Thus Madame de la Perrière, farmer-general, had suffered for more than a year from a disease which, if correctly described, would seem to have been rheumatoid arthritis. She had rheumatic pains all over the body : "les doigts se courberent, et il vint des nodus à toutes les articulations." After following the magnetic treatment throughout the summer of 1783, her hands returned to their natural state and all her symptoms disappeared (p. 22).

M. Perruchot (p. 28) writes that he had suffered from gout for three years. One day Deslon happened to call and found him in bed with a severe attack of gout in the foot. He was magnetised and experienced immediate relief. That evening he dressed himself and went out to pay calls.

Antoine Santon (p. 28), valet de chambre to the Count d'Artois, had suffered for six months from rheumatism in the right arm, which prevented him from making use of the limb. Three days' treatment from Deslon sufficed to banish the pain and to restore the use of the arm. Palpitation of the heart, from which he had suffered for four years, was cured at the same time.

Desanclos, a ferryman, had suffered for four years from rheumatism, which had prevented him from doing his work. At the time of writing he had been three weeks under treatment and already found his pains much less, and that he could move his arms and legs more freely.

M. Leclerc (p. 40) was so rheumatic that he could not put on his shoes. After some months' treatment his pain has practically disappeared. He is now in superb health (*se porte comme un royaume*).

Madame Parceval (p. 51), widow of a farmer-general, had been for six months unable to move her arm from rheumatism. She was persuaded by her children to try the effects of Magnetism, and after ten minutes' treatment was able to move the arm with little pain, and that evening undressed herself and did her hair without assistance for the first time for six months. After two more visits the pain was entirely cured.

M. de Landresse (p. 59) had suffered for some years from gouty rheumatism, which attacked particularly the joints of the hips, knees, and feet. Later the disease attacked the hands, and finally the eyes. Ordinary treatment gave him little relief, and he finally came to consult Deslon. The treatment, which had lasted four months, is still proceeding ; but already he is able to say " these four months have given me a new life."

An interesting case is that of M. Chauvet, a priest (p. 51). In the early summer of 1778 he had a severe attack of rheumatism which confined him to his bed for three months. Since that date he had never been entirely free from rheumatic pains in one or other arm, often sufficiently severe to prevent him from moving it. In September, 1783, some friend persuaded him to try Animal Magnetism. He went, and was half persuaded that Deslon was a charlatan when he saw the physician point his index finger at the arm affected and approach his foot to that of his patient. But his opinion changed when, Deslon having placed his hand on the patient's shoulder-blade, there followed immediately a profuse perspiration on the whole left side of the body (where he felt the pain), and on that only. His collar was glued to his skin, and his friends saw drops of sweat rolling down his face. His pain left him at that moment, and he is able a year later to write that he no longer knows what rheumatism is.

Gabriel d'Effet (p. 39) had suffered for ten days from a sprained shoulder, the pain from which kept him awake at night. He was unable to do his work. After four days' treatment he was able to return to work.

Françoise Lamotte (p. 41) had been unable to use her arm for thirteen months. The Magnetic treatment, which is still proceeding, has restored the use of her arm and improved her general health.

Besides the case of the Countess de la Blache, already described, there are several instances of tumours being affected. Magdelon Prin (p. 43), a portress, had had since the age of fifteen tumours of the size of an egg on her leg and thigh. They had hitherto resisted all medical or surgical treatment, but they disappeared after ten weeks' treatment by M. Deslon.

Dame Gaddant (p. 76), housekeeper to Madame d'Avignon, had suffered seven years from a tumour (*squirre*) nearly as big as a head, also from dropsy and other maladies. After treatment by Animal Magnetism for nearly a year her general health was restored, and her tumour had entirely disappeared.

The Marquise de Grasse (p. 68) suffered for fifteen months from " glands " in the breast. Ordinary remedies had proved of little use, when not actually harmful. But a desultory course of treatment by Animal Magnetism, spread over five months, had already reduced the swellings to half their former size. Treatment apparently proceeding.

There are a few cases in which Magnetism is said to have exerted a beneficial effect on diseases of the eye—inflammation, films, ulcers, blindness " *du lait repandu.*" But though Mesmer himself claimed on more than one occasion to have given sight to the blind, there is no case amongst this set of records sufficiently striking to be worth quoting.

Jean Gastal, a scullion (p. 43), reports a curious case. On a *fête* day a packet of fireworks (*fusées*), which he was carrying in the pocket of his apron, had exploded. He tried to stop the explosion by pressing the box between his thighs, but made matters worse. He was severely burnt on the lower part of the body. Deslon on the spot magnetised the thighs, and on the morrow Jean was able to remove the scab and find the skin underneath quite healed. But he had been reluctant to allow the lower part of the body, which had suffered less injury, to be magnetised, and this part was not healed for three weeks.[1]

---

[1] Compare Delbœuf's experiment. By the application of a red-hot iron bar he produced on each arm of his subject a burn of the same

We have two cases of "putrid fever." In the first case (M. Gueffier, p. 37) bleeding was followed by delirium, and, the disease taking an unfavourable turn, the doctor in attendance told the relatives to prepare for the worst. Deslon was called in. In the night following the first treatment the delirium left the patient, and the worst symptoms disappeared; a fortnight later he was able to eat meat.

In Madame Bové's case (p. 37) the putrid fever was complicated by other ailments, and the physician, in despair, himself called in Deslon. Immediate relief was experienced, and fifteen days later the cure was assured.

Of diseases of the abdominal viscera, or of ailments diagnosed as such, two or three cases have been already quoted. One more will suffice.

M. de la Vaultière (p. 47), commandant of the Gardes de la Marine at Brest, had been out of health for six years. In April, 1783, he contracted a serious ailment of the bladder. The attacks came on at the end of each month, causing fever and intense pain, for which temporary relief was sought by bleeding, the patient parting with fifteen or sixteen ounces of blood at a time. Finally, as a last resource, M. de la Vaultière came to Deslon on the 26th of December, in expectation of the usual monthly attack. Magnetism procured relief, and after four months' treatment he was able to leave Paris and return to his duties in better health than he had enjoyed for six years.

The Marquis de Rochegude (p. 46) sustained in January, 1782, a stroke which enfeebled all the left side and rendered the left arm powerless. Mesmer treated it by Magnetism and bleeding alternately, and he was cured in twenty-four hours. A fresh attack a year later was cured by Magnetism alone in a few days. A third and more severe attack, in April, 1784, required four months' treatment. But the patient was completely cured, except for a slight difficulty in speaking.

dimensions. He suggested that the burn on the right should be painless; not only was the injury painless, but it healed much more rapidly and with less inflammation than the other (quoted by Bramwell, *Hypnotism*, p. 84; see also p. 368).

A case typical in many respects is that of M. Gerbier, advocate (p. 53). He had been in ill-health for years. He suffered from catarrh, which persisted for months together ; his nerves were in a sad state, his slumbers broken, his digestion so feeble that he was reduced to a vegetarian diet. After some months' treatment his health underwent a wonderful change for the better. His nerves troubled him no more, he found that he could eat and digest what he liked, and his tendency to catarrh appears to have been stopped altogether. He has enjoyed the best of health for two years.

It is useless and would be tedious to multiply testimonies. From the cases already cited the reader can gain a fair idea of the whole. Of the 115 persons whose cases are here recorded nearly half profess themselves to have been completely cured, and of the remainder all but six experienced sensible relief under the treatment. The six exceptions were persons who had not been under treatment for more than a few weeks, and who still continued to attend in the hope of a cure.

No doubt the list included some who were *malades imaginaires*. Further, as already pointed out, the large majority of the testimonies cited necessarily proceeded from persons still attending the Baquet, or who had ceased to attend for a relatively brief period. It may be contended, therefore, that the permanence of the cures in these cases had not been demonstrated. A certain amount of exaggeration, no doubt, must also be allowed for. Partly from gratitude, partly from love of sensation, partly from the mere wish to believe, many patients would describe their cure as more complete than the facts would warrant. But whatever deductions are made on these and other accounts, it would be futile to deny the fact that a large number of persons, some of them suffering from grave disorders, which had resisted all the ordinary means of cure, did find substantial and frequently permanent relief at the hands of Mesmer and his colleagues. To whatever cause we may ascribe the results, the results themselves are certainly of the highest importance. The patients are almost unanimous in rejecting, some with delicate irony, some with emphatically expressed contempt, the suggestion that the cures were due to imagination, and in attributing the results to the magnetic fluid directed by the rod or finger of the operating physician, and many curious proofs are offered of the reality of the agency.

As said, most of the accounts relate to the years 1782–1784, and, whatever may have been the case in the first three or four years of Animal Magnetism, and whatever may have been the case at this time in Mesmer's own practice, it would seem that the crisis at this time played a quite subordinate part in Deslon's treatment. Of the 115 cases here considered, eleven only, all women, are recorded as having experienced the crisis. Of the remainder, a considerable minority experienced no effect from the treatment beyond that produced upon their health.

The state of induced somnambulism—the eponymous fact of modern hypnotism—which was to play so large a part in the subsequent history of Animal Magnetism, was observed for the first time in 1784, the year in which these records were written, by Puységur at Busancy. But his account of the phenomenon had scarcely penetrated beyond the circle of his intimates ; and it is not until the following year, 1785, that somnambulism became a common feature of the magnetic treatment. In the present records the treatment is said in a few instances to have induced sleep, which the observers do not appear to have distinguished from ordinary sleep. In many cases a marked tendency to drowsiness was observed.

But the majority record certain physical symptoms which were held to indicate the actual operation of the fluid. Of these physical symptoms the most constant are a feeling of agreeable warmth—occasionally of coldness—following the touch or direction of the operator's finger. This would often be accompanied or succeeded by shivering, or other feelings vaguely described as " an agitation of the blood," " fermentation of humours," &c. Frequently there would be a tickling or pricking in the part affected. This is specially noticed in cases of diseased eyes. In one case of a " weeping " eye the weeping ceased during the process of magnetisation. The pricking or tickling of the diseased part frequently increased to positive pain, in accordance with the belief that a painful crisis was in most cases necessary to the cure of the malady. We have seen, in a case already quoted, that Dr. Patillon entreated one of his patients to endure the pain a little longer, in order not to interfere with the cure. Many of the patients explain that the first effect of the magnetic treatment was to increase their pains and oppress still further the laboured breathing; in one case total blindness overtook the diseased eye as a preliminary to cure. Two of the patients were unaware that their troubles were due to congested spleen, until Deslon's apocalyptic finger made them feel severe pain in that organ, painless before. One witness found that Animal Magnetism renewed the pain of a sprained thumb, healed many years ago. M. Quinquet remarks that the operating physician seemed, as if by enchantment, to make the pain follow in obedience to his healing touch from one part of the body to another (p. 66). The gradual descent of the pain recorded by Dr. Patillon in one of his cases is described by two or three other witnesses. The descent of the pain from the head or other parts to the extremities, as a preliminary to its final expulsion from the body, was, it may be pointed out, a marked feature in the treatment pursued by the spiritualist healers, Valentine Greatrakes and J. J. Gassner.

The actual impact of the fluid is claimed to have been felt in some cases. M. Rossi (p. 57) records that after having waited for some months in vain, experiencing nothing beyond the improvement in his health, he at last felt a subtle fluid pour from the iron rod and fall upon his face. The Marquis de Chateaurenaud testifies that, when magnetised by a physician without his knowledge, he first felt an oppression in the head and then fainted. The Countess de la Saumés gives an interesting account of her first interview with Deslon. She was brought to his consulting-room by her father.

"In talking to him of my symptoms I looked upon him as a physician, and hadn't the least suspicion that he was magnetising me. He asked permission to touch an 'obstruction' in my liver, which was very sensitive. After he had held his hand for a few minutes on my side, I was on the point of fainting. I did not know to what to attribute my feeling, but supposed that M. Deslon was pressing too hard. I asked him to withdraw his hand. A moment later he directed his finger towards me. I experienced the same sensation, coupled with extreme heat."

Her friends then told her who M. Deslon was (she was apparently up to this point ignorant of his identity), and explained to her that she was being magnetised. She was much astonished (p. 73).

It will be seen that Mesmer claimed for Animal Magnetism not simply a healing influence, but a direct physical effect upon the human body. According to his theory the " Magnetiser " wielded a subtle fluid, akin to, yet distinguishable from, the other subtle fluids—electricity, magnetism, vital heat, &c.—with which the science of the day was acquainted. Before proceeding to treat of Mesmer's later life and the reception which he met with at the hands of the medical faculty and the scientific authorities generally, it will be convenient to set forth the pedigree of the new-born doctrine of Animal Magnetism, and to glance briefly at some other circumstances which had their influence in shaping his career.

CHAPTER II

THE MAGNETIC SYSTEM

The Faith-healers—Mesmer's debt to Gassner—Sympathetic or Magnetic medicine—Sir Kenelm Digby's Weapon Salve, and his explanation of its virtues—Paracelsus on Mummy and the *Magnes Microcosmi* —Van Helmont's account of the Sympathetic system : further developed by Fludd and Maxwell—Mesmer's propositions : his doctrine wholly derived from his predecessors, but with a difference.

A DEMONSTRATION of the power of healing without drugs or processes of surgery was no new thing even in eighteenth-century Paris. In all ages and in all countries there have been persons who, living, have claimed such power for themselves, or have been credited with such power after death by their worshippers. But such cures had before the time of Mesmer been attributed generally to some peculiar sanctity in the healer, allied with peculiar strength of faith in the sufferer. Often the diseases themselves had been ascribed to the action of demons. Even in the Sympathetic or Magnetic system of medicine the process of healing was considered primarily as a spiritual affair. It was still to the Eternal Creative Spirit of the universe that Fludd and Maxwell ascribed the cure of wounds and diseases.

Mesmer was the first to rationalise the process and explain it as wholly due to the operation of an indifferent mechanical force. He was also the first who, without claiming peculiar sanctity for himself, or avowedly exacting faith from his patient, was able to heal as effectually and on at least as large a scale as any saint or inspired healer who had gone before. There had, in fact, within the hundred years which immediately preceded the commencement of Mesmer's career, been three remarkable exhibitions of healing in England, France, and Germany respectively. To Mesmer and his contemporaries Valentine Greatrakes was probably little more than a name. But amongst Mesmer's older patients there may have been some who had been eye-witnesses of the cures which took place round the tomb of the Jansenist Deacon Paris in 1731, and to all they would probably be familiar by report. To the most recent of these healers, the Suabian priest J. J. Gassner, Mesmer probably owed many features of his practice. The five or six years ending with 1777—when he was forced by ecclesiastical interdict and Imperial decree to quit Ratisbon—were those in which Gassner reached the zenith of his fame. During these years he resided chiefly at Ratisbon; but he travelled about and visited many towns in Bavaria, healing by his word and touch. Mesmer, as already said, prior to his arrival in Paris in 1778, had for some years journeyed about Europe, amongst other countries in Suabia and Bavaria. If he did not actually meet Gassner—and it is stated that he did—he must have heard of his fame, and been conversant with his methods of operation. A noticeable point in Gassner's treatment was that, as a preliminary to undertaking a cure, he would cause to be reproduced in the patient the pains and other symptoms of the disease. The exorcism by which he sought to expel the demon (to whose presence in the patient he attributed the disease) generally produced strong convulsions; and the cure commenced only when they were calmed. Again, Gassner constantly chased the pain from one part of the body to another, finally chasing it out, by his command, from the fingers or toes. All these features are characteristic of Mesmer's early treatment, though, as we shall see, they soon disappeared in the practice of his successors.

But if Mesmer seems to have borrowed from the Faith-healers some of his practical methods and, what was of more importance, the self-confidence essential to success, he unquestionably found his philosophy ready-made.

To most English readers, no doubt, the Sympathetic or Magnetic system is best known through the writings of the ingenious and versatile Sir Kenelm Digby. Digby was by occupation privateer and philosopher, in religion Catholic and Protestant, by turn; himself the son of a man who had been executed for high treason to his sovereign, he devoted himself to the successors of that sovereign during his exile, and became the Chancellor of the Queen, Henrietta Maria. He was one of the earliest members of the Royal Society, and, according to his contemporary, Evelyn, " an arrant mountebank." In a lecture delivered in Montpellier he gives an account of his powder of sympathy and of the remarkable cures effected by it.[1] One of Digby's acquaintances, James Howell, author of the well-known *Letters*, had been wounded in the hand in the course of parting two friends who were about to fight a duel. Four or five days later the wound showed serious symptoms. Howell asked Digby whether he could do anything for him. Digby asked for something which had the blood of the wound on it, and Howell sent for the garter with which the hand had first been bound up. Digby then dissolved some powdered vitriol (the powder of sympathy) in a basin of water, and, whilst Howell's back was turned, placed the garter in the water. Howell suddenly exclaimed that he felt no more pain. " Methinks that a pleasing kind of freshness, as it were a wet cold napkin, did spread over my hand which hath taken away the inflammation which tormented me before." Later in the evening Digby took the garter out of the water and dried it before the fire. Presently came Howell's servant running to say that his master's hand was much worse—" the heat was such as if his hand were between coals of fire." Digby replaced the bandage in the water, and the servant on his return found his master free from pain. The wound was entirely healed in five or six days. It should be pointed out that this is Digby's own account of the matter; that we have no evidence beyond his word for the cure; and that a con-

[1] *A Late Discourse* . . . by Sir Kenelm Digby, translated from the Latin by R. White (London, 1658).

temporary calls him "the very Pliny of our age for lying."[1]

However, the incident, whether real or fictitious, will serve to illustrate the theory. Briefly, Digby's explanation of the matter is something of this kind. All bodies consist of infinitely divisible particles, which are constantly flying off and travelling through the air, as we may perceive in the case of musk and other odorous substances. The chief agent in their disintegration and conveyance is light, which is always darting and bounding about like a tennis ball, and is constantly loosening the surface of the bodies on which it falls and carrying away with it some of the loosened particles. The wind is nothing else than the rush of these small particles loosened from their parent bodies by the action of the sun : Digby had himself seen a wind thus born in an Alpine pass at sunrise. Now, these flying particles are subject to certain laws of attraction. Like attracts like, as we see that fire and all hot bodies attract air. The greater attracts the less ; so fire draws out the pain from a burn ; so the body, being the greater, attracts to itself the blood spilt by the sword. And herein enters the final principle : that the body attracts not only its own proper particles, but any particles conjoined with them. Hence it follows that the atoms of blood on the bandage or sword, transported by the air, and especially by the sun's rays, drawing with them the volatile and balsamic spirits of vitriol, are attracted by the wound and take up their proper place there, bringing with them the conjoined balsamic and healing spirits. Conversely, if you burn cow's milk in the fire, the cow's udder will ulcerate.

Digby gives some other illustrations of the working of this principle in medicine, rustic lore, and the minor magical arts. But, after all, even apart from the dubious testimony of his contemporaries, Digby is not our best guide in the matter. He did not belong to the central tradition ; he was simply an amateur playing with the subject. Paracelsus is commonly reputed to be the founder of the Magnetic system. He is

[1] Stubbes, quoted in Chambers's *Encyclopædia*, under " Digby."

said to have employed the actual magnet in medicine, recommending its use, inasmuch as it attracted martial humours, in fluxes, inflammatory diseases, hysteria, and epilepsy. But for the most part Paracelsus applies the term "magnetic," by a metaphor, to all action at a distance real or presumed, between bodies of all kinds on our earth. In medicine the principal mediator of this action is mummy. Of mummy there are various kinds, but the most precious is the moss which grows on the skull of the criminal hanging on the gallows :—

"For from such there is a gentle siccation that expungeth the watery humour, without destroying the oyle and spirituall, which is cherished by the heavenly Luminaries and strengthened continually by the affluence and appulses of the celestiall Spirits, whence it may properly be called by the name of Constellated or Celestiall Mumie." [1]

In places not sufficiently favoured with criminals and gibbets a scarcely less efficient mummy might be constructed at small expense from the blood, hair, nail-clippings, and the waste products generally of the human body. This is the true *Magnes Microcosmi*, and rightly used is competent for the cure of all diseases. Mummy so prepared from the living body might be given to an animal to eat, and the disease of the original owner so transferred to the unoffending dog or pig, even as the leprosy of Naaman the Syrian passed over and was transplanted into Gehazi. Or, better still, let the mummy of the sick person be mixed with earth, and place in the earth so prepared seeds or plants bearing the "signature" of the disease, or of the part affected, and as the plant grows it will suck up the mummial spirits and the sick man will be cured. If the disease be jaundice, you should sow linseed or hempseed; if pleurisy, plant St. John's wort ; if there be oppilations of the liver, take rue, liver wort, or maidenhair ; if of the lungs, take nettles, vernacle, or lung wort; if of the spleen, stone wort or germander.

Paracelsus's writings are, however, unsystematic, and his

[1] *Medicina Diastatica, or Sympatheticall Mumie* . . . Abstracted from the works of Dr. Theophr. Paracelsus by Andrea Tentzelius, translated by F. Parkhurst (London, 1653).

prescriptions are, no doubt by design, obscure. The clearest authoritative exposition of the Magnetic system was given two or three generations after the founder by Van Helmont. One Goclenius, a professor of medicine at Marpurg, had, early in the seventeenth century, published as his inaugural thesis a treatise on the Weapon Salve (*De unguento armario*). To this a Jesuit Father named Roberti had replied in *A Short Anatomy of Goclenius' Treatise on the Magnetic Cure of Wounds*. Goclenius, waxing warmer, countered this attack with *The Articulation of the Magnetic Philosophy, Contrasted with the Miserable Anatomy of John Roberti*.[1] Roberti retorted with a final treatise entitled *Goclenius Convicted out of his own Mouth, or the Downfall of the Magnetic Cure and the Weapon Salve*.[2] At this stage the dispute was referred to Van Helmont, one of the most famous physicians and chemists of the day. Van Helmont took advantage of the opportunity to give his own interpretation of the Magnetic philosophy. He begins by pointing out that Roberti is clearly in the wrong. The Jesuit called all these things diabolical only because he couldn't understand them. But "whosoever attributes a natural effect, so created by God . . so bestowed on the creatures, unto the Devil, he estrangeth the honour due to the Creator."[3] Let the divine inquire concerning God, but leave it to the naturalist to make inquiries concerning nature. But if Roberti was in the wrong, Goclenius cannot be said to be wholly in the right. He has proved himself an embarrassed and indiscreet champion. He has confounded sympathy with witchcraft, and both with Magnetism, not understanding that they are diverse manifestations of the same power. Further, misinterpreting Paracelsus, in his treatment of the Weapon Salve he has confused the two cases, when the weapon is bloodied and when it is not. In the former case a sympa-

---

[1] *Synarthrosis Magnetica, opposita infaustæ Anatomiæ Johannis Roberti: Theatrum Sympatheticum* (Nüremberg, 1672), p. 237.

[2] *Goclenius Heautontimorumenos, id est curationis magneticæ et unguenti armarii ruina*, id. p. 309.

[3] Van Helmont's *Workes*, translated (London, 1664), p. 793.

thetic unguent will suffice. But in the second we need a much more powerful treatment—to wit, the magnetic armary, of which the fat of bulls is the chief ingredient. For the bull dies exulting in revenge more than any other animal; and hence his fat yields a more violent, efficacious, and Taurine impression. Again, Goclenius has blundered badly in his account of *usnea*, the moss from the skull of a criminal. He attributes its special virtues to the fact that in the process of strangling the vital spirits enter the skull. But practical experience, says Van Helmont, shows that moss from the skull of a man broken on the wheel or suffering any other violent death is equally efficacious. In fact, *usnea*, rightly named the seminal offspring of Heaven, consists as it were in the excretions and superfluities of the stars, and derives its magnetism at once from the mummial virtue of the bones and from "the circular Tract of the Heavenly Bodies."

It will be seen that Van Helmont conceives of the Magnetic or Sympathetic healing as of a natural process. It needs no rites or ceremonies; "it doth not so much as fore-require the Imagination, Confidence, or Belief, nor Leave to be required from the wounded party." In controverting Roberti, indeed, he expressly says that "it is not suitable to the customs of Naturalists to dispute from naked authorities; they rely upon experience." As fair samples of the facts of experience which were relied upon by the Magnetists to prove the existence of action at a distance we may quote the following. Lightning will not strike a house or a stable which has been smeared with the fat of a sea-calf; "the experience is trivial and frequent." If a sapphire be rubbed upon a carbuncle (*i.e.*, a boil, not the jewel of that name) and then removed to a distance from the patient, it will suck the poison from the swelling. If the leaves of asarabacca are plucked upwards they will cause the patient to vomit, if downwards they will purge him. The eyes of the basilisk or catablepa can kill a man at a distance of 1,000 yards and more. Eagles are attracted to the carcass, as indicated in the Scriptures, instantaneously. It cannot be by sight or smell, it must therefore be by magnetic power. Again, he tells a curious tale—since repeated with local variations by each of his successors—of a certain rich merchant of Brussels who had the misfortune to lose his nose. At length he found in Italy a poor man, a porter, who was willing to part with some of his flesh to form a new nose. But thirteen months later the Belgian, having then returned to his own country, found his nose putrefying, and, in effect, it dropped off. He afterwards discovered that at that exact date the Italian porter had died. The borrowed flesh had shared in the corruption of its original body, hundreds of miles away.

All these observations are cited by Van Helmont. From Digby we learn in addition that if you hold a gold coin in your mouth, it will be discoloured if you put your big toe into a vessel of mercury ; and that you may wash your hands in a silver basin by collecting moonbeams in it.[1] Tentzelius adds that when vines shoot forth their branches old wines work anew in the vessel and their lees rise and are troubled ; that a venison pasty grows rank at the rutting season, and sweetens later ; that the fat and flesh of a bear kept in a closed trough increases at the same time " when as the Beares lying down in their den in the Winter time do wax fat." [2]

Now, all these facts, says Van Helmont, and others like them, prove an influence of sublunaries on each other like the influence of the magnet on the iron ; and this influence in all cases alike is called Magnetism. The influence is not of a corporeal nature. The light of the sun, the influence of the heavens, the sight of the basilisk, the stupefaction darting forth of the cramp-fish, the attraction of the magnet itself, are dispersed upon the object at a distance, " not by communion of a substantial evaporation, but by the medium of an unperceivable Light." The exact nature of the communication it is not easy to understand. The influence of the stars is, of course, matter of common knowledge :—

"Ye grant that material Nature doth daily draw down Forces by its magnetism from the superiour Orbs . . . and that the Heavens do in

---

[1] *Op. cit.*, pp. 43 and 111.　　[2] *Medicina Diastatica*, pp. 21, *seqq.*

D

exchange invisibly allure something from the inferiour bodies, that there may be a free and mutual passage and a harmonious concord of the members with the whole universe."

Nay, all particular created beings have their own heaven within them, or, as Fludd put it later, "Man containeth in himself no otherwise his heavens, circles, poles, and stars than the great world doth." [1] And these particular heavens do at ordinary times govern themselves according to the harmony of the superior tributary motion. But sick persons have by the persuasion of their proper heaven wandered from the motion of the universal heaven. And because of this want of harmony they feel more keenly than those in health the changes of the seasons and all the celestial motions.

And that brings us to the heart of the mystery. Man was originally made in the likeness of God, and able, like God, to create and effect all things *per nutum*, by his mere beck or will. But all this magical power now "sleeps, since the knowledge of the apple was eaten." It can, however, be roused by various means. In some Satan can excite it to action and by his diabolical cunning make the witch believe that the power comes from him, which is really the witch's own. For if the witch kills a man, it is by virtue of the magical power which sleeps in us all. Again, prayer and fasting will overcome the drowsiness of the flesh, and release the " nimble, active, heavenly and ready power towards God." By similar means there may be induced a state of ecstasy, as in a case recorded by Martin del Rio, which Van Helmont quotes—a young lad, "transported with violent cogitation of seeing his mother," actually succeeded in seeing her at a distance, and gave many signs of his true presence with her.

So, again, ill-health or corruption may release this seminal virtue. Thus when a wound is made,

" it happens that the blood in the Wound freshly made, by reason of the said foreign quality (the entrance of the air) doth now enter into the beginning of some kind of corruption (which blood, being also then

---

[1] *Mosaicall Philosophy* (London, 1659), p. 221.

received on the Weapon or splinter thereof, is besmeared with the magnetick Unguent), the which entrance of corruption mediating, the ecstatical power lurking potentially in the blood is brought forth into action, which power, because it is an exiled returner unto its own body, by reason of the hidden Ecstasie, hence that blood bears an individual respect unto the blood of its whole body. Then indeed the magnet or attractive faculty is busied in operating in the Unguent; and through the mediation of the ecstatical power (for so I call it for want of an Etymologie) sucks out the hurtful quality from the lips of the wound, and at length through the Mummial, Balsamick and attractive virtue contained in the Unguent, the magnetism is perfect."

The Magnetic philosophy was developed and systematised by Robert Fludd in his *Philosophia Moysaica* (1637) and by the Scotch physician Maxwell in his treatise *De Medicina Magnetica* (1679). From the stars, the human body and from all substances in the universe, according to these philosophers, there radiate beams which reciprocally affect all other bodies. But the influence of the stars is original and predominant.

" Every astrall influence in the Creature," says Fludd, "doth by a natural inclination, and that Sympathetically, aspect the Star or celestiall Fountain from which it did spring ; and likewise the Star in Heaven, by a paternal respect, doth send down his influence to feed and nourish his like filiall fire and force in the Creature here below." [1]

Again, Maxwell says "the Stars bind the vital spirit to the proper body by light and heat, and pour it into the same by the same means." [2] Seeds contain a more liberal portion of the vital spirit than anything else, and in their growth they attract more and more in its descent from the heavens.

The later philosophers followed Van Helmont in conceiving of these rays as being, like light itself, of inconceivable tenuity.[3] But the rays themselves were only the vehicle of

---

[1] *Mosaicall Philosophy* (1659), p. 223.

[2] Stellæ vitalem spiritum corpori disposito ligant per lucem et calorem, eidemque iisdem mediis infundunt."

[3] Maxwell, however, says, " ab omni corpore radii corporales fluunt," but *corporales* does not apparently here mean " material."

the indwelling spirit, which directed all their operations and gave them their virtue. Thus Fludd :—

"The Etheriall Sperm or Astralicall influences are of a far subtiler condition than is the vehicle of visible light. Yea, verily they are so thin, so mobile, so penetrating, and so lively . . . that they continually penetrate even unto the center or universal bosom of the earth, where they generate metals of sundry kinds, as the antient philosophers do justifie. . . . It is not the starry light which penetrateth so deeply, or operateth so universally, but the Eternal Centrall Spirit."

But if a hard mineral stone, immovable and stupid, can act on other bodies at a distance, much more man's heavenly spirit, being more subtle than the loadstone, can send forth "the astralicall beams of his vertue" even unto the throne of Divinity. It was a necessary consequence of this doctrine that, in Maxwell's words, he who had learnt to strengthen his individual spirit by means of the universal spirit, could prolong his life to an indefinite time (*in ævum*) unless the stars were unfavourable. Again, having learnt how to employ the universal spirit, the physician could stay all manner of corruption in his patient's body, and give to the individual spirit dominion over disease.[1] Again, by like means the physician might affect his patient "at any reasonable but limited and unknown distance." Thus Paracelsus :—

"By the magic power of the will a person on this side of the ocean may make a person on the other side hear what is said on this side . . . the ethereal body of a man may know what another man thinks at a distance of 100 miles or more."[2]

Fludd expresses the same idea more generally :—

"How, by relation of naturall things unto one another, they do, after a corporall contact or touch is made between them, operate wonderfully, and that by a Magneticall concent and Spirituall continuity . . . by a mutuall operation at an unknown distance."[3]

---

[1] *Op. cit.*, p. 92, *cf.* p. 94. "Medicamentum universale nihil aliud est quam spiritus vitalis in subjectum debitum multiplicatus."

[2] *Philosoph.*, *Sag.* i. cap. 60. Quoted by Hartmann, *Life of Theophrastus Bombastes*, p. 296.

[3] *Op. cit.*, p. 252.

And Maxwell definitely applies the principle to the relation between physician and patient :—

"Qui spiritum vitalem particularem efficere novit, corpus, cujus spiritus est, curare potest ad quamcunque distantiam, imploratâ spiritus universalis ope." [1]

The later interpreters laid more stress than Paracelsus and Van Helmont had done upon the dual and reciprocal action of the forces directing the universe. The attractive and repulsive action of the magnet corresponded to the alternation of light and darkness, heat and cold, the flux and reflux of the tides, centrifugal and centripetal action, the mystery of the sexes. Man himself was a magnet and contained his own poles or points of reciprocal attraction and repulsion. Let a man be placed, says Fludd, with his face to the east : his right hand will then correspond with the earth's right or southern pole, and the cold, dark spleen will be turned to the cold, dark north. But Fludd's view on this point was not universally accepted, and philosophers, while agreeing that the human body was in the likeness of a magnet, differed as to the exact disposition of the poles.

If we compare Fludd's explanation of the magnetic cure of wounds with the passage already quoted from Van Helmont, we shall see more clearly how the doctrine had developed.

"If, after the wound is made, a portion of the wound's externall blood, with his inward spirits, or the internall spirits onely, that have penetrated into the weapon, or any other thing which have searched the depth of the wound, be conveyed from the wound at any reason- able but unlimited and unknown distance, unto an Oyntment, whose property is Balsamick, and agreeing specifically with the nature of the creature so wounded, the Oyntment so animated by those spirits will become forthwith magneticall, and apply with a magneticall aspect and regard unto those beamy Spirits which stream forth invisibly from the wound, being directed thereto by the Spirituall bloody spirits in the weapon or other thing which hath received or included them : and the lively and southern beams, streaming and flowing from the wound, will with the northern attraction of the

---

[1] *Op. cit., Aphorism* 69.

Oyntment, so magnetically animated, concur and unite themselves with the northern and congealed, or fixt, bloody spirits contained in the oyntment, and stir them to act southernly, that is, from the center to the circumference; so that by this reciprocall action, union or continuity, a lively southern beam will act and revive the chill, fixt or northern beams which do animate the oyntment with a magneticall vertue, and quickened spirits of the oyntment, animated by the spirits of them both, and directed by the spirits which were first transplanted into it, doth impart by the said union or continuity his balsamick and sanative vertue unto the spirits in the wound, being first magnetically attracted, and they afterwards by an unseparable harmony, transfer it back into the wound. And this is the reason of that Sympatheticall or anti-patheticall reference and respect, which is by experience observed to be between the Oyntment and the wound."

But however their explanations of the process may differ, all the Magnetic philosophers were agreed that if the wound were carefully washed and wrapped up in clean linen, whilst the weapon which did the mischief was suitably anointed, the wound would heal. And in this, curiously enough, they find themselves in agreement with modern science. For the treatment prescribed differs little from that followed by the surgeon of to-day—barring the anointing of the sword.

Mesmer's own statement of his doctrine is contained in a series of twenty-seven propositions drawn up in 1779, of which the following may be quoted :—

1. Il existe une influence mutuelle entre les corps célestes, la terre et les corps animés.

2. Un fluide universellement répandu et continué de manière à ne souffrir aucun vuide, dont la subtileté ne permet aucune comparaison, et qui, de sa nature, est susceptible de recevoir, propager et communiquer toutes les impressions du mouvement, est le moyen de cette influence.

3. Cette action réciproque est soumise à des loix méchaniques, inconnues jusqu'a présent.

4. Il résulte de cette action, des effets alternatifs qui peuvent être considérés comme un flux et reflux.

6. C'est par cette opération (la plus universelle de celles que la nature nous offre) que les relations d'activité s'exercent entre les corps célestes, la terre et ses parties constitutives.

9. Il se manifeste, particulièrement dans le corps humain, des propriétés analogues à celles de l'aimant; on y distingue des pôles également divers et opposés qui peuvent être communiqués, changés, détruits et renforcés; le phénomène même de l'inclinaison y est observé.

10. La propriété du corps animal qui le rend susceptible de l'influence des corps célestes et de l'action réciproque de ceux qui l'environnent, manifestée par son analogie avec l'aimant, m'a déterminé à la nommer *Magnétisme animal.*

14. Son action a lieu à une distance éloignée, sans le secours d'aucun corps intermédiaire.

15. Elle est augmentée et réfléchie par les glaces comme la lumière.

16. Elle est communiquée, propagée, et augmentée par le son.

21. Ce système fournira de nouveaux éclaircissements sur la nature du feu et de la lumière, ainsi que dans la théorie de l'attraction, du flux et reflux de l'aimant et de l'électricité.

22. Il fera connoitre que l'aimant et l'électricité artificielle, n'ont à l'égard des maladies, que des propriétés communes avec plusieurs autres agents que la nature nous offre ; et que s'il est resulté quelques effets utiles de l'administration de ceux-là, ils sont dus au Magnétisme-animal.

23. On reconnoitra par les faits, d'après les règles pratiques que j'établerai, que ce principe peut guérir immédiatement les maladies des nerfs, et médiatement les autres.

24. Qu'avec son secours le médécin est éclairé sur l'usage des médicaments ; qu'il perfectionne leur action, et qu'il provoque et dirige les crises salutaires, de manière à s'en rendre le mâitre.

The reader who will compare Mesmer's propositions with the account above given of the Magnetic system will see that the whole of the Viennese physician's doctrine is implicitly contained in the writings of his predecessors.[1] But there is one subtle difference. To Van Helmont the Magnetic system is still primarily a spiritual affair, a link between the heavens and the earth. Man can only obtain a complete mastery over the powers which sleep in his own nature by assimilating his will to the Divine Will. In the writings of Maxwell and Fludd greater stress is laid upon the material operations of the fluid ; the theory tends to become less mystical and more scientific. But neither quite loses sight of the spiritual aspect of the matter. It

[1] A detailed comparison of Mesmer's ideas with those of earlier mystics, including, besides those mentioned in the text, Kircher, Borel, and others, is given in Thouret's *Recherches et doutes sur le Magnétisme animal* (Paris, 1784). See also Bertrand, *Du Magnétisme animal en France* (Paris, 1826), pp. 13-18. Nearly every item in Mesmer's statement of his doctrine can be paralleled from the writings of his predecessors.

is not the starry light, says Fludd, "which operateth so universally, but the Eternal Centrall Spirit." And Maxwell gives an even more emphatic expression to the Spiritualist view. Thus runs his first Aphorism :—

"The world is quickened by the original and supreme Mind, containing in itself the seminal causes of all things, which proceeding from the splendour of the Ideas in the original Mind, are as it were instruments by which this great body is moved, and links in the golden chain of Providence.[1]

But in Mesmer's exposition this spiritual aspect of the doctrine has entirely disappeared. For him the Magnetic system is purely a question of matter and motion. So far, no doubt, his doctrine was better adapted to catch the ears of his contemporaries. The Paris of the Age of Reason—at least, that part of it which was not versed in the physical sciences—might be expected to believe in a Universal Fluid without examining too closely the evidence for its existence. But they would not have hearkened so gladly to a revival of the scarcely more baseless mysticism of the previous century.

[1] "Mundus animatus est animâ primâ et supremâ intellectuali, in se rationes rerum seminarias possidente, quae a splendore idearum intellectus primi procedentes sunt quasi instrumenta, per quae corpus hoc magnum agitur, et sunt quasi nexus catenae aureæ providentiæ."

CHAPTER III

THE FIRST FRENCH COMMISSION

Mesmer's relations with the Academy of Sciences, and with the Royal Society of Medicine—Three doctors of the Faculty inquire into Mesmer's treatment—Deslon's application to the Faculty on Mesmer's behalf—De Vauzèsmes' speech—The case of M. Busson—Rejection of Mesmer's proposals, and ultimate expulsion of Deslon from the Faculty—Mesmer refuses a substantial pension from the Government —His pupils form a Society of Harmony—Berthollet's letter—Two Commissions of Inquiry appointed by Government—Their Reports— What they saw and what they did not see—Report of De Jussieu.

IT is clear that when Mesmer came to Paris in February, 1778, the reports which had preceded him were not so universally unfavourable as some writers would have us believe.[1] Even if to the medical profession generally he was an impudent charlatan, driven in disgrace from the country of his birth, or adoption, that opinion was by no means universal amongst men of enlightenment. It may be admitted that the crowd of fashionable folk who thronged his reception-rooms almost from the moment of his arrival

---

[1] The chief authority for the first four years of Mesmer's career in Paris, from 1778 to 1781, is his *Précis historique des Faits relatifs au Magnétisme animal*, which appeared in the course of 1781, and carries the narrative as far as the April of that year. The account is well documented, and may, no doubt, be relied upon so far as the external facts are concerned. Indeed, the authors of the *Histoire académique* (1841), Burdin and Dubois, have based their account upon the *Précis*, and as they were themselves members of the Royal Academy of Medicine, at whose instance the history was undertaken, they were in a position to check Mesmer's statements, at least as regards his relations with that body.

counted for little. But his claims from the outset found recognition in quarters more worthy of consideration. M. Leroy, Director of the Academy of Sciences, came on several occasions to examine Mesmer's methods of treatment, and was sufficiently impressed to bring the matter before a meeting of the Academy. The meeting, the exact date of which is not given, apparently took place in the spring or early summer of 1778. According to Mesmer's statement of his position, it was not so much a new method of treating disease, but a new physical force which he claimed to have discovered. He had, he tells us, no intention of practising in Paris, and only undertook to effect cures at the solicitation of the numerous patients who flocked to his consulting-rooms. It was as a physicist rather than as a physician that he asked to be recognised. It was true that the newly discovered magnetic fluid had proved in his hands of immense benefit in therapeutics, and the numerous cures effected by the treatment were no doubt calculated to impress the vulgar; but they were little likely to convince the experts. "Cette espèce de preuve," he says, "paroît sans replique; c'est une erreur. Rien ne prouve démonstrativement que le Médecin ou la Médecine guérissent les maladies." [1]

The paper, then, which Mesmer, through the intervention of M. Leroy, presented to the Academy of Sciences contained, no doubt, a statement of his doctrine of a Universal Fluid as set forth in the propositions quoted in the last chapter. [2] Such a belated echo of mediæval mysticism, even when it masqueraded as Science, was little likely to impress scientific Paris at the end of the eighteenth century. The Academy before which the last of the alchemists advertised his pretended discovery included amongst its members, to name no others, Lavoisier, who was even then laying the foundations of the new chemistry, and Benjamin Franklin, who had

---

[1] *Précis*, p. 37. The passage was later quoted in Bailly's Report as a justification of the attitude of the Commissioners.
[2] The propositions in the form in which we now have them were first published in Mesmer's *Mémoire sur la découverte*, &c. (1779).

a generation before played a similar part in the kindred science of electricity. Mesmer's vanity was wounded because the Academy refused to listen to Leroy and suggested that he should leave Mesmer's communication lying on the table, for any to read who would. His vanity was even yet more seriously hurt when at the close of the meeting some of the members asked to see a demonstration of the new force. Mesmer stigmatised the request as " childish "—the epithet proves him a true son of the Middle Ages. For him, no doubt, the symmetry and simplicity of his theory was its own sufficient proof. But he at length consented to magnetise one of the members, M. A——. M. A—— professed—apparently in mockery—to feel thrills in his hands and subtle currents coursing along his arms. But Mesmer claims that he succeeded in bringing on an attack of asthma some time before it was due, and subsequently, after blindfolding, he passed his finger under the subject's nostrils, and by " reversing the poles " made him smell sulphur or not, at his will. A similar experiment, he tells us, succeeded with a glass of water.

It was by such effects as these, by the physical sensations accompanying the treatment—by the transfer of a pain from head to stomach, from stomach to abdomen and back again to head—rather than by cures which must always remain of dubious interpretation, that Mesmer thought to establish his vaunted discovery.

When Leroy and his colleagues undertook to explain all these sensations as due simply to imagination, Mesmer was confounded. He forgot his resolve not to leave his great discovery to the uncertain arbitrament of the consulting-room, his reluctance to embroil himself with the medical faculty, and he decided against his better judgment to offer the proofs demanded of him. A new medical society had recently been founded in Paris—the Royal Society of Medicine.[1] To this body had been entrusted the duty of licensing patent medi-

---

[1] Though in existence for some time previously, the new body was not formally constituted by letters patent, according to Mesmer (p. 56), until August, 1778.

cines; and they naturally conceived that it was within their province to examine into a new method of treatment. Several of the members—Mauduit, Andrey, Desperrières, and the Abbé Tessier—called upon Mesmer and persuaded him to submit his cases for examination. It was arranged —according to Mesmer's version of the agreement—that every patient who was to be made the subject of a test should be examined, before his treatment, by a doctor of the Faculty, not necessarily a member of the Royal Society. In conformity with this arrangement Mesmer presented to Messrs. Mauduit and Andrey a young girl, the demoiselle L——, who was certified by several physicians and surgeons to be suffering from epilepsy. The two representatives of the Royal Society, not satisfied with a simple inspection of the patient and the certificates offered, some from obscure provincial doctors, wished to inform themselves by further tests of the nature of the disease. Mesmer refused. Nevertheless, at the beginning of May, 1778, he betook himself with several patients to the village of Creteil, two leagues from Paris, and from thence wrote to M. Vicq d'Azir, Secretary of the Royal Society, announcing his intention at a later period, when the cures were completed, of inviting a Commission from that Society to testify to the facts. Meanwhile, in compliance with the understanding above referred to, Mesmer enclosed, for the inspection of the Society, certificates, or diagnoses (*consultations*), signed by doctors of the Faculty. The Secretary in reply intimates that a Commission had already been appointed, in accordance with the Society's understanding of the arrangement, to follow Mesmer's treatment. He is now instructed to withdraw the Commission, to return Mesmer's documents, without breaking the seal of the envelope in which they were enclosed, and to intimate that the Society could not undertake to certify the cure of maladies the existence of which in the first instance it had not been enabled to ascertain.

Mesmer replied to this letter on the 12th of May, 1778. He professed himself desirous at all costs to establish the truth;

and he would have welcomed the proposed visit of the Commissioners, " if I thought that maladies so serious as those which I proposed to treat could be satisfactorily diagnosed by a single inspection, and on the sole statement of the patients themselves." MM. Mauduit and Andrey, members of the Royal Society, agree with him on this point, for when Dame L—— presented her daughter to them, that they might diagnose her ailments,

" these gentlemen replied that they could see that the young woman made convulsive movements, but that these movements were not sufficient in themselves to prove anything. I have taken then, Monsieur, of all possible courses that which seemed the most certain, and at the same time most in accordance with the intentions of the Royal Society, in requiring from the patients, who were good enough to give me their confidence, attestations or diagnoses drawn up and signed by members of the Faculty, and I sent these documents to the Society, in order that it might be in a position to form a judgment as to the cures effected, when time and circumstances permitted of my presenting my patients for examination."

The letter was an adroit move. It was calculated, as indeed Mesmer practically admits, to enlist on his side the Faculty against the new body, whose existence and claims were naturally the subject of considerable jealousy. How far the misunderstanding was wilful on Mesmer's part it is difficult to say. But his account of the matter leaves the impression of a man of boundless self-confidence, of confidence also in the efficacy of his new treatment, but one little likely to be over scrupulous in gaining his ends ; ready to impute the basest motives to his adversaries, and skilled in the arts of sophistry to justify himself not only in the eyes of his disciples, but even in his own. He is the typical case of a man who believes in a half-truth because he chooses to believe, and by his force of will becomes himself the chief of his own dupes.

For the rest, Mesmer's position is intelligible and even in a measure justifiable. If the Royal Society had had their way their selection would probably have been confined to well-marked cases of organic disease ; they would, no doubt, have excluded all ill-defined ailments, and especially all cases in which the symptoms could wholly or in part be attributed to nerves or hysteria. In other words, they would have excluded some nine-tenths of the cures. A modern physician, acquainted with the marvellous effects of hypnotism in some cases of nervous and hysterical ailments, would recognise that a test carried on under such conditions would have been an unfair one. But as against Mesmer's claim, that his treatment worked by physical means alone, and was independent of the patient's imagination, such a process of selection would not have been unfair. If it is desired to test the action of a new physical force, it is clearly essential to eliminate as far as possible the operation of all disturbing agencies, such as "nerves" and imagination.

Receiving no answer to his letter of the 12th of May, Mesmer wrote again to the Royal Society in August. The reply was a definite refusal on the part of the Society to have anything to do with alleged cures the antecedent conditions of which they had not been permitted to investigate. A similar application to the Academy of Sciences remained unanswered. After August, 1778, Mesmer's personal relations with the Academy and the Royal Society were broken off. In September he returned to Paris, retaining the charge of only four patients, and set to work to write his *Memoirs on the Discovery of Animal Magnetism*, which appeared early in the following year. At this period Mesmer made the acquaintance of the celebrated astronomer Bailly, who was subsequently to sit in judgment on his pretensions. Of Bailly's candour and modesty Mesmer speaks in the highest terms. But the most immediately profitable of his new acquaintances was Deslon, physician to the Count d'Artois. Deslon very soon became almost as enthusiastic for the new treatment as Mesmer himself. He arranged that three doctors of the Faculty—Bertrand, Malloët, and Sollier—should pay fortnightly visits to Mesmer's establishment and report on the results of the treatment. The inquiry went on for seven months, but the visiting physicians were not satisfied. Mesmer's account of the manner in which they dealt with the cases submitted to them may be quoted as illustrative of the difficulties in the way of an investigation of this kind, and of the attitude persisted in for generations by the medical profession.

Case 1.—A paralytic who had lost sensation and warmth in the lower half of the body. After eight days' treatment by Mesmer, warmth and sensation were restored.

The restoration of warmth and sensibility does not in itself indicate a cure, said M. Malloët. Moreover, the results may be due to nature alone.

Case. 2.—Affected with paralysis on the entire right side. Was carried to his treatment on a litter. After two months was so far recovered as to discard the litter and walk to the treatment.

The physicians saw nothing remarkable in this case beyond the fact that the hand had made better progress than the foot.

Case 3.—A young girl nearly blind as a sequel to tumours in the breast. After six weeks' treatment her sight was completely restored.

The physicians were agreed that the girl could now see, but were not so sure that six weeks previously she had been blind.

Case 4.—A soldier "obstrue," in his own words, "au point de ne plus penser qu'à la mort"; a month later "ne pense plus qu'à la vie."

The physicians thought that the change might have been brought about by natural causes.

Case 5.—A young girl emaciated by scrofula had already lost the sight of one eye ; the other was covered with ulcers and attacked by a "hernia." Six weeks later she had put on flesh, her eye was free from ulcers, and she could see perfectly with it ; the scrofulous swellings were considerably reduced.

"Wherein," said the physicians, "is the proof that Nature has been aided by Animal Magnetism?"

At their instance Mesmer made repeated experiments, but failed to convince the three physicians that Animal Magnetism could produce any physical effects independently of the imagination of the patient ; and the inquiry came to an inconclusive termination some time in the summer of 1780.

Deslon published in the course of this year his *Observations on Animal Magnetism*, and two or three pamphlets appeared attacking the subject. In the autumn of the same year—1780 —Mesmer, with the aid of Deslon, made a further bid for official recognition. He addressed a Memorial to the Faculty of Medicine, proposing that the Faculty, or Mesmer and the

Faculty jointly, should select twenty-four patients; that the twenty-four patients should then be assigned, by lot, twelve to be treated by Mesmer, twelve by the ordinary practice, and their condition at the end of a reasonable period compared. The whole experiment should be under the joint supervision and control of a committee chosen by the Faculty, Mesmer himself, and Commissioners appointed for the purpose by the Government, the members of which should not belong to any medical body. The Government was to be asked to bear the expense of the experiment. Deslon applied to the Dean of the Faculty to summon a General Meeting, to which he might submit Mesmer's proposals. But some of Deslon's colleagues at the same time took the opportunity of asking for a General Meeting to denounce Deslon for unprofessional conduct. A meeting on the twofold application was appointed for September 18, 1780. The proceedings were begun by a speech from M. Roussel de Vauzèsmes, a brilliant young physician and a bitter opponent of the new treatment. He began by reminding the assembled doctors that in the history of medicine there had been many quacks, who had enjoyed brief notoriety by vaunting a secret remedy. Mesmer's career would, no doubt, have been as short-lived as the rest if he had not unfortunately succeeded in allying with himself a physician of some standing, and a Doctor Regent of the Faculty. He then gave an unflattering sketch of Mesmer's career prior to his coming to Paris. He demonstrated Mesmer's palpable ignorance of physics, and the empty and unscientific nature of his theory of Animal Magnetism.

The speaker then proceeded to accuse Deslon of conduct unworthy of the dignity of his profession, in allying himself with a charlatan who professed to cure by means of a secret universal remedy. Further, Deslon had insulted the scientific world in general and the Faculty in particular; and, lastly, he had propounded principles repugnant to sound medical theory, and had supported them by a recital of impossible cures. De Vauzèsmes went on to deal with Deslon's book, criticising its unprofessional language, and holding up some of the alleged cures to ridicule. In some cases he succeeded in showing that the accounts given of the symptoms were probably exaggerated ; in two cases he was himself acquainted with the patients, and asserted that the cases had been misrepresented by Deslon.

Mesmer had won considerable fame at this time—September, 1780—by the alleged cure of M. Busson, physician to the Countess d'Artois, and as the cure had been publicly announced only a few days before the meeting, de Vauzèsmes felt bound to give his account of the case. M. Busson was attacked by a nasal polypus of enormous proportions. Six physicians, including one of Mesmer's chief opponents, de Horne, had in consultation decided that an operation was inadvisable, but they were unanimously of opinion, according to de Vauzèsmes' that it was possible that a favourable suppuration (*fonte heureuse*) might occur, and the polypus thus disappear in the course of nature.[1] This is de Vauzèsmes, account of the matter. But Burdin and Dubois (*Hist. Acad.*, p. 21) expressly say " les chirurgiens et les médecins les plus habiles la déclarèrent incurable, annonçant que s'il arrivait une fonte, ce serait une fonte de mauvais caractère." What did those six doctors really say ? That we shall probably never know. But it is worth noting that at the time when de Vauzèsmes was speaking M. Busson was alive, and proclaiming himself cured. De Vauzèsmes, therefore, was concerned to show that the improvement in health was due entirely to the recuperative force of nature, and that it had actually been predicted as not improbable. But M. Busson unfortunately died a few days after de Vauzèsmes' speech. The authors of the *Academic History*, writing sixty years after the event, tell us that the attendant physicians and surgeons had foreseen the unfavourable issue ! The judicious reader will, no doubt, conclude that the misrepresentations and perversions of fact in this century-long controversy are not all on the side of the Animal Magnetists.

Deslon's justification of his conduct was ingeniously conceived. He gave a sketch of his relations with Mesmer. The

---

[1] *Précis historique*, p. 150.

two men became acquainted just at the time when Mesmer had definitely broken off his relations with the Academy of Sciences and the Royal Society of Medicine. The first-named body had neglected and practically ignored him. But the Royal Society had gone further; it was impossible for it to ignore a matter so directly within its province as a new discovery in therapeutics. But after undertaking to examine it had, ostensibly because of a technical informality, but actuated really by wounded vanity, broken its engagement, and so put itself wholly in the wrong. Deslon was as anxious as Mesmer that the Magnetic treatment should be fully examined by competent judges, and he felt that the Faculty were the proper persons to undertake the task. But he pointed out that it would not have been judicious to invoke the aid of the Faculty at the date of his first acquaintance with Mesmer, September, 1778. If the Faculty had at that date pronounced in favour of Mesmer's treatment, the Royal Society, which had already usurped so many of the former privileges of the Faculty, would have welcomed the opportunity for still further crushing and humiliating it, and might have done so safely since Mesmer was at that time alone and almost friendless; he had not been sufficiently long in Paris for the benefits of his treatment to be known as they were now known to the public at large. But the last two years had given Mesmer an assured standing, and furnished many incontrovertible proofs of the beneficial nature of his treatment. MM. Malloët, Bertrand, and Sollier were witnesses; and if they had not spoken in favour of Mesmer, they had not ventured to deny the reality of the cures which they had witnessed. The Faculty, said he, had now the opportunity of repairing the serious error committed by the Royal Society, and incidentally of strengthening their own position as against their rivals. It was equally their duty and their interest to endorse Mesmer's claims and to press them upon the consideration of the Government, to whom alone Mesmer was willing to make known his secret.

Deslon, after making his speech, retired whilst the Faculty

deliberated. He was recalled to hear the decision of the meeting, which was couched in four resolutions—

1. A warning to him to be more circumspect in future.

2. Suspension for a year of his power to vote in the meetings.

3. Erasure of his name from the list of Doctors Regent if he had not at the end of a year disavowed his *Observations on Animal Magnetism.*

4. Rejection of Mesmer's proposals.

A year later, when the time came for Deslon's name to be struck off the rolls, he presented himself before the Faculty and boldly proclaimed himself not merely a follower of the Magnetic treatment, but the possessor of his master's secret. Many of his colleagues were tainted with the heresy. Some thirty doctors lay under suspicion, and the Council of the Faculty summoned them to its presence one by one and called upon them to sign, under pain of degradation, an undertaking that they would have nothing to do with Animal Magnetism either in their practice or in their writings. Several of the thirty suspects refused to sign and shared Deslon's fate.[1]

The Royal Society of Medicine had expressed their willingness to investigate, and had only withdrawn from their undertaking when Mesmer had refused to comply with the conditions which seemed to them essential. They were, no doubt, technically justified in their attitude. And in any case, in 1778, the matter was of less importance. Mesmer had yet his reputation to make in Paris. But two years later, when his halls of reception were thronged and all Paris was ringing with his cures, when more than one physician of distinction had been convinced, the need for investigation could scarcely be ignored. It was at this time that the Faculty of Medicine, without even calling for a report from those of their members who had been following the treatment for months, without any facts before them to justify their procedure, and moved apparently solely by the violently partisan denunciation of one of their body who had himself little, if any, first-hand

[1] Bertrand, *Du Magnétisme animal en France,* p. 49.

acquaintance with the facts—it was under such circumstances that the Faculty of Paris not only refused to investigate, but resolved to punish the man who had invited them to discharge a plain duty.[1]

Failing to win the support of any learned Society, Mesmer now resolved to approach the Government direct. He numbered among his patients and partisans many of the nobility and the clergy; the Queen herself was known to be not unfavourable to the pretensions of her fellow-countryman. Negotiations were opened in the first instance through the intermediation of Deslon with Laffonne, physician to their Majesties. A Commission was suggested, but the project, after considerable delay, fell through. Mesmer then threatened to leave Paris and betake himself to Spa. The Queen caused a message to be conveyed to him asking him in the interests of humanity not to desert his patients. Shortly afterwards definite proposals were put before Mesmer by the Government. He was offered a yearly pension of 20,000 livres and a further sum of 10,000 livres to enable him to rent suitable premises for carrying on his treatment. In return he was to instruct in his system three pupils nominated by the Government. Mesmer had privately intimated that instead of an annual rental he would prefer that a certain château, with its demesne, should be placed at his disposal. The Minister, in making the offer above mentioned, intimated that the question of making any further concessions must depend upon the report furnished by the three pupils[2] nominated by the Government. Mesmer professed to find the terms unworthy of the dignity of his great discovery. If the King's advisers did not believe in that discovery, said he, they ought not to offer him so much as 30,000 livres a

[1] Even the authors of the *Academic History* condemn the conduct of the Faculty : "Celle-ci eut le grand tort, l'immense tort de vouloir juger les faits annoncés par Mesmer sans se donner la peine de les examiner préalablement" (p. 13):

[2] Élèves. The word, it should be added, is Mesmer's own. The original proposal, which Mesmer gives in its official form, had suggested the appointment of Commissioners. To meet Mesmer's objection this part of the proposal was withdrawn and pupils were proposed instead.

year. If they did believe in it, the sum was absurdly inadequate. In a letter to the Queen he explained that the austerity of his principles imperiously forbade him to accept the proffered terms. But to her Majesty, he suggests, 400,000 or 500,000 livres more or less would be nothing ; the welfare of the people is everything. His discovery ought to be welcomed and himself recompensed with a munificence worthy of the grandeur of the monarch whom he wished to serve. Meanwhile, in order apparently to afford the Government time for repentance, he promised the Queen that he would not carry out his threat of leaving France until the 18th of September, 1781—the anniversary of the rejection of his proposals by the Faculty.

If Mesmer had calculated on forcing the hand of the Government, he was disappointed. His greed was perhaps too apparent, and no further offer was received from the Minister.

After the end of the year he retired for a time to Spa, where some of his wealthy patients followed him. There he learnt that Deslon after his departure had set up in Paris on his own account an establishment for treatment by Magnetism and that he claimed to have discovered the great secret on which Mesmer set so high a price. Mesmer, we are told, was in despair at what he deemed to be Deslon's treachery. Some of his patients and disciples took the opportunity for making an arrangement with Mesmer. He was to reveal the secret of his discovery to his pupils and to give them a complete course of instruction in the practice of Animal Magnetism. Each pupil undertook to pay 100 louis (2,400 livres), and Mesmer appears to have received a guarantee that the total sum paid him should be not less than 240,000 livres (somewhere about £10,000). In the event he received more than 340,000 livres. The pupils formed themselves into a Society of Harmony and proposed to pass on the lessons which they had learnt and to instruct others in the principles and practice of the new healing. Mesmer vehemently opposed this project. He maintained that they had signed a formal undertaking not to instruct others or to undertake any public treatment of the sick without his express permission. As the price of that permission he required that they should establish centres of Magnetic treatment throughout the provinces and should hand over to him half the fees which they received. Many of his pupils were men of great wealth and position. The first list of members includes four dukes, eight marquises (one of whom was Lafayette), many other noblemen, ambassadors, landed proprietors, officers in the army, abbés, besides many doctors.[1] Naturally they had no desire to become Mesmer's agents. Many of them did not propose to practise for money; the knowledge they had acquired was to be given freely for the benefit of suffering humanity. In the event the discussion became extremely bitter. It was ended by the Society of Harmony meeting and resolving that they were not bound by the agreement upon which Mesmer relied, and thenceforth the members, of whom the Marquis de Puységur was one, held themselves at liberty freely to use the knowledge which they had acquired. The explanation of the misunderstanding shows Mesmer's greed in a most unpleasant light. According to Bertrand, the earliest pupils, eager to begin their course, had, as said, guaranteed to Mesmer the price of one hundred subscriptions. But as it was evident that if any of these earlier pupils prematurely revealed the secret the guarantors would run the risk of losing their money it was agreed, in their own interests, to bind themselves to secrecy until the subscription list was complete. It is scarcely conceivable in any event that the pupils, who were men of honour, should have deliberately cheated Mesmer, or, on the other hand, seeing that many of them were men of affairs, that they should have paid a large sum for a secret which they were unable to use.[2] For the rest, it is noteworthy, as Deleuze has pointed out, that in the midst of this embittered controversy we do not hear that one of the 100 or 150 pupils complained that he had bought the secret too dear. Their eagerness to impart its benefits to

---

[1] See Dureau, *Notes bibliographiques* (1869), p. 32.
[2] Bertrand, *Du Magnétisme animal en France*, p. 57.

others is in itself the strongest proof of the value they set upon it. For them, at any rate, Mesmer's great discovery was not a sham. One exception should be made, however, to this statement. The distinguished chemist Berthollet, himself a Doctor Regent of the Faculty of Medicine, attended Mesmer's course of instruction in the spring of 1784. On the 1st of May he made the following declaration :—

"After having attended more than half of M. Mesmer's course ; after having been admitted to the halls of treatment and of crises, where I have employed myself in making observations and experiments, I declare that I have found no ground for believing in the existence of the agent called by M. Mesmer Animal Magnetism ; that I consider the doctrine taught to us in the course irreconcilable with some of the best established facts in the system of the universe and in the animal economy ; that I have seen nothing in the convulsions, the spasms—in short, in the cures alleged to be produced by the magnetic passes—which could not be attributed entirely to the *imagination*, to the mechanical effect of friction on regions well supplied with nerves, and to that law, long since recognised, which causes an animal to tend to imitate, even involuntarily, the movements of another animal which it sees, trying to place itself in the same position—a law so frequently illustrated by epidemic convulsions. I declare finally that I regard the theory of Animal Magnetism and the practice based upon it as perfectly chimerical ; and I am willing that this declaration should be made use of in any way that may be found desirable.

"BERTHOLLET."

At the very time when Berthollet issued this manifesto an inquisition on the claims of Animal Magnetism was already proceeding. Disquieted at the rapid progress made by the new treatment amongst all classes of society, and notably amongst fashionable folk, alike in Paris and in the provinces, the Government on March 12, 1784, appointed two Commissions to inquire into the matter—one chosen from the Faculty, one from the Royal Society. On the application of the first-named body five members of the Academy of Sciences were joined in the Commission, with four medical representatives. The five members were Benjamin Franklin, Leroy, Bailly, de Bory, and Lavoisier. The four doctors of the Faculty were Majault, Sallin, D'Arcet, and Guillotin. The Commission from the Royal Society pursued its investigations concurrently but independently, and the two Reports were presented almost simultaneously. It was naturally the Report of the first-named Commission, which included some of the most distinguished savants of the day, the Report itself drawn up with great literary skill by Bailly, that drew the public attention. The Report was signed on August 11th, and was immediately printed and circulated throughout the kingdom.

Bailly and his colleagues begin by quoting from Mesmer's propositions (above, p. 38) a description of the fluid into the existence and properties of which it was their duty to inquire. The investigations were to be conducted on Deslon's patients, as Deslon himself accepted Mesmer's statement of the theory of Animal Magnetism.[1] The Commissioners point out that the effects produced by the alleged fluid may be, for the purpose of the inquiry, divided under three heads : (1) the physical effects, (2) the immediate physiological effects produced on the organism of the patient, (3) the therapeutic effects.

1. As regards the first point, they satisfied themselves, by means of an electrometer and an iron needle, that the Baquet was innocent of either electricity or magnetism of the " mineral " kind. No strictly physical proof of the fluid could be obtained. But amongst the patients some professed occasionally to see the fluid streaming from the end of the operator's finger or to feel an impression of cold or heat where the healing stream fell upon the skin. No doubt the Commissioners were perfectly justified in summarily dismissing these statements as of no account. But they would have been wiser not to have given their reasons. Bailly and his colleagues gravely pronounced that the visible emanations were simply the transpiration from the operator's skin, that the feeling of cold was due to the movement of the air caused by the operator's finger, and the impression of heat was

---

[1] The Commissioners do not give their reasons for choosing to study the treatment under the guidance of Deslon rather than of Mesmer himself. Probably the real reason could not be stated so as to avoid giving offence.

simply due to the communication of animal heat from the operator. If this statement was made, as it appears to have been, in the first intention, and not merely as an ironical device for dismissing the allegations in question, it is quite clear that the Commissioners had not taken the trouble to make themselves acquainted at first hand with the subject under discussion, and had so far neglected their duties. A modern student of the subject knows well enough that the explanation given by the Commissioners was irrelevant and ridiculous. All these subjective effects and others more re-markable can safely be ascribed to expectation and imagi-nation on the part of the patient.

3. As regards the therapeutic effects, the Commissioners decided that it would be useless to employ them as a test of the magnetic fluid. In the first place, they pointed out, we know too little about the human economy and about the effect of drugs, to be able with certainty to ascribe any given effect to a given cause. We constantly see what is appar-ently the same disease cured by drugs and treatments of precisely opposite potencies. In the second place, as Mesmer had himself admitted, cures prove nothing, since we can never eliminate the *vis medicatrix naturæ*. To establish any conclusion by the experimental method would require an infinity of lives, and perhaps " the experience of several centuries." As a subsidiary argument they add that it would annoy the distinguished patients who sat round the Baquet to be importuned with questions as to their symptoms.

As the matter was of urgent importance, and time would not permit of the alleged cures being adequately tested, the Commissioners conceived themselves limited to testing the existence of the alleged fluid by its immediate physiological effects, such as pain, shivering, convulsions, stimulation of secretions, &c.—in a word, the crisis with all its accompani-ments and consequents. Their task thus simplified, the Commissioners found little difficulty in showing that the symptoms of the crisis, and the physiological effects of the treatment generally, when not the direct result of

the mechanical processes employed, or the effect of unconscious imitation, could safely be attributed to the imagination
of the patients.   They made several control experiments.
The Commissioners themselves submitted to the treatment,
and selected several other patients, some from the ranks of the
people, some from the higher classes of society, for treatment.
Of fourteen sick persons, nine experienced no effect whatever, and in other cases the effect produced was equivocal.   A
man with an inflamed eye, for instance, felt pain under the
treatment, not in the injured eye, as he should have done
according to the theory, but in the eye which was sound.
The sick children who were magnetised experienced no
effects, because they did not know what to expect.   Again,
the Commissioners found that M. Jumelin, who held a theory
different from Mesmer and Deslon, produced precisely similar
effects, though he took no pains to observe the distinction of
poles in the human body, a precaution which was essential
on the theory of Animal Magnetism.   Finally, they made
several experiments on persons blindfolded, or placed in
front of closed doors, behind which, unknown to the patient,
the operator took his stand.   Sometimes they told the patient
under such conditions that she was being magnetised when
she was not ; sometimes they magnetised her without her
knowledge.   In each case the result followed, not on the
fact, but on the expectation of the patient ; if she believed
herself to be operated upon, she fell into a crisis ; if her
expectation was not excited, she remained calm.   One
experiment of the kind was made at Passy in presence of
Benjamin Franklin, whose health would not permit him to
make the journey to Paris.   Deslon was taken into the
garden, and there magnetised an apricot-tree standing at
a considerable distance from any other tree.   A patient of
his own, a boy of 12, was then introduced, blindfolded.   The
boy was led up to four trees in succession.   He began to
sweat profusely on contact with the first tree, and fell into a
violent crisis at the fourth—never having approached within 24
feet of the tree actually magnetised.   Deslon was compelled
to attribute the result to the natural magnetism of the trees,

reinforced by his own presence (at some distance from the boy) in the orchard !

The Commissioners further point out that imitation undoubtedly played a large part in spreading the more violent movements observed in the crisis; and that the strong and frequently long-continued pressure applied to the region of the stomach and the intestines was in itself a sufficient cause of many of the accompaniments of the crisis; and that from this cause there was reason to fear serious danger both to health and morals. The Report concludes as follows :—

"The Commissioners having found that the Animal Magnetic fluid cannot be perceived by any of our senses, that it has no action either on themselves or on the patients whom they have presented for treatment; being satisfied that the touches and pressure employed are the cause of changes in the organism which are rarely of a favourable character, and are liable to produce a deplorable effect on the imagination; having finally shown by conclusive experiments that the imagination without the aid of Magnetism can produce convulsions, and that Magnetism without the imagination can produce nothing; they have come to the unanimous conclusion, on the question submitted to them of the existence and utility of Animal Magnetism, that there is no proof of the existence of the Animal Magnetic fluid; that this fluid, having no existence, has in consequence no utility; but that the violent effects which are observed in the public treatment are caused by the touches of the operator, the excited imagination of the patient, and by the involuntary instinct of imitation. At the same time they feel compelled to utter a serious warning: that the touches and the repeated stimulation of the imagination in the production of the crisis may prove harmful; that the spectacle of the crisis is equally dangerous, because of the risk of imitation which seems to be a law of nature; and that in consequence all public treatment by Magnetism must in the long run have deplorable consequences."

In a confidential Report to the Government the Commission emphasised the moral dangers likely to result from the practice of Animal Magnetism as at present carried on. The danger is all the greater, they point out, because both physician and patient may be unconscious of its existence.

The Report of the Commission nominated from the Royal Society of Medicine, which appeared five days later, on

August 16th, was to the same effect. Here also great stress was laid upon the mischievous effects likely to follow from the crisis, both on the health of the individual and, by the contagion of example, on others. The Royal Society had not, however, felt itself precluded from making observations on the state of the patients under treatment by Deslon ; they give in brief the result of four months' experience. The patients are divided into three classes :—

1. Les malades dont les maux étaient évidents et avaient une cause connue.

2. Ceux dont les maux légers consistaient en des affections vagues, sans cause déterminée.

3. Les melancoliques.

To the lay mind the classification is not exhaustive. Even in the present state of medical science it is possible for a man to be seriously and unmistakably ill without any agreement of the doctors as to the precise cause, or to have a comparatively slight ailment of a perfectly definite and recognised character. And, as will be seen from the account given in Chapter I., there were at the time of the Commission's visits many patients of both these classes undergoing treatment and being cured. However the Commissioners report that as regards the first class—definite maladies—they observed no case of cure, or even appreciable improvement. The third class, melancholia, is dismissed in a sentence. But of the second class many professed to find their health better, their digestion improved, &c.

These results the Commissioners attribute to three causes —hope, regular exercise, and abstinence from the remedies which they had previously taken. The last is a strange reason to proceed from the mouth of a committee of doctors. But no doubt there was some truth in the reason given, especially if we remember that amongst the remedies thus discontinued were included in some cases the cupping-glass and the moxa.

One of the five Commissioners chosen from the Royal Society of Medicine, M. de Jussieu, issued a separate Report on his own account. His Report is noteworthy in several respects. As will be shown later, he proved himself a better observer than his colleagues. Moreover, his conclusion on the curative effect of the treatment differs from theirs. He agrees that the repeated crises are probably injurious to the patient in many cases, especially in phthisis. He finds it almost impossible from his own observation to establish any real improvement in the majority of the cases treated. But in some cases he is satisfied that favourable changes had occurred during the few weeks or months in which he was able to watch the treatment. Amongst these were several patients whose eyes were affected. In one instance, the eyes of the patient were covered—"a la suite d'un lait repandu"—with films so thick that the iris could not be discerned when she first came for treatment in May. The disease had lasted for five years. After treatment for a few weeks the outlines of the iris could be seen and the patient could distinguish colours and make out some objects held three inches from her eyes. In another case a washerwoman had injured her arm in lifting a heavy tub; she had tried various treatments without relief for more than a year. When she came to Deslon the whole shoulder was swollen and painful, and she could not move the arm at either the shoulder or the elbow-joint. The hand and fingers she could move with some difficulty. The pain in her shoulder was continuous, and interfered with her sleep. In the first few days of the treatment the pain was lessened, and some hours of quiet sleep ensued each night. The last time that de Jussieu saw her, after five weeks' treatment, the case had made such progress that the patient could lift her hand to her head.

De Jussieu's conclusion is that imagination, unwonted exercise, freedom from drugs, and the other incidental advantages of the Magnetic treatment, are not in themselves sufficient to account for all the facts observed. He finds traces of some real and continuous cause operating, and he is inclined to identify this cause with the animal heat. But the animal heat which de Jussieu imagines is an agent almost as transcendental and far-reaching as Mesmer's magnetic fluid. The important point in his theory, which distinguishes it from Mesmer's conception, as expressed in the propositions, of an indifferent mechanical fluid, is that he conceives the operation of the animal heat—the principle of vitality—to be directed and intensified by the will.   In the recognition of the human element we find the beginnings of the true scientific explanation.

CHAPTER IV

THE DISCOVERY OF SOMNAMBULISM

Shortcomings of Bailly's Report—A thing which does not exist may yet be useful—Replies : *Doutes d'un Provincial*—The case of Court de Gébelin—Reports from provincial doctors. The Marquis de Puységur —His discovery of Somnambulism—Somnambulic diagnosis and " predictions "—The theory of a vital fluid—The tree at Busancy. Mesmer's real secret—Believe and Will—Observations of Tardy de Montravel, Pététin, Deleuze—Influence of the magnetic fluid in stimulating the intellectual functions.

PERHAPS the worst that can be said of Bailly's Report is that the Commission insisted on too narrow an interpretation of their mandate. The task imposed upon them by Government was obviously distasteful, and they were glad to rid themselves of it as speedily as was consistent with their duty.   Mesmer, whatever else we may believe him to have been, was unquestionably a quack and a charlatan.   His belief in his vaunted discovery was, no doubt, genuine, but his enthusiasm was certainly not altogether disinterested.   The throng of fashionable folk displaying their hysterical antics round the magnetic trough was a spectacle as futile to science as it was repulsive to common sense. *The distinguished patients could not be questioned too closely without risk of annoying them.* This one sentence serves to illustrate the attitude of the Commission.   The thing to them was not a matter for serious investigation, but a fashionable craze, one more folly of the idle rich, of the representatives of the Court, the old nobility, and the clergy— all the elements in the State which were most repugnant to the spirit of the new age, even then swelling to the flood that should sweep them away.

Moreover, the theory of Animal Magnetism bore on the face of it the proof of its pedigree. It was easy enough to show that this belated survival from the pre-scientific ages was as vain a thing as the secret of Hermes Trismegistus, and that the pretended proofs existed only in the imagination of its dupes. But if the "magnetic" fluid did not exist, the Commissioners were dispensed from fulfilling the second part of their commission—the inquiry into its utility. "A thing which does not exist," said they, "can have no utility." The logic seems incontrovertible. But one remembers that science has been defined as insatiable curiosity, and it would have been better for their reputation if Bailly and his colleagues had not allowed their intellectual fastidiousness to stifle their natural instincts. It may have been true that many of the patients owed their improved health to having escaped from the ordinary medical treatment of the day, and that, in any case, medical science is not to be judged by results. But these were dangerous admissions for doctors to make. Some one maliciously remarked that it seemed to follow that medicine and the art of healing were two distinct sciences, without any necessary connection between them.[1] After all, it is the duty of the physician to cure disease, and if imagination could be proved to effect that end, it might have been worth while to inquire how so beneficial an agency could best be directed. The Commissioners might then have discovered that a thing which does not exist may yet possess utility.

It is impossible to acquit the Commissioners of prejudice in the manner in which they fulfilled their task—the prejudice not only of doctors faced with the pretensions of quackery, but of men, informed by the new spirit of enlightenment and freedom, confronted with the futilities of the old order and the follies of mediæval superstition.

It may be pointed out, · further, that there was a curious infelicity in the use made by the Commissioners of the word

[1] Bergasse, *Considérations sur le Magnétisme animal*, p. 21.

"imagination." The purely subjective sensations experienced by some of the patients—the stream of light from the operator's fingers, the feelings of heat and cold, the smell of sulphur—all these were ascribed by them to physical causes, though the most superficial investigation of the actual facts would have sufficed to convince them that the effects did not correspond to the causes alleged. The word "imagination" might appropriately have occurred in this connection, where the Commissioners, unhappily for their own reputation, did not employ it. For these sensations began and ended in the imagination. They corresponded to no external reality and perished in the moment of their birth. When we have said that they were imaginary, we have said all that needs to be said. But when the Commissioners ascribed the crises and the cures to the imagination the explanation is obviously incomplete. It may be that here also the starting-point was to be sought in the imagination. But the process did not end there. The effects produced—whether transitory convulsions or salutary functional changes—were real and frequently of a more or less permanent character. In dismissing them from consideration as merely due to the imagination the Commissioners were paying themselves with words.

The numerous replies and commentaries which appeared in the course of the few months immediately following the publication of the reports naturally concerned themselves mainly with this question of the reality of the cures. One of these, the *Supplément aux deux Rapports*, as shown in Chapter I., furnished a notable list of cures actually effected under the Magnetic treatment. Naturally enough those who had been cured repudiated, some with elaborate irony, some with emphatically expressed contempt, the Commissioners' explanation that the cures were due to imagination. Says one:—

"Si c'est à l'illusion que je dois la santé dont je crois jouir, je supplie humblement les savants, qui voyent si clair, de ne le pas détruire ; qu'ils illuminent l'univers, qu'ils me laissent mon erreur, et qu'ils permettent à ma simplicité, à ma faiblesse et a mon ignorance de faire usage d'un *agent invisible et qui n'existe pas, mais qui me guérit*" (p. 30).

F

No doubt Deslon's patients were deceived in their belief in the invisible fluid. But this error was more venial and probably less mischievous than the incuriosity of the Commissioners. After all, whatever the explanation, they had been cured.

But the most famous and probably not the least effective of the replies was the *Doutes d'un Provincial*, whose author is understood to have been M. Servan, formerly advocate-general to the Parlement of Grenoble.[1] He had himself found relief through Animal Magnetism after twenty years' ineffectual treatment by ordinary medicine, and on this he based his claim to be heard. He begins by correcting the Commissioners on one or two matters of fact. Their Report gives the impression that the convulsive crises were a general feature of the cure ; but in the provinces, the author asserts, out of fifty patients not more than five or six will experience convulsions, and those of a sufficiently mild type. In the eyes of the provincial, again, the sneer at the distinguished patients seems curiously out of place. His heart has been warmed by seeing gathered round the Baquet persons of all ranks of society—" le spectacle de l'égalité originelle des hommes et de la bienveillance que je veux leur croire naturelle." For the rest he criticises with shrewdness and humour the conduct of the inquiry by the Commission, especially their refusal to judge Animal Magnetism by its cures, and their insistence on the production of immediate physiological results. In his view the facts and the reasonings of the Report are alike distorted by pro-fessional prejudice. On first reading, he tells the Com-missioners, he doubted what he had seen with his own eyes ; then he began to doubt what the Commissioners had seen—" ensuite j'allai jusqu' à douter sur ce que vous aviez voulu voir." And this delicate inquiry into the pretensions of a rival system had been entrusted, he points out, to the hands of medical men, members of the profession which had obstinately refused to accept the proofs of the circulation of the blood ; which had rejected the use of emetics ; which had

[1] Deleuze, *Histoire Critique,* ii. 58.

treated as rubbish the quinine for which they now ransacked a whole continent; which had made itself the laughing-stock of Europe and Asia by opposing the practice of inoculation; which, in a word, had consistently set its face against every new thing—condemning in its day even the *petits pains* which every doctor now consumes for breakfast. Suppose, the provincial suggests, that the inquiry had been concerned with the practice of medicine instead of with that of Animal Magnetism; that the action of drugs had been judged in every case by their immediate effects; and that in the treatment of cases every result which could be attributed to the imagination or to Nature had been eliminated; suppose, in a word, that the Commissioners themselves had been the subject of inquiry, and the judges had been chosen from the ranks of their own patients—"juste ciel, quel rapport ils eussent pu faire!"

Finally, the provincial asks indulgence as one who has suffered much for twenty years at the hands of doctors; they had failed to cure either the ills of Nature or the ills wrought by their own remedies. You have sought to dismiss Animal Magnetism, he says to the Commissioners, as an illusion: "Non, Messieurs, non. Vous n'avez point assez apprécié même une chimère qui nous garantit de vos funestes réalités: sous ce point de vue, le Magnétisme animal étoit en physique la plus utile des erreurs, comme peutêtre l'instinct de la bienveillance l'est en morale."

The other side of the question is presented in a Report drawn up by Thouret, and read before the Royal Society of Medicine early in November of the same year, 1784.[1] The Report is based upon communications received from medical men in the provinces relating to the spread of Animal Magnetism. Already we find centres of treatment established in many of the more considerable towns in France. Naturally the medical correspondents of the Royal Society of Medicine have no good to say of the new treatment. If they were inclined to look upon it with favour they would certainly not have betrayed their unprofessional

[1] Reprinted by Burdin and Dubois in the *Hist. acad.*, pp. 190–236.

weakness at headquarters. The Report is of value precisely because these interested witnesses have so few definite facts to urge against the treatment. The instances cited are mostly on the principle already demonstrated in the case of Court de Gébelin—"heads I win, tails you lose." Court de Gébelin, author of *Le Monde primitif*, having been seriously ill for six months, and finding no relief in ordinary medicine, went to Mesmer in March, 1783, and soon afterwards sent a circular letter to the subscribers to his book, announcing his complete restoration to health. The physicians were unanimous in asserting that de Gébelin had never been really ill. A year later he had to return to Mesmer for further treatment, and died in May, 1784, from kidney disease. The physicians were now agreed that he had never been really cured. Thus M. Thers relates the treatment of a case of dropsy by Magnetism. The cure was complete at the end of July and the patient died in October. He infers that the cure was only apparent, and that even the appearance was due to the milk diet prescribed. Another, a full-blooded patient—*sujet a une humeur vague*— who was undergoing treatment by cautery, was persuaded to give up the cautery and try the Baquet. He died in a few days of apoplexy. The inference is that the substitution of Animal Magnetism for the beneficent processes of orthodox medicine proved fatal to the patient. There is but one serious testimony against Animal Magnetism, and for that M. Thouret had to go as far as Malta. He learns from an Italian physician that six physicians and surgeons in that island had selected for observation twenty-five patients who were undergoing treatment by Magnetism. The selection included persons blind from birth, cases of "obstruction," rheumatism, epilepsy, hypochondria, paralysis, hysteria, and cancer in the breast. After seventy days' treatment some were found to be worse ; some remained the same ; a few declared themselves better, but afterwards relapsed into a worse state than before. It is obvious that such a statement from prejudiced witnesses, dealing with patients selected by themselves, is worth very little. The comparative method suggested by Mesmer would at least have yielded results less open to question.   For the rest, the doctors who came forward to give their testimony are contented with vague statements; they have never seen any real cures, though the public unfortunately still flock to the Baquet, and the treatment has the regrettable effect of giving their patients a distaste for ordinary medical practice—*e.g.*, the cautery!   One witness, however, M. Pujol, more candid than the rest, not only admits the reality of some of the cures, but admits also that they cannot be attributed wholly to the *vis medicatrix naturæ*.   It is the enthusiasm that Mesmer inspires, said he, which effects these cures.   " C'est la précisément la base du mesmérisme et tout le secret du magnétisme animal."

M. Pujol, no doubt, came very near the truth, as near as the facts then known would permit.   For at that date there was no evidence of any special psychological effects produced by the mesmeric treatment.   Probably what will most strike the modern student, in reading the Reports of 1784, is that the Commissioners, in the course of the five months over which their inquiry extended, found so little to excite their curiosity. Apart from its curative effects, and its influence on the animal functions, hypnotism at the present day, as the audience of any itinerant lecturer can testify, offers many features of a most surprising kind.   Amongst the more salient of these effects are perversion of sensation and somnambulism.   Under the influence of suggestion the operator can cause a good subject to see, taste, or feel whatever he chooses, or at his will can suspend sensation altogether.   Many of us have seen a boy inhaling pepper or ammonia under the belief that it was lavender-water, without sneezing or watering of the eyes ; or, again, have seen the subject suffer the pressure of a finger on his eyeball without movement of any kind, and endure the contact of a flame or a smart electric shock without betraying any sign of discomfort.   But facts such as these the Commissioners of 1784 apparently had no opportunity of observing. Indeed, the existence of induced anæsthesia does not seem to have attracted notice until a much later period.   It was demonstrated in Paris hospitals in 1820 and 1821, but it was still a theme of hot debate in our own country thirty years later, and it was not finally accepted as a fact until the revival of hypnotism in the present generation.

But if the contempt which the Commissioners were at no pains to disguise had left them free to observe, they might have made, as one of their number actually did, a discovery of another kind. The state of induced somnambulism had been recognised, at the time of the Commission's investigation, only by one observer, Puységur, and his observations were not made public property until after the appearance of the Reports. But from the frequent occurrence in the course of 1785 of the somnambulic trance, it seems probable that the state, though unrecognised, was not uncommon even before that date. And de Jussieu actually records in his Report, though without appreciating its significance, a case observed by himself :—

"A young man who was frequently in a state of crisis became in that state quite silent, and would go quickly through the hall, often touching the patients. These regular touches of his often brought about a crisis, of which he would take control without allowing any one to interfere. When he returned to his normal condition he would talk again, but he did not remember anything that had taken place, and no longer knew how to magnetise. I draw no conclusion from this fact, of which I was a witness on several occasions."

If the other Commissioners had proved themselves as free from prejudice as their colleague, the Reports of 1784 might have been more fruitful. The discovery of the state of artificial somnambulism and of the remarkable effects of hypnotic suggestion would have been no unworthy addition even to Lavoisier's fame.

Whatever effect the Reports of 1784 may have had in dis-crediting Animal Magnetism in the eyes of the Faculty and the "intellectuals" generally, they seem to have done little to check its progress in the country at large. Already Mesmer is said to have instructed 300 pupils, most of them physicians or men of science, and Deslon claimed 160 medical pupils.[1] The Central Society of Harmony at about this date

[1] *Supplément aux deux Rapports*, p. 80.

numbered 430 persons, of whom 90 were physicians.[1] Most
towns in France of any importance, except, indeed, as the
authors of the *Histoire académique* tell us, the University
towns, had in 1784 a centre for Magnetic treatment.[2] The
fame of Mesmer had indeed spread over the civilised world,
and we hear of societies for studying Animal Magnetism
being founded at Turin, Berne, Malta, and in the French
West Indies.[3] It had also spread to Germany and Sweden.
Some of the provincial Societies of Harmony attained to
considerable proportions ; that at Strasbourg, founded in
1785 by Puységur, appears to have lasted at any rate to the
Revolution, and published three volumes of *Proceedings*.

The Marquis de Puységur was one of those who had paid
his hundred louis to learn what Mesmer had to teach. In the
early spring of 1784, after having attended the Master's
course of instructions, but having failed, as he tells us later,
to apprehend the great secret, he retired to his own estate of
Busancy, near Soissons, proposing, though without any great
hope of a favourable result, to employ the methods he had
learnt for the relief of the suffering. From the first he viewed
with dislike and suspicion the crisis attended with violent
convulsions which he had witnessed at Mesmer's establishment, and deplored the discredit which the spectacle of this
enfer à convulsions, as he calls it, had brought upon the
practice of Animal Magnetism.

He attributes these violent crises in the first instance to
the circumstance that Mesmer had too many patients to look
after single-handed, and was obliged, therefore, to allow the
crisis to work itself out without the guidance and the quieting
influence of the operator.[4] Accident revealed to Puységur
other characteristics of the crisis which the convulsions and
general disorder of the Salle aux Crises had served to mask.

[1] Dureau, *op. cit.*, p. 33.

[2] *Hist. acad.*, p. 218.

[3] Bergasse, *Considérations sur le Magnétisme animal*.

[4] *Mémoires pour servir*, &c. (second edition), p. 110. The first edition
appeared in December, 1784, and Puységur, therefore, in his condemnation of the crisis, anticipated Bailly and his colleagues, just as in
his discovery of somnambulism he anticipated de Jussieu.

His first patients were two women on his estate, who were suffering from toothache. His success in curing them without crisis, and after manipulation in each case for a few minutes only, encouraged him to essay the treatment of a young peasant of twenty-three named Victor, who had been confined to his bed for four days with inflammation of the lungs (*fluxion de poitrine*). Puységur visited the patient at 8 p.m., and found the fever already diminishing :—

"After having made him get up," he writes to a correspondent, "I magnetised him. What was my surprise, after seven or eight minutes, to see the man go to sleep quietly in my arms, without any convulsion or pain. I accelerated the crisis and brought on delirium ; he talked, discussed his business aloud. When it seemed to me that his thoughts were affecting him for the worse I tried to divert them to lighter themes ; the attempt cost me no great trouble ; I soon saw him quite happy in the belief that he was shooting for a prize, dancing at a fête, and so on."

Puységur was struck by the fact that this simple-minded peasant, "*le plus borné du pays*," who in the natural state hardly knew how to converse with his superiors, assumed in the trance an altogether different character. He was able even to speak freely and in appropriate language. In his normal state he could find no words to express his gratitude to Puységur and the Marquise, but when somnambulic his tongue was loosed. Further, his intelligence was enhanced : "quand il est en crise, je ne connois rien de plus *profond*, de plus *prudent* et de plus *clairvoyant*." Puységur soon found to his astonishment that his patient when awake could recollect nothing of what had taken place in the trance. One day Victor had in the trance spoken freely of his personal affairs, and had entrusted to Puységur's keeping a paper of some importance. The following day Puységur found him in a state of some distress, and learnt on questioning him that he had been searching vainly all day for this very paper. Another patient, a young Parisian student of nineteen, refused to believe that he had really walked about in the state of somnambulism, and, to test the matter, tied himself with elaborately knotted ropes to his chair. As soon as he was entranced Puységur made him untie the ropes and seat himself in another chair, and was much astonished at the young fellow's incredulous stare when he came to himself.

"The line of demarcation," says he, "is so complete that these two states may almost be described as two different existences. I have noticed that in the magnetic state the patients have a clear recollection of all their doings in the normal state ; but in the normal state they can recall nothing of what has taken place in the magnetic condition."[1]

The state of induced somnambulism, with the remarkable division of memory described by Puységur, is, of course, fully recognised at the present day, though it has taken more than three generations to establish its existence. But Puységur found in his somnambulic patients many wonderful faculties of a more dubious kind. Most of them, he tells us. were able to diagnose the nature of their ailments, to prescribe the appropriate treatment, and to foretell the course of the disease and the date of the final cure. A single illustration must suffice. Henri Joseph Claude Joly was a young man of nineteen. Up to the age of seventeen he had been a student at the College of Louis le Grand, in Paris, until his increasing deafness—due to a severe illness in his childhood —forced him to relinquish his studies. He came to Puységur for treatment on Wednesday, October 13, 1784. He went into trance on the 14th. On the 15th he began to tell Puységur about the nature of his ailment and its probable course. He explained that he had a gathering (*depôt*) in his head, and would suffer much before it could be discharged. If it discharged into the throat he would die, but if by the nose, he would be cured and would regain his hearing. He was not at the moment—the third day of the treatment— sufficiently advanced to say more. On the Sunday evening, however, he felt that the gathering was dividing in half, and announced that it would discharge by the nose in two portions—one on the Monday, the second sŏmewhat later. In effect, on his return from a ride on the following day, Joly announced that there had been a copious discharge of matter

[1] *Mémoires pour Servir* (ed. of 1809), vol. i. p. 103.

from his nose. On the Wednesday morning, in the trance, he announced that the second discharge would take place by the nose on Thursday evening, but that he would suffer much in the interval, and would have severe crises every two hours. The predicted crises, which took the form of violent convulsions, punctually fulfilled themselves, somewhat to Puységur's alarm, every two hours (with the intermission of some hours at night, whilst the patient slept). The crisis due at 7 p.m. on Thursday came half an hour late, and shortly after it had ceased Puységur and his friends, who were watching in the room next to that in which the patient lay in bed, were aroused by a slight movement, and found that the predicted discharge was just taking place. From that moment the patient was cured, and left with the intention of resuming his studies. The existence of the ailment and the completeness of the cure in this case are formally attested, under the municipal seal of Dormans in Champagne, the patient's native place, by the mayor of the town and many of the principal inhabitants, including several seigneurs, curés, councillors, and a procureur fiscal.

Another remarkable faculty which Puységur claimed for his somnambulists was that of being able to diagnose and prescribe for the ailments of others. Victor, the first somnambule, was employed regularly by Puységur in consultation on the other patients ; Puységur almost regrets his cure, since it will mean the loss of his advice. But other somnambulic clairvoyants were soon found to take his place. Joly, who was frequently employed in this way during the few days of his own treatment, explained to Puységur that his diagnosis was founded on actual sensations experienced by himself in the part of his body corresponding to the part affected in the others. In the same way, he explained, the power of predicting the course of his own malady rested not on any process of reasoning, but on what might be called presentiment (*pressensation*).

An illustration may be quoted to show how this claim to diagnose maladies impressed spectators. M. Cloquet, a collector of taxes in Soissons, had at Puységur's request come over in June to see the Magnetic treatment. After watching for some time the somnambules going about and prescribing for the patients, he resolved to test the matter on his own account :—

" I got one of the 'doctors' (sc. somnambules) to touch me," he writes. "She was a woman of about fifty. I had certainly told no one the nature of my ailment. After paying particular attention to my head, the woman said that I often suffered pain there, and that I had constantly a buzzing in my ears—this was true. A young man who had been an incredulous spectator of my experiment then submitted himself for examination. He was told that he suffered from the stomach, and that he had obstructions (*engorgements*) in the abdomen, arising from an illness which he had had some years previously. All this, he told us, was correct. But, not content with this soothsayer, he went straight away to another 'doctor,' 20 feet distant, and was told exactly the same. I never saw anybody so dumfounded with astonish-ment as this young man, who had assuredly come to ridicule rather than to be convinced." [1]

For all those who accepted Animal Magnetism there was at this date but one theory, variously modified, to account for the phenomena—the theory of a fluid. By Jumelin and de Jussieu this fluid was identified with the vital heat, or rather with the cause of vital heat. But in de Jussieu's detailed statement his theory seems to be well nigh as all-embracing as Mesmer's own. The principle which gives movement to the whole Universe, he says, becomes manifest in a living body by the vital heat. And it is from the efforts to produce equilibrium of this fluid that all the manifesta-tions of Animal Magnetism are due. Puységur re-states the theory, but it is essentially the same. The earth and all the celestial bodies, he writes, rotating continually in the midst of the universal fluid, continually generate electricity. This electricity is modified according to the nature of the sub-stance which receives it, and especially bv the human body, which may be described as the most perfect electric machine in existence.[2] This is the principle of movement in all

[1] From a contemporary letter, quoted by Bertrand, *Du Magnétisme animal*, p. 222.

[2] *Mémoires* (2nd ed.), 1809, vol. i. p. 25. The first edition was pub-lished in 1784.

nature—the principle of chemical affinity, the principle of reproduction in the vegetable and animal kingdom. He illustrates its special action in disease by various metaphors. A sick person in the state of somnambulism is like a magnetic needle replaced on its pivot. Or, again, the healthy man is like a vase in connection with an inexhaustible reservoir of the fluid. The channel of connection is unobstructed, and the vase is always full to the utmost limit of its capacity. In the sick man the channel with the universal is obstructed. The magnetist opens a channel between himself and the sick man, who then receives his fill, while the level in the other remains unaltered. The fluid itself Puységur is inclined to identify with dephlogisticated air, the recent discovery which had set the scientific world in a ferment.

Acting on the idea that it was only necessary to open a channel in order to set the fluid in motion, Puységur proceeded to magnetise a large tree, to serve as a Baquet, and attached to it a cord for the patients to fasten round their bodies. The experiment was a great success. Writing on the 17th of May to his brother, he says that more than 130 persons had congregated round it that morning: " The tree is the best Baquet possible ; every leaf radiates health ; and all who come experience its salutary influence." M. Cloquet, already quoted, gives us a contemporary picture. Says he :—

" Picture to yourself the village *place*. In the middle is an elm, with a spring of clear water at its foot. It is a huge old tree, but still green and vigorous ; it is a tree held in respect by the elders, who are wont to meet at its foot on holiday mornings to talk over the crops and the market prospects. It is a tree dear to the young folk, who assemble there in summer evenings for their rustic dances. This tree, magnetised from time immemorial by the love of pleasure, is now magnetised by the love of humanity. M. Puységur and his brother have given it a healing virtue which penetrates everywhere."

He goes on to describe the stone benches, on which the patients sit round the tree ; the encircling rope ; the chain made by interlacing thumbs ; and, the climax of the drama, Puységur choosing out some of the patients, and sending them into the somnambulic state by the touch of his hand or the direction of his magic wand.

But Puységur soon saw reason to modify the purely physical theory which we find set out in Mesmer's own writings. In his address at the foundation of the Society of Harmony at Strasbourg in 1785 he tells us that after attending Mesmer's expensive course of instruction he departed almost as ignorant as he came. He had learnt the theory of Animal Magnetism and the kinship of man with the planets, but no more. His brother, who had attended the same course, had soon discovered the real principle at work, but felt himself bound in honour to Mesmer to guard the secret. It was Puységur's first somnambule, Victor, who revealed to him the mystery. The whole secret of Animal Magnetism, Puységur assured his hearers, lay in these two words—*Croyez et Veuillez*—Believe and Will.[1] In his later work the doctrine of a universal fluid has become already only a working hypothesis. It may or may not be true. The one thing which is certain is the existence of a force by which the soul can work upon the bodily organism. As God directs and sustains the motion of the planets, so man directs and sustains the motion of his own body. Further, by the exercise of his will, the magnetist can influence the principle of life in another. "Animal Magnetism does not consist in the action of one body upon another, but in the action of the thought upon the vital principle of the body."[2] Its action upon the patient consists in reinforcing this vital principle in his organism. For this reason it is not necessary for the operator to know the nature of the malady, or even the internal anatomy of the body. It is enough that he should have a firm will to influence the principle of life. It is thought which moves matter, even as the Strasbourg Society inscribed on the walls of its hall of treatment Virgil's mighty line—

" Mens agitat molem et magno se corpore miscet."

---

[1] *Du Magnétisme animal* (Paris, 1807). See esp. pp. 30, 142, 149.
[2] *Ibid.*, p. 163.

This recognition of the part played by the will in the process of Magnetism was, then, the great secret on which Mesmer set so high a price, and which, if we believe Puységur, he refused to surrender to those who had paid the price. But the book in which Puységur announced this modification of his theory was not published until 1807 ; and most of his contemporaries, not only in 1785, but later, even if they shared his views on the need of a directing will, emphasised by preference the physical side of the theory. They accumulated proofs of the analogy of the fluid operating in Animal Magnetism with that supposed to emanate from the mineral magnet and with the other fluids known to the science of the day—electric, light and heat bearing. Some somnambules could see the fluid radiating as a brilliant shaft of light from the person of the operator ; one of Tardy de Montravel's subjects saw his hair shining like threads of gold. They would see it radiating from trees and other living objects, and would note differences in colour and brightness according to the diverse sources. There was a magnetic effluence from the sun, and yet another differing in glory from the earth. The fluid could be seen passing into water or milk ; the liquid would then become luminous ; magnetised milk could be retained by a stomach which would at once reject all other forms of nourishment. Iron was found to conduct the magnetic current; glass, Puységur found, would even augment it ; wax or copper dispersed it, and silver reflected it back upon the rod. Mesmer had already discovered that the fluid was reflected by a mirror ; and we know from old ecclesiastical carvings that the baleful stream from the eyes of the basilisk could by means of a mirror be turned back on the reptile to its own destruction. But Tardy de Montravel bettered this observation. It was not the glass of the mirror, which was already proved to act as a conductor, but the metal backing which operated in the reflection.[1]

Of other phenomena described by the early Magnetists many were grouped under the general name of *rapport*. The idea of a reciprocal influence between physician and patient,

[1] *Essai sur la Théorie du Somnambulisme magnétique*, 1785.

as shown in a previous chapter, was a prominent feature in the sympathetic system. Mesmer's early disciples, inheriting the older tradition, naturally found proofs of *rapport* amongst their subjects ; for in this study, whether we call it by the name of Animal Magnetism, Hypnotism, or Suggestion, the student always finds what he looks for. As soon as the practice of Magnetism passed from the public phase, with which it began in Mesmer's Salle aux Crises, and individual treatment became the rule, *rapport* became prominent. The magnetic subject, it was soon found, could hear no voice but that of the operator, could feel no touch and obey no influence but his. Puységur, indeed, gives the existence of exclusive *rapport* between operator and subject as the surest test of the magnetic state.[1]

Other surprising phenomena attested by the early Magnetists are ascribed to the same fluid. The subject, it was found, in the somnambulic state would obey the slightest gesture or even the silent will of the operator. She would move about the room and stay her steps, in accordance with his unexpressed desire. She would go up to an object and touch it if the operator merely directed his eyes towards it.[2] Some of the spectators asserted that Puységur claimed this "magnetic mobility" as due to thought-reading on the part of the subject. "Not at all," said Puységur ; "when Madeleine obeys my silent will, it is the fluid directed by my will that causes the movement; she is herself only an animated magnet."[3]

One of Tardy's subjects would go through the town with her eyes closed, and guide herself safely. Further, when in the trance she would examine objects handed to her by placing them on the pit of the stomach. Her sense of hearing was also transferred to the same region ; and Tardy found it necessary to address his remarks to the epigastrium. Tardy is unable, however, to hit upon a satisfactory explanation of this curious phenomenon.[4]

[1] *Mémoires*, &c., vol. i. p. 192. See also Tardy, *op. cit.*, p. 67.
[2] Puységur, *Du Magnétisme animal*, p. 20.
[3] *Mémoires*, vol. ii. pp. 12, 15, &c.
[4] *Op. cit.*, p. 66, &c.

No limit was assigned by the early Magnetists to the operation of the fluid. Some of the peasants who came to see Puységur at Busancy fell into a crisis as soon as they set out on the road when still a great way off. A manifest proof, says Puységur, of the efficacy of the will in directing the fluid even at a considerable distance.[1] In October, 1785, one Beatrix, a captain of artillery stationed at Metz, was directed by one of his patients to magnetise her at midnight when she was asleep in her own house. The husband, who carefully watched the while, inferred, from the remarks made by his wife and her movements, that she was in a veritable crisis. Captain Beatrix is quite satisfied that the crisis was due to his own magnetism from a distance, and Puységur is inclined to agree.[2]

Yet another theory of the physical forces at work in the induced trance was advanced at a somewhat later period by a medical man who rejects the term " Animal Magnetism " altogether. J. H. Désiré Petetin, a doctor practising at Lyons, was perpetual president of the Medical Society of that city, and held several appointments from the Government. Shortly after his death, in February, 1808, was published his book, *Électricité animale*, in which he records observations which he had made for many years past on several cases of spontaneous catalepsy. The disease is, of course, a rare one, and it is remarkable, as Bertrand has pointed out, that a single provincial practitioner should have come across no fewer than eight cases in one district. It is but one more illustration of the truth that in this region the student always finds what he seeks. In no other field of human activity can the imagination with equal truth be styled creative. For the rest, Petetin's patients would, no doubt, nowadays be classed as hysterical—they were all women, mostly under twenty years of age.

The phenomena which Petetin's subjects presented were very remarkable. In the cataleptic state the patient generally remains motionless, and gives often hardly any sign of life at

[1] Quoted by Bertrand, *Du Magnétisme animal en France*, p. xxi.
[2] Letter to Puységur, quoted in *Du Magnétisme animal* (1807), p. 279.

all, pulse and respiration being alike almost imperceptible. Petetin found that his patients, though they would show no signs of intelligence if questions were directed in the usual way to their ears, would answer either by voice or gesture if the speaker addressed himself to the pit of the stomach, the tips of the fingers, or sometimes even the toes. Not only so, but they would appear to taste, smell, and even see with those parts of the body. Petetin gives details of several occasions on which his patients were able to describe medals, letters, playing cards, and other small objects placed under the bedclothes on the epigastric region, or even hidden in the pockets of the interlocutor. His explanation of these curious manifestations is again a purely physical one, and rests on a theory of Animal Electricity which, from our standpoint, does not differ essentially from the hypothesis of Animal Magnetism. His observations seemed to afford him abundant proof that the phenomena depended on electrical action. He gives a list of simple experiments to demonstrate the electrical attraction and repulsion exercised by the physician's hand on that of the patient. (p. 293). Again, he found that the most convenient way to speak to the patient was for the interlocutor to place one hand on the stomach (duly covered with clothes) and to address his remarks to the finger-tips of his free hand. The human body being of course a conductor, the patient would then hear and reply. The same results would follow if the operator stood at the remote end of a chain of persons holding each other's hands, of whom the last only touched the patient. But if a stick of wax or a plate of glass were placed in the circuit, communication at once ceased. Again, the patient would not hear music played close to her by any person not actually touching her. But if the performer were connected with the patient by a moistened thread, she would hear music even in a distant part of the house, and would respond to questions addressed to the far end of the thread.

The experiments in "seeing" with the pit of the stomach on one occasion, Petetin tells us, so amazed and affrighted the spectators that calm was not restored until, by showing that objects wrapped up in wax or silk could not be " seen," he satisfied them that the phenomena had a natural cause and were not due to the intervention of demons.

Petetin's explanation of the transference of sensation to the pit of the stomach is that the vital fluid, when driven by the disease or the operator's hand from the external organs of sensation, is concentrated upon the brain and nervous system.[1] As an illustration of the increased vitality of the brain which results in certain patients, he mentions the case of a girl of sixteen upon whose memory he made in the course of an attack of spontaneous somnambulism the following experiment. Holding his finger over the patient's stomach, he read to her, *sans articuler*, a piece of poetry, with which she was not acquainted, consisting of more than fifty verses. She then immediately at his request declaimed the piece without a single mistake. Her memory in the normal state was not above the average, and to learn the piece by heart would probably, he tells us, have cost her two days' work (p. 256).

Another notable figure in the history of Animal Magnetism at this date was Deleuze, author of the *Histoire critique*, which made its appearance in 1813.

---

[1] The supposed faculty of seeing, hearing, and smelling with the pit of the stomach can in most cases be explained as due to the heightened sensibility of the special senses, which is a not infrequent accompaniment of the trance, or to enhanced susceptibility to gestures or changes of tone. It is noteworthy that most of Petetin's experiments in " seeing" were conducted with patients who were unable to speak, and that the test consisted in addressing to them a long string of questions. Thus : " Is this which I hold in my hand made of metal ? " " Yes." " Is it silver ?—gold ?—lead ?—antimony ?—manganese ? " " No." " Is it platinum?" " Yes." The almost inevitable sub-conscious change of tone would be enough to give the required cue. And in the only case of the kind where the question was asked by a person ignorant of the proper answer no response was elicited (p. 188).

But one of Petetin's patients retained in the cataleptic state the use of her voice, and it is not easy to explain some of the results which he records as having witnessed in her case. If accurately reported, the results may have been due to thought-transference.

Deleuze had before the Revolution been Assistant Naturalist at the Jardin des Plantes, and was the author of one or two works on science and philosophy. Though he was not a medical man his scientific training gives his testimony some importance. His first acquaintance with Animal Magnetism dated from 1785, and by many years' experience he satisfied himself of the truth of the facts recorded by Puységur and others. We miss, indeed, the fine cosmic flavour which distinguished the writings of Mesmer himself and some of his earliest disciples. For Deleuze Animal Magnetism is no longer " un rapproche-ment de deux sciences connues, l'astronomie et la méde-cine." He cannot see what the planets have to say in the matter. But he is convinced of the existence of the magnetic fluid. His somnambules had seen it raying from his fingers ; many had smelt it and found the odour agreeable, and had tasted it in magnetised water or milk.

Moreover, Deleuze had satisfied himself, by direct experiment, of the existence and physical properties of the fluid. It is not, he points out, apparently identical with the electric fluid, though both are probably modifications of a universal medium. It has many analogies with nerve-force. It forms an atmosphere round each of us, which does not make its presence continually felt, only because it is necessary, for any sensible effect to be produced, that it should be concentrated and directed by the will. How it is that the will directs the fluid we know as little as how our will moves our own organism. *C'est un fait primitif*: we cannot go behind it.

In Deleuze, as already in Puységur, we find an increasing recognition of the human element in the process of " Mag-netism." We have no longer to deal with the indifferent mechanical fluid which Mesmer's famous propositions described. The fluid, whatever its inorganic analogies, is pre-eminently vital. It is set in motion, directed, and controlled by the will. Deleuze is inclined to invert Puységur's maxim and say, " *Veuillez et Croyez*," arguing on the lines of latter-day Pragmatism that belief will follow on will. As marking the radical difference between Deleuze's attitude and that of the modern hypnotist, it is interesting to note that whilst he regards both will and faith as necessary to the operator, he does not regard either as essential on the part of the patient.[1] Obstinate incredulity may retard and obstruct, but cannot ultimately prevail against a fluid which is real enough to be reflected by glass, and to make its presence felt even through opaque substances. It is in accordance with this conception of Animal Magnetism as a definite physical agent that Deleuze attributes painful effects to it in some diseases. Generally speaking, it has a tonic action, and may be usefully employed when stimulating agents are indicated. But when the system is already irritated and excited—as by poisons, for example— he finds that the effect of Magnetism is to increase the irritation and the suffering, and frequently to bring on convulsions. Again, in many diseases where it can be usefully employed its first effect is generally to increase the pain and accelerate the crisis.

Again, like his predecessors, Deleuze explains the subject's clairvoyance and her obedience to the silently expressed will of her Magnetiser, as physical effects of the fluid accumulated in the nervous system. He gives an interesting illustration of the exaltation of memory in the trance. He had put into the somnambulic state one of his friends, a young man of about two-and-twenty. The patient had some time previously spent two years in Crete, but had forgotten the language spoken there. At Deleuze's instance he set himself in the trance to recall the books which he had read during his stay, and succeeded in reciting (apparently in French), "precisely as if he were reading it off," about two pages of "Narcissa," from Young's *Night Thoughts.* Deleuze adds: "Je suis bien sûr qu' étant éveillé il ne savait pas les *Nuits d'Young* par cœur. Je crois même que personne ne les sait en prose française, et d'ailleurs il ne faisait de la littérature qu'un amusement."[2]

[1] Edition of 1819, vol i. p. 141.   [2] *Ibid.*, vol. i. p. 236.

In another case his patient suffered from a form of aphasia. She was hemiplegic on the right side ; she had lost the power of reading ; could not count beyond three ; and in her speech could use no pronouns, and was unable to conjugate her verbs. Thus she said "*souhaiter bon jour*" instead of "*je vous souhaite.*" After treating her for a few weeks Deleuze restored the power of counting, and of reading, by spelling the words. In her speech, though she still employed the infinitive, she had resumed the use of pronouns. At this stage the cure was unhappily interrupted by the Revolution, and Deleuze lost sight of the patient.[1]

With Deleuze the first epoch of Animal Magnetism may be said to end. For both the authors whose writings have just been considered, though their views were not published until much later, belong to the pre-revolutionary period. Deleuze owed his interest in the subject to the experiments at Busancy, and made his first observations in 1785. Petetin's book, published in 1808, deals with experiences beginning many years before. He was treating one of his cataleptic patients throughout the siege of Lyons in 1792 ; we hear the guns of the besieging force echoing through his pages ; he was himself called away from his professional duties to take his place under fire ; and the recovery of his patient was seriously retarded by the sanguinary reprisals exacted by the army of the National Convention. But the Revolution had almost stopped the progress of Animal Magnetism altogether. The Societies of Harmony had dissolved. Most of the members were amongst the *emigrés* ; and the study itself was for a time discredited in the eyes of all good Republicans from its association with the old *régime*. It earned further discredit from the fact that many of Mesmer's early disciples were among those who afterwards became the followers and disciples of Cagliostro. Up to the end of 1788 there had been a steady flow of books and pamphlets on the subject. But the next twenty years, according to

[1] Edition of 1819, vol i. pp. 238–239.

Dureau's Bibliography of the books published in France, furnished barely as many items, all told.   It is not until the Restoration, in fact, that we find Animal Magnetism fully restored to favour.   The Magnetists and the Jesuits, as one writer puts it, returned in company with the returning *emigrés* : " La France féodale, qui ne vivait que de souvenirs, aurait volontiers redemandé au nouveau Paris et les baquets de Mesmer, et les marquises en convulsions." [1]

In fact, as we shall see in the next chapter, the Baquet and the crisis had gone for ever, but new marvels were found to take their place.

[1] *Hist. acad.*, p. 256.

CHAPTER V

HEALING BY SUGGESTION

Progress of Animal Magnetism after the Restoration in France—Demonstrations of anæsthesia and clairvoyance—Views of Bertrand: he attributes many of the phenomena to suggestion—His description of the trance and its characteristics—His explanation of "prediction" —He is disposed to believe in clairvoyance and thought-transference.

THE appearance in 1813 of Deleuze's *Histoire critique* marks, as has been said, the close of an epoch. From that date onwards we are watching the incubation of a new science. For, indeed, not only Paris, but the whole country was now busied with the marvels of the magnetic trance. A bi-monthly journal, the *Annales du Magnétisme animal*, had been started in 1814, which after a short interruption reappeared as the *Bibliothèque du Magnétisme animal*. This came to an end in 1819, and was replaced by the *Archives du Magnétisme animal*, under the editorship of Baron d'Henin de Cuvillers. There were, moreover, professional clairvoyants as we learn from frequent references in writings of this period, who seem to have found in the practice of clairvoyant diagnosis and treatment of disease a lucrative occupation. The Abbé Faria claimed that he had entranced more than five thousand persons. Nor was the interest in the subject confined to France. The Academy of Berlin in 1821 proposed a prize for the best essay on the subject—a prize for which Bertrand would have contended, but unluckily his essay arrived too late.[1] In Russia a Commission appointed by

[1] *Du Magnétisme animal*, p. 248.

the Emperor in 1815 had reported in its favour. In Prussia and Denmark the efficacy of Magnetism had been recognised, and its exercise confined by law to members of the medical profession. In fact, throughout Northern Europe, but especially in Germany, the new treatment seems to have been widely practised. It was only the land of the immortal Newton "qui dans la culture des sciences, suivant la marche sévère de l'expérience et de l'observation, a dédaigné jusqu'a présent de s'occuper de magnétisme." [1]

It was not long before the new treatment penetrated even into the Paris hospitals. In 1819 a young physician, Alexander Bertrand, who had been initiated by Deleuze, gave a course of lectures on Animal Magnetism. They were so successful and so largely attended that he gave another course in the following year. In the same year—1820—M. Husson, chief of the staff of the Hôtel Dieu, invited an amateur, Baron Dupotet de Sennevoy, twenty-five years later editor of the *Journal du Magnétisme*, to treat one of the patients in the hospital. Mdlle. Samson, age seventeen, belonged to that hysterical type, heirs, in Janet's phrase, of *la misère psychologique*, which seems almost peculiar to the Paris hospitals. At the third attempt she yielded to the Magnetic treatment and fell into a refreshing sleep, from which she could not be roused. In the somnambulic state she gave some account of her malady. She could see her stomach filled with small pimples (*boutons*), some red, some white ; at the side of her heart there was a receptacle (*poche*) full of blood, and a fine thread which made her heart beat. The pimples she pronounced incurable ; but she prescribed for the malady of the heart, and rapidly improved in health. [2]

M. Husson, desiring to obtain proof of the reality of the magnetic influence apart from the imagination of the patient, arranged for Dupotet to be concealed in a cupboard and to

---

[1] Foissac, *Rapports et Discussions* (Paris, 1833), p. 41.
[2] *Ibid.*, p. 275 ; *Hist. académique*, p. 259. The pouch full of blood and the small thread which made the heart beat seem like imperfect reminiscences of a first lesson in anatomy. But Mdlle. Samson seems to have looked upon these structures as part of the disease.

magnetise her from thence unseen, at a given signal. The experiment succeeded on three or four consecutive occasions. But Bertrand, who was present, suggested that, as all the trials had taken place at the hour when the patient had been accustomed to be magnetised, the results might be due to expectation. A control experiment was therefore instituted. Dupotet was asked to absent himself; but the same company assembled, the same procedure was followed, and a mock signal was given. The patient did not fall asleep.

As a further control experiment Dupotet was introduced into the ward at seven o'clock one evening, and sent Mdlle. Samson to sleep from a distance, at a given signal. Despite the precautions taken, however, to conceal Dupotet's presence, Bertrand was not satisfied. M. Husson, the chief of the staff, contrary to his usual routine, had come into the ward just before the experiment, and in passing the patient's bed had asked whether she was asleep yet. The circumstance might have aroused her suspicions, and it seemed possible that a shadow cast by the lamp might have betrayed Dupotet's person, behind a curtain, a few feet off. To Bertrand, therefore, the experiment seemed inconclusive. But M. Husson and the other medical witnesses held his objection to be over-scrupulous.

It is not a little remarkable that at a time when anæsthetic drugs were wholly unknown the induction of anæsthesia in the trance appears not to have attracted the attention of the early Magnetists. They do, indeed—*e.g.*, in the Reports of 1784 and the discussions which followed—take note of the numbness in the limbs which occasionally accompanied the trance, but this was commonly attributed to the constrained attitude or, as by Deleuze, to the fact that the lower limbs were generally not included in the passes, and thus escaped the vitalising influence of the fluid (*Histoire critique*, vol. i. p. 149). This singular omission is, of course, but another illustration—if another is needed—of the fact that in this region the observer finds what he looks for. But at this date the phenomenon seems to have been on its way to recognition. In the year following the experiments at the Hôtel Dieu a demonstration of anæsthesia was given on two patients in the wards of St. Madeleine and St. Agnes, under the direction of the chief, M. Recamier. A moxa was used in each case, composed of a cubical piece of agaric measuring rather less than an inch (*dix lignes en tous sens*). The scars produced involved the whole thickness of the skin, but the patients gave no signs of feeling. In another case a flask of ammonia was held to the patient's nostrils for fifteen minutes without any effect being produced. Further experiments were made on another subject, Mdlle. Pétronille, at the Salpêtrière. Amongst the phenomena supposed to have been demonstrated in this case were clairvoyance of the patient's own diseased organs, the power of predicting her own crises, of prescribing for her own ailments, and so on. The witnesses in this case included a brilliant young physician, Georget, author of a book on the *Physiology of the Nervous System.* In a second edition of that book he devotes a chapter to his experiences in Magnetism. His early death prevented his pursuing the study ; but he left behind him a remarkable testimony to the effect produced on him by what he had seen. In a paper, which came to light only after his death, he declared that when he published the first edition of his book he was a materialist, but the remarkable manifestations of somnambulism "ne me permirent plus de douter de l'existence en nous et hors de nous d'un principe intelligent, tout à fait différent des existences matérielles."[1] Another physician who attested the marvels of Animal Magnetism, and especially clairvoyance (*e.g.,* of a watch held behind the head), was Professor Rostan, author of the article on the subject in the *Dictionary of Medicine.*

But with one exception the medical witnesses of this time count for little in the history of the science. They had been attracted by the superficial marvels of the trance ; they lacked the ability, or perhaps the opportunity, to pursue their investigations below the surface. From an uninstructed contempt for Animal Magnetism as a relic of mediæval superstition they had swung round to an equally uncritical

[1] Foissac, *Rapports et Discussions* (1833), p. 290.

acceptance, marvels and all. All were ready to believe in physical action at a distance; Rostan even put forward a theory of a subtle nerve atmosphere, "having a great analogy with electricity," which is simply Animal Magnetism under a new name. Some, like Georget, went so far as to find in the marvels of clairvoyance proof of a spiritual universe.

But Alexander Bertrand had patiently pursued his investigations, correcting year by year his first crude impressions in the light of later experience, and in his books we pass at a step from the mediæval to the modern world. For Bertrand Animal Magnetism was a chimera. The various phenomena observed by his predecessors—the magnetic crisis; the sensations of heat and cold; the influence of the Baquet and the iron rod; the tree at Busancy; the stream of light seen by Tardy's somnambules; the conduction by iron, the reflection from mirrors, the dissipation by copper; the effects of wax, silk, wet cards, &c., as observed by Petetin— the whole machinery on which the earlier writers relied as demonstrating the existence of a fluid—celestial, magnetic, or electric—he sweeps away in a word by showing that the results were due to the imagination of the subject, preternormally alive to the least suggestion, by word, look, gesture, or even unexpressed thought, from the operator. It is not necessary to follow Bertrand in detail through the steps of his argument. His theory of suggestion is the modern theory, and by it, as we know, are explained most of the phenomena which to the earlier observers appeared most inexplicable. Indeed, it is surprising how modern Bertrand's book is. It might have issued within the last decade from the Hôpital Civil at Nancy. It would need but a slight change in names, dates, and other unessential particulars to make it fit the times. For the three stages of the magnetic crisis, as observed in the Paris of 120 years ago—perturbation, " coction," and evacuation— [1] we should substitute the three classic stages of *la grande hystérie*, as observed in the Paris of yesterday; and for the names of Petetin and Deleuze those, say, of Charcot and Gilles de la Tourette. The transfer

[1] See Puységur, *Du Magnétisme animal*, p. 140.

of diseases, the influence of magnets and metals, the presence
of a nerve atmosphere, have all been demonstrated as con-
clusively within recent years at the Salpêtrière or the Charité
as they were more than a hundred years ago at Busancy or
Lyons ; whilst the most brilliant results of Tardy de Montravel have been outshone in modern Paris by Dr. Luys,
Colonel de Rochas, M. Baraduc, and M. Emile Boirac. For
modern scientific appliances have enabled these later observers
to claim that they can photograph the fluid which the earlier
writers could only take on trust from their somnambules.
And, to complete the parallel, the scientific world, and the
mass of medical men in this country, at any rate, were until
recently no more concerned about the whole business than
they had been sixty or a hundred and twenty years ago. As
has been said of another subject :—

> " Hic liber est in quo quærit sua dogmata quisque
> Invenit et pariter dogmata quisque sua."

Bertrand, it will be seen, anticipated Braid by one and
Bernheim by two generations.[1] For him the magnetic trance
is not the result of a mysterious force acting from the outside,
but a particular psychological, or, if you will, pathological,
condition induced by various exciting causes within the
organism. He begins by relating the artificial trance with
spontaneous noctambulism, the somnambulic states associated
with certain diseases, and the states of ecstasy epidemic from
time to time in religious communities. He then proceeds to
analyse the phenomena presented, and enumerates twelve
principal characteristics of the state of induced somnambulism,

---

[1] The Abbé Faria had for some years before this date given public
séances, apparently much like the demonstrations of popular lecturers
on Mesmerism at the present day, at which he had made his subjects
drink water for lemonade, see phantoms of absent friends, &c. In
1819 he had published a book, De la Cause du Sommeil lucide, in which
he maintained that the phenomena of the trance were to be attributed
neither to a fluid nor to the will of the operator, but to self-suggestion
on the part of the patient. But Faria had no medical training, and he
seems to have had even less influence on educated opinion than
Bertrand.

for all of which he finds more or less exact parallels amongst the records of delirium and the outbreaks of spontaneous ecstasy described in certain religious epidemics, such as the Tremblers of the Cevennes, the Nuns of Loudun, and the Convulsionaries at the tomb of the Archdeacon Paris. These characteristics are :—

1. Division of memory between trance and normal life.
2. Appreciation of time.
3. Anæsthesia.
4. Exaltation of imagination,
5. And of the intellectual faculties.
6. Instinct for remedies.
7. Prevision.
8. Moral inertia.
9. Communication of the symptoms of maladies.
10. Thought-transference.
11. Seeing without eyes.
12. A peculiar influence exercised by the somnambulist on his own organism.

Of the first five items on the list little need be said, since they are sufficiently recognised by modern students. The existence of the state of artificial somnambulism, with the subsequent oblivion dividing it from the waking life and the other characteristics above enumerated, though persistently denied or ignored for several generations, is too well established at the present time for its reality to be called into question.

Just as Bertrand has explained the curious physical phenomena recorded by his predecessors as due simply to the exaltation of the imagination in the trance, so he attributes to exaltation of memory and of the intelligence generally in the state of ecstasy some of the marvels recorded by religious chroniclers, especially the speaking and understanding of foreign tongues by demoniacs. By moral inertia (10) Bertrand aims at describing the passivity and want of initiative generally characteristic of the induced trance. Under the heading (12) the special influence of the somnambule on her own organism are included, as will be shown later, the phenomena of pseudo-prevision, as described in the last chapter, and, generally speaking, the control over involuntary organic processes.

But the remaining five items are not yet admitted by modern science, and for the most part probably never will be. It will be observed that Bertrand does not include amongst the powers claimed for somnambulists that clairvoyance of the interior which was so fully illustrated by Puységur's patients, and in which even Georget seems to have been disposed to believe. The marvels described in the last chapter were seen, so to speak, through the eyes of the contemporary observers. It will be convenient now to consider them in the light thrown upon them by Bertrand himself, and by more modern investigators. On the state of somnambulism itself the observations of Puységur and his contemporaries may, as said, be taken as substantially accurate. It is after this point that our difficulties begin. As regards the alleged seeing of the interior organism, it is to be noted that the descriptions given of the diseases and of the nature of the cure are in most cases ridiculous and show complete ignorance of anatomy. Most of Puységur's patients traced the cause of their disease to an internal abscess (*depôt*); and this abscess, whatever its situation, was to discharge itself by the intestinal canal, the nose, the mouth, or ear, and the patient would be immediately cured. The abscess which caused young Joly's deafness discharged by the nose; we hear of another patient who suffered from an abscess in the hand, which discharged itself through the ear, by means of a canal which he discerned to connect the little finger with the head![1] A man whose work consisted in sifting wheat saw a mass of dust caked together in his stomach as the cause of his woes.[2] Yet another, after his abscess had discharged, saw its outer covering (*poche*) in the form of a fine membrane, firmly attached to the nerves, and his cure was not completed until the membrane had disengaged itself.[3]

---

[1] Bertrand, *Traité du Somnambulisme*, p. 69.
[2] Puységur, *Mémoires*, vol. ii. p. 70.   [3] *Id.*, vol. i. p. 125.

There is no need to accuse these clairvoyants of bad
faith ; we see, no doubt, in their preposterous anatomy
the spontaneous expression of the confused ideas current
amongst the uneducated at this date. But if the diagnosis of
the disease was not due to clairvoyance, we certainly need
not ascribe the prediction of the results to a *pressensation
particulière.* When Puységur's patients foretold much
suffering for themselves and the occurrence of several severe
crises as the preliminary to a cure, we can see that in these
predictions they were again reflecting their environment.
The orthodox medical practice of the time encouraged the
use of violent remedies—its chief and almost its only weapons
were purges, emetics, and bleeding. Mesmer had taught his
pupils to seek salvation through violent convulsions and the
intensification of the painful symptoms of the malady.
Puységur in one place expresses a doubt whether a patient
had been really healed "because he had not yet experienced
the painful crises which, I imagine, are essential to the cure
of so grave a malady." [1]

There are several peculiarities, as Bertrand points out, in
these "predictions." In the first place, the convulsions and
other crises generally occurred punctually on the stroke of the
clock, and lasted as a rule for a measured time—half an hour,
an hour, two hours, &c. Again, the predictions were
singularly eclectic in their subject-matter. They were concerned with such incidents as sleep, convulsions, dumbness,
catalepsy, spitting of blood, bleeding from the nose, and so on.
But they never foretold the occurrence of serious organic
disease. Bertrand mentions a case where a patient afflicted
with paralysis of the left leg announced, amongst other
predictions, that some months hence she would be affected
with paralysis of the tongue and be unable to speak for a
week. The prediction was punctually fulfilled. But long
before the time fell due the patient was found to be in an
advanced stage of pulmonary phthisis, the presence of which
not only the attendant physician but her own clairvoyance
had failed to detect. That is a curiously limited clairvoyance

[1] Puységur, *Mémoires*, vol. i. p. 65.

which enabled the sick woman to foresee months beforehand the occurrence of a transient functional disability, but could not enable her to detect the fatal disease which had already seriously affected her organism.

It is not, in fact, to precognition but to predetermination that the results are to be ascribed. The patient himself set his organism to explode in the predicted fit of convulsions, to bleed from the nose, or, as in the last cited case, to lapse into hysterical dumbness, and it was himself who attended to the fulfilment of the prediction. And here another question arises. So far as most of the effects are concerned there is no reason to question the good faith of the subject. The convulsions, the dumbness, the temporary paralysis of the limbs were no doubt all the effect of unconscious self-suggestion. Similar effects have been produced again and again in the history of hypnotism, where there were no reasons to suspect the good faith of the subject. But Puységur was a grand seigneur ; he was rich and his favour was no doubt worth conciliating ; he was a brave soldier, ready to be carried away by enthusiasm, a man of transparent honesty himself, and slow to suspect others of bad faith. Above all, he was no physician.

Some of the things related by him are very difficult to accept. Curiously enough, the instance which, as he tells the story, caused most suspicion at the time is one in which it is not difficult to credit the good faith of the patient, and that precisely because of the circumstance which at the time seemed most suggestive of trickery. Victor, Puységur's first somnambule, some months later happened to sustain a serious fall, which left him with pains in the head. He experienced some relief from bleeding, but announced in the clairvoyant state that there was some blood still remaining in the head (" *qu'il lui restait encore du sang dans la tête* "), and that his cure would be completed by bleeding from the left nostril, which would occur spontaneously at a given hour a day or two later. Puységur thought to convince some of his incredulous friends by inviting them to witness the fulfilment of the prediction. At the appointed time the bleeding from the left

nostril duly took place; but the spectators remained uncon-
vinced, because the blood was pure, and not mixed with
matter, as would have been the case if discharged from an
abscess. On the assumption that the effect was due to
self-suggestion, pure blood is precisely what we should have
anticipated.

But of all the facts recorded by Puységur and other contemporary observers the most open to suspicion is the
alleged discharge of diseased matter by improbable routes,
from hypothetical abscesses. The analogy which leaps to the
mind is that of witchcraft. The hysterical or merely mischievous children, who were the chief denouncers of witches
in this country, frequently enhanced the effect of their fits
and convulsions by fraudulent means. They would vomit
strange substances previously secreted in the mouth for the
purpose; they were detected colouring their urine with ink,
employing soap to simulate frothy saliva in pretended
epileptic attacks, and so on. It is true that in the case of
young Joly, recorded in the last chapter, we have credible
and abundant testimony to the reality of his cure; and we
have no reason to suspect the genuineness of his somnambulism. But all that does not afford a sufficient guarantee
against trickery, and the circumstances, as shown, would have
admitted of trickery being practised. It is precisely the
difficulty of distinguishing between the real, the imaginary,
and the fraudulent which for three or four generations
repelled the majority of thinking men from the investigation
of Mesmerism, and which still causes many medical men to
hold aloof from the newly christened science of Hypnotism.

Modern observers, however, claim to have produced by
suggestion bleeding from the nose or even from the skin;
several cases are known in which the secretion of milk has
been restored by suggestion. There are cases recorded by
modern French hypnotists in which blisters and suppuration
have been so caused. Effects of this kind, indeed, do not
appear to have been observed outside France, and Dr.
Bramwell, after criticising the precautions taken, regards the
evidence for blistering by suggestion as by no means

H

conclusive.[1] On the other hand, it should be borne in mind that the patients who are the subjects of experiment in French hospitals are apparently far more amenable to suggestion than those commonly accessible to English or German physicians. Further, it is probable that the effect of spontaneous self-suggestion working, as in the case of Puységur's patients, through several days or even weeks, may have been more powerful to affect the organism than any suggestion made for experimental purposes by the hospital physician.

Bertrand cites from his own experience a case which gives rise to mixed reflections. One of his patients announced to him that in eight days' time she would be suffering from a swollen face, inflamed (*infiltrées*) eyelids, and scratches on the face such as might be made with a pin. The results were in accordance with the "prediction." The scratches here obviously suggest trickery ; but it is more difficult to see how the inflammation of the eyelids could have been produced fraudulently.[2]

Amongst the pseudo-phenomena, then, which melted away under the powerful solvent of Bertrand's analysis we may place the alleged clairvoyance of the interior of the human body and the power to foresee the course of a disease.[3] But

---

[1] *Hypnotism* (1903), p. 84.

[2] *Traité du Somnambulisme*, p. 176 ; *Du Magnétisme animal en France*, p. 420.

[3] In his earlier work, *Traité du Somnambulisme*, published in 1823, Bertrand had not sufficient experience to determine the true significance of these "predictions," and he suggested tentatively that they might be attributed to an instinctive perception of organic processes, antecedently not more incredible than the instinct which guides the bird in its nesting and migration. But in his *Du Magnétisme animal en France*, published in 1826, he expressly repudiates the former explanation, and ascribes all the phenomena to predetermination (*i.e.*, self-suggestion). He maintains (1) "que nous ne pouvons positivement déterminer les limites dans lesquelles peut s'étendre cette influence singulière (*i.e.*, predetermination) des somnambules sur leur organisation ; (2) qu'on ne peut nier que dans la plupart des cas les prédictions ne soient réellement la cause de l'effet produit " (*Du Magnétisme animal en France*, p. 420). After this plain statement it is surprising to find that the authors of the *Histoire académique* (p. 271) ridicule Bertrand

the four remaining faculties, viz., instinct for remedies, communication of symptoms, thought-transference, and clairvoyance, which Bertrand claims, though somewhat doubtfully, for somnambulism, require more attention. He thinks it probable, though his own experience does not qualify him to pronounce a decided opinion, that some somnambules can indicate the remedies appropriate to their maladies, just as the lower animals can seek out their appropriate food ; and he would explain the faculty in each case as being instinctive. Of the ability of the somnambule in certain cases to divine the ailments of others, without visible means of diagnosis, he has no doubt; and he gives three examples from his own practice. He brought to a somnambule a patient of his own whom she had never seen. The chief affection in this case was asthma. The somnambule, after being placed in *rapport* with the invalid, shortly presented all the symptoms of a severe asthmatical attack ; she then proceeded to describe with great accuracy various minor ailments and pains, and finally a skin affection in a particular part of the body of which there were no external signs, and the existence of which was unknown even to Bertrand himself.

He made two similar observations on another somnambule. The second I give in his own words :—

" Voici une troisieme observation, faite sur la même somnambule, et qui ne paraîtra pas moins remarquable que les précédentes. Je n'avais pas préparé cette épreuve : le hasard me la fournit. J'étais auprès de la somnambule, que je magnétisais endormie sur son lit, quand je vis entrer un de mes amis accompagné d'un jeune homme blessé depuis peu de temps en duel, et qui avait reçu une balle dans la tête ; il était encore malade de sa blessure, et venait pour consulter. On me le dit à voix basse, sans parler du genre de la blessure ; et comme la somnambule parut disposée à donner la consultation qu'on lui demandait, je la

---

for believing in the power of somnambules to " predict " crises, and cite the very page from which the above quotation is taken in support of their contention. It is not only magnetic somnambules who force upon us the perplexing choice between the fictions of the imagination and those of wilful deception. No doubt MM. Burdin and Dubois may be acquitted of the graver charge, but imagination of this kind in the authors of academic history is in itself almost criminal.

mis en rapport avec le blessé, et me bornai à lui demander de déclarer ce qu'il avait. (Je n'ai pas besoin de dire avec quel soin on doit éviter de faire aux somnambules des questions qui puissent leur indiquer les résponses qu'ils doivent faire.) Elle parut chercher un instant, puis elle dit en s'adressant le parole à ellemême : " Non, non, ce n'est pas possible ; si un homme avait eu une balle dans la tête, il serait mort."—" Eh bien ! " lui dis-je, " que voyez-vous donc ?"—" Il faut *qu'il* se trompe," me dit-elle ; "*il* me dit que monsieur a une balle dans la tête." [1] Je l'assurai que ce qu'elle disait était vrai, et lui demandai si elle pouvait voir par où la balle était entrée, et quel trajet elle avait parcouru. La somnambule réfléchit encore un instant, puis ouvrit la bouche, et indiqua avec le doigt que la balle etait entrée par la bouche, et avait pénétré jusqu'à la partie postérieure du cou ; ce qui était encore vrai. Enfin elle poussa l'exactitude jusqu'à indiquer quelqués-unes des dents qui manquaient dans la bouche, et que la balle avait brisées.

Cette observation ne me laissa rien désirer, puisque d'ailleurs j'étais sûr que la somnambule n'avait eu d'avance aucune connaissance de la personne qu'on lui avait amenêe, et qu'elle n'avait pas ouvert les yeux depuis l'instant où le blessé était entré dans la chambre. Au reste, quand elle l'aurait vu, la balle étant entrée dans la bouche sans faire aucune lésion aux tégumens extérieurs, il lui aurait été impossible d'acquérir d'un coup-d'œil toutes les connaissances qu'elle montra sur la nature de la blessure.[2]

If the somnambule's diagnoses in these three cases were not due to subconscious interpretations of external indications too slight to attract the waking attention, her success may perhaps be attributed to telepathy. But the cases described by the earlier writers are not sufficiently detailed or sufficiently numerous to justify any certain conclusion.

In thought-transference (*communication des pensées*) Bertrand is disposed to believe because of the abundant testimony to be found in the religious chronicles referred to. As an illustration of the general belief in earlier times in such a faculty, he points out that the ability to read the thoughts of those around was regarded by the Church as the touchstone of demoniac possession. Further, though he had himself witnessed no clear instance of its operation, he thinks the testimony of his contemporaries too strong to be set aside.

[1] "*Il* "= not the patient, but the inner voice which seemed to the somnambule to speak from her stomach.

[2] *Traité*, &c., pp. 232–234.

He is inclined to explain by thought-transference the "magnetic mobility" which Puységur observed in Madeleine and other subjects, and the action at distance which some of his contemporaries claim to have witnessed.

Again, he finds it difficult to refuse credence to a faculty of vision at close quarters without the aid of the eyes. Not only is such a faculty attested by Petetin's experiments, but amongst Bertrand's contemporaries there were several persons who had witnessed instances of its apparent operation.[1] This question of clairvoyance at close quarters will be further considered in the next chapter. Recent research has not brought any confirmation of the belief. And two points with regard to it may be noted here. In the first place, none of those who have expressed their belief in the possibility of vision by the pit of the stomach or the back of the head or the toes or fingers have ever attempted to explain how the alleged transference of visual sensibility to the nerves supplying those parts of the body could possibly supply the place of the complicated optical instrument which in normal life furnishes us with the means of seeing. Let it be assumed that under certain conditions in certain somnambules the skin of the toes or the back of the head may become as sensitive to light as the surface of the retina. Would that explain how the somnambule could read a printed book with her toes or the back of her head? Even the retina—which has, after all, had a lifelong training in the business—is assisted in its task by adjustable lenses and curtains and what not. Where in these cases of abnormal vision do we find the necessary apparatus for focussing the divergent rays? If, then, the observers who testify to this power of clairvoyance had boldly claimed it as a possession of the soul itself, unhampered by any clumsy corporeal apparatus, their position would at least be intelligible. But Petetin claimed this marvellous power for a mere fluid, a mechanical emanation;

---

[1] In addition to Petetin and Deleuze, Georget, and Rostan, Bertrand cites the testimony of Despines, a physician of Aix, another doctor, Delpit, and the case of Baron Strombeck's somnambule, described in Chapter XI. (*Du Magnétisme animal en France*, pp. 445-466).

and even Bertrand does not seem to have realised the almost insuperable difficulties in the way of an explanation in terms of physics or physiology. But Bertrand in particular appears to have been misled by a false analogy. At the commencement of his *Traité du Somnambulisme* he cites from the article on Somnambulism in the *Encyclopædia* an account of a young ecclesiastic who in the somnambulic state could write sermons with his eyes closed. When a piece of cardboard was interposed between his eyes and the paper, so as effectually to exclude vision by normal means, it was observed that he still continued to write and, as before, would go back over the writing and insert corrections and additions in their proper place. Bertrand ascribes this phenomenon to a new kind of *vision*. But it is not vision at all; it is probably, as recent investigations have shown, to be explained by a special development of the muscular sense.

To conclude this brief retrospect of the phenomena recorded at this epoch in connection with the induced trance, we may note that in the literature of this date we meet with the earliest instances of the post-hypnotic fulfilment of injunctions given in the trance, a phase of the subject which has attained much prominence in recent times from its interest both for psychology and therapeutics. On one occasion Bertrand told a somnambule to remember on waking a song which had been sung. To another somnambule he gave the command that she should willingly submit to cold baths which had been prescribed for her, and from which she had hitherto shrunk. Both suggestions were fulfilled.[1] Again, a case is recorded in the *Annales du Magnétisme*.[2] A young girl was told in the trance that she should go at a certain hour to a particular house and ask for the magnetiser. When the appointed time came the girl, who was awake and in her normal state, felt the impulse to go to the house, but knowing nothing of the preceding circumstances, thought it altogether unreasonable. She nevertheless obeyed it.

[1] *Traité du Somnambulisme*, p. 285.   [2] Vol. vi. p. 272.

CHAPTER VI

LATER FRENCH COMMISSIONS

Discussion at the Academy of Medicine in 1825—a committee of investigation appointed—Their subjects: Céline, Mdlle. Samson, Paul Villagrand—Their Report endorses prevision and clairvoyance—Anæsthesia in trance—the case of Madame Plantin, and of Oudet's patient: reception by the Academy of reports on these two cases—The Academy in 1837 appoints another Commission to investigate the subject—Their Report unfavourable—Burdin's prize for clairvoyance—Experiments with Mdlle. Pigeaire, Teste's subject, Mdlle. Prudence, and others—The prize not awarded.

THE experiments made in 1820 and 1821 in the Hôtel Dieu, the Salpêtrière, and other public institutions had alarmed the General Council of the Hospitals ; and a decree was issued forbidding the further practice of Animal Magnetism in any of the State hospitals. Of Bertrand we have no news after the publication of his second book in 1826. He died a few years later. There seemed then some danger that the whole question of the induced trance and the attendant phenomena might be left to be investigated by uninstructed laymen and exploited by professional quacks. However, in 1825 a young doctor, P. Foissac, approached the Medical Section of the Royal Academy of Medicine and offered to provide somnambules if they would appoint a Commission to investigate the subject. The Section proceeded in the matter with due circumspection. They appointed a committee of five to consider the question whether it was suitable for the Academy to concern itself with the question or no. On December 13, 1825, this Committee reported by the mouth of M. Husson, and recommended the Section to undertake the inquiry. The reading of the preliminary report was followed by a heated discussion, which was prolonged over the next three sittings. There is no need to analyse the debate in detail. The arguments of the opponents are by now sufficiently familiar. In the course of the fourscore years which have intervened they have been reproduced, *mutatis mutandis*, in the annals of every medical society in the civilised world. Some of the speakers had studied the subject for years, and were convinced that all the phenomena reported, "or at least nine-tenths of them," were due to illusion and jugglery. It was pointed out that the whole subject had been investigated by the Commissions of 1784; there was no need to reopen a *chose jugée*. Moreover, it was clear that Mesmer was a quack and Puységur a man without scientific training; from Germany and the Scandinavian countries, where the doctrine was most rife, had notoriously proceeded too many extravagant systems and erroneous beliefs alike in medicine and philosophy. Let the system be judged by its results; the German physicians could not show a higher proportion of cures than the French. Even if there were anything in it—and some of those who opposed the appointment of the Commission (M. Récamier, for instance, who had, in 1821, witnessed the painless application of a moxa in the Salle Sainte Madeleine) were willing to admit so much—it would be beneath the dignity of the Academy to undertake the inquiry, for the subject had fallen into the hands of quacks and charlatans, who made a lucrative living out of their alleged clairvoyance. Nay, the very appointment of an academic Commission would be taken as endorsing the pretensions of these pernicious impostors, and would unsettle the minds of the rising generation, delivering them over to mediæval superstition. Moreover, it was a very difficult subject to investigate, since so many of the phenomena depended on the good faith of the subject; and if all that was said of it proved true, it would still not be of the smallest use in medicine—let the physicists or somebody else take it up. Conversely, another argued that it was not a subject for inquiry either by physicists or physiologists, since the alleged manifestations transcended all the laws of Nature, and an Academy of Medicine was not competent to investigate the properties of the soul. Last, and most singular argument of all, there were such grave moral dangers arising from the abuse of the magnetic influence that it would be most undesirable for any responsible body of trained investigators to have anything to do with such a disagreeable business.

The supporters of the motion had, as may be imagined, the best of the argument; they had also the majority of the votes; the recommendation was finally carried by thirty-five to twenty-five, and a Commission was appointed on February 28, 1826.

The Commission as finally constituted consisted of MM. Leroux, Bourdois de la Mothe, Double, Magendie, Guersent, Thilleye, Marc, Itard, Fouquier, Gueneau de Mussy, and Husson. MM. Magendie and Double, however, at an early period withdrew from the Commission; the final Report was signed by all the nine remaining members.

The Commission began its labours by experimenting with Foissac's somnambule Céline, but at that period obtained with her no results of value. They then turned their attention to the hospitals; but after a few observations had been made on patients in the Hôtel Dieu and the Charité the Council General of the Hospitals again interposed and forbade them to continue. The Commissioners were thus forced to depend upon private sources; and unfortunately few subjects appear to have been forthcoming. The inquiry dragged on for about five years, during which period experiments were made upon no more than twelve or fourteen persons who gave unmistakable proofs of being amenable to the magnetic influence.

No doubt the Commissioners were seriously hampered by being precluded from making observations in the hospitals. Further, no member of the Commission was able himself to magnetise, and they were thus unable to pursue their investigations in their private practice. Forced to rely upon the assistance of Foissac and Dupotet, their field of investigation was naturally restricted to the subjects presented to them by these two gentlemen, most of them selected apparently for the exhibition of sensational effects. And, indeed, the Commissioners appear generally to have allowed themselves to be guided in their lines of inquiry by these two enthusiastic amateurs of the marvellous. For, notwithstanding the difficulties, it is impossible to suppose that the Commissioners could not, if they had wished, have found a more profitable field for their investigation. Bertrand's second book, containing the fruit of his later researches and his mature reflections, was published at the outset of the Commission's five years' inquiry. Bertrand had given cogent reasons for ascribing all the phenomena which the Commission had to investigate either to the imagination of the patient or to a peculiar psychological state induced by psychological causes. And he had shown that this peculiar psychological state possessed many characteristics in common with delirium and religious ecstasy on the one hand, and with spontaneous noctambulism on the other. It was probably open to the Commission to have enlisted Bertrand's aid in their inquiry. It was certainly open to them to have profited by his experience, to have repeated his observations, to have verified his conclusions. But they did nothing of the kind. Bertrand's name is not mentioned, and his theories are dismissed in a single line of the Report.

The Commission was obsessed, as all their predecessors had been obsessed, with the idea of a mysterious external agent as the active cause of all the phenomena. Confining themselves strictly to the physiological side of the inquiry, they do not, indeed, presume to define this agent as a fluid, celestial, magnetic, or vital. But their whole Report is based upon the preconception of something passing from operator to subject in the process of magnetisation; and the very vagueness of their conception enables them to discuss with a light heart such marvels as prediction of the future and vision without the aid of eyes. This presumption necessarily guided the whole course of their inquiry, which was directed to discovering incontrovertible proofs of the action of this hypothetical influence. Generally speaking, they found that the influence was conveyed by actual contact or by passes, but in some cases they claimed to have demonstrated its effect to have been produced by the mere will of the operator, without the knowledge of the subject. The Commissioners, mainly, no doubt, because of their scanty opportunities for observation, scarcely touch on the question of the curative influence of Magnetism. They found that healthy subjects are rarely subject to the influence. Of the sick, most experience only slight or equivocal results, such as could readily be attributed to normal causes. But in a few cases the state of somnambulism was induced. They pass lightly over, or completely neglect, most of the unsensational, but none the less significant, characteristics of this state, already described by Bertrand. They briefly record, however, experiments and observations tending to prove *rapport* with the magnetiser and complete insensibility to all other sounds except his voice : insensibility to pain, oblivion on waking, and in one case extraordinary increase of muscular power. The patient in this case, a young law student named Paul Villagrand, who had suffered for more than eighteen months from paralysis of the left side, was unable, in the normal state, using both hands, to mark more than 31 kilogrammes on the dynamometer. On one occasion in the somnambulic state, to prove his strength, he lifted one of the Commissioners and whirled him round, and then pressed the dynamometer until the scale marked 160 kilogrammes.

Amongst the more dubious phenomena which the Commission reported as proved are influence at a distance without the knowledge of the subject, intuition of the diseases of others, the prediction, months ahead, of epileptic fits, and vision with closed eyes. The material available for the research, as said, was rather meagre ; and two at least of the somnambules, Mdlle. Céline and Mdlle. Samson, were trained subjects, and not above the suspicion of fraud. The Committee showed little judgment in their experiments and extreme rashness in their conclusions. They completely ignored the reasons given by Bertrand for adopting an alternative explanation of the alleged power of prevision, and deliberately chose the more sensational interpretation, which Bertrand's mature experience had caused him to reject. In any case the data on which their conclusions were founded were quite insufficient. The alleged phenomena of prevision had been observed in two cases only. One subject only— Mdlle. Céline—had proved her ability to diagnose and prescribe for the ailments of others. The greatest marvel of all —clairvoyance—had been demonstrated only in two cases.

The Report was read before the Academy in June, 1831, by M. Husson, who had been deputed by the Commission to draw it up. It was not likely that a document which set forth on so narrow a basis of fact such astounding conclusions would gain the favour of the medical world, when the careful and long-continued observations and sober reasoning of Bertrand had failed to win a hearing. Some of those present desired an opportunity for discussing it, but Husson objected on the ground that, as the work of the Commissioners consisted of rigorous experiments, there was nothing to discuss, unless, indeed, the intelligence or the integrity of the Commissioners themselves were to be called in question.[1] This statement is sufficient in itself to show how unfitted the Commissioners were to discharge their task. Some writers, indeed, have proposed to throw the whole burden on Husson, alleging that the rest of the Commissioners made themselves responsible only for the accurate statement of the facts, Husson, as reported, for the conclusions based upon them.[2] But this contention is hardly consistent with the fact that the whole of the Commissioners append their signatures without

[1] "Que le travail de la Commission reposant tout entière sur des expériences rigoreuses, il ne pouvait donner lieu à aucune espèce de discussion, à moins qu'on n'attaquât les lumières ou la moralité des Commissaires" (Foissac, *op. cit.*, p. 209). The Academy declining to publish the Report, that task was undertaken by Foissac, who also published a summary of the several discussions on the subject. Husson himself corrected the proofs of Foissac's book, so far at least as relates to his own share in the matter. So the Foissac Report, from which the statement in the text is quoted, may be taken as authoritative.

[2] *Hist. acad.*, pp. 332 and 435, *note.*

reserve to the Report. Whatever the explanation, Husson successfully evaded all attempts to bring about a discussion on the subject of the Report, and the Academy took no further action in the matter.

This ill-considered Report, no doubt, did much to hinder the recognition of the subject amongst men of common-sense generally. The line taken by the authors of the *Histoire académique* in dealing with the subject is a sufficient indication of the attitude of the official medical world. MM. Burdin and Dubois pour out their contempt indiscriminately on everything connected with Animal Magnetism ; the very existence of the state of artificial somnambulism and the induction of anæsthesia share in the general discredit.[1]

The practice of Animal Magnetism and the induction of somnambulism were not, however, left solely to enthusiastic amateurs and professional clairvoyants. Among the younger members of the medical profession there were some who made use of the auxiliary placed within their reach ; and through the action of one of them, a young physician named Hamard, the subject again came before the Academy at the beginning of 1837. Amongst the instances cited by the Commission of 1826-1831 to prove insensibility to pain was a case of which

---

[1] The treatment of the Report and the reporter by the authors of the *Hist. acad.* can scarcely recommend itself to the judicious reader. MM. Burdin and Dubois, not content with criticising every observation and controverting every argument in the Report, expend a large amount of petty spite in ridiculing the language employed by the reporter. One of their comments may be quoted, no sillier or more spiteful than the similar notes which they append to almost every page of their account. The Report states that the somnambule will occasionally be deaf to the loudest sounds, such as the clanging of a copper vessel, "*la chute d'un meuble,*" &c. To which statement the *Histoire académique* appends a note : "M. Husson a voulu ici mettre un certain choix dans les termes, ennoblir ses détails ; mais le fait est qu'il s'agit tout simplement d'une bûche qu'il a jetée par terre" (p. 439). The comment is not only small-minded and silly, but incorrect. In the account of the actual experiment as given by the joint authors themselves (p. 387) we find "le rapporteur jeta sur le parquet *une table et une bûche.*"

they had not themselves been witnesses, but which had been reported at the time to the Section of Surgery of the Academy. Madame Plantin, aged 64, was suffering from an ulcerated cancer in the right breast, of some years' standing. M. Cloquet was called in in April, 1829, to operate, and the patient's medical attendant, M. Chapelain, desired, with M. Cloquet's consent, to put her into the somnambulic trance during the operation of extirpating the tumour. The experiment was a complete success. The patient prepared herself for the operation and seated herself in the chair, without being held or bound. The operation lasted ten or twelve minutes, and the patient remained throughout perfectly calm, betraying no sign of pain or uneasiness, and conversing quietly with the operator. The pulse and breathing remained unchanged. The patient was not wakened from the trance until two days later. She then retained no recollection of the operation, but on seeing her children and hearing what had taken place became so profoundly affected that it was thought prudent again to induce the trance. The Section had been sufficiently interested in M. Cloquet's report to appoint a committee of inquiry. But the relatives refused to allow the Committee, or any member of it, to see the patient, who, in fact, died of pleurisy within three weeks of the operation. The Committee, however, assisted at the autopsy, and reported that the clairvoyant's statement that her liver was diseased proved to be incorrect. Apparently the Committee and the Section considered that this circumstance dispensed them from the necessity of paying any further attention to the matter. A woman who was capable of telling a falsehood about her own liver was clearly not to be trusted when she pretended to feel no pain during a surgical operation.

M. Cloquet's case, as said, had taken place in 1829. But in 1836 the young doctor Hamard invited a member of the Academy, M. Oudet, to extract a tooth from a somnambulic patient. The operation was successfully performed ; it made some noise in the Press, but M. Oudet refrained from reporting it to the Academy. Some weeks later, in January, 1837, in reply to a challenge from a colleague, he explained that he had deliberately kept silence, fearing to involve the Academy in a fruitless discussion, "car les faits ne se discutent pas, on les accepte ou on les rejette, il n'y a pas de troisième parti à prendre." To satisfy his colleagues' wishes, however, he consented to speak, but he warned them that he was not prepared to discuss the question of Magnetism, and that he must confine himself strictly to the rôle of an historian. What follows is curiously significant of the reluctance of medical men to imperil their reputation by even the remotest contact with Animal Magnetism. From Oudet's speech it must have been inferred that he was himself going to describe to his colleagues what he had seen and done—for how else could he play the part of an historian? Perhaps at the actual meeting of the Academy he did so; but in the official bulletin of the Society we find, not a speech by Oudet, but a report by the magnetiser, Hamard, given "with the approval of M. Oudet."[1]

The patient was a woman of twenty-five, exceptionally nervous and sensitive to pain. She showed the utmost dread of the operation when it was proposed to her, and almost had an attack of convulsions. Hamard succeeded, however, in inducing the trance; the patient's insensibility was tested by the ordinary processes, by pricking her severely in several places with a pin, and by holding her finger for some seconds in the flame of a candle. In reply to a direct question Oudet testified that the skin was burnt by the flame. The tooth was then extracted, but the patient did not seem to know what had happened, and took no notice of the suggestion that she should wash out her mouth. Awakened from the trance she was astonished and relieved to find that her tooth was gone.

Here were two plain statements of fact. It is curious to see the effect of them upon the *élite* of the medical profession in France. Two or three doctors described in their own practice operations at which the patients by mere force of will had suppressed all signs of pain; the authors of the *Histoire académique* recall that in the Conscription recruits would frequently feign epileptic fits and maintain their

---

[1] *Hist. acad.*, p. 453.

simulated insensibility through tolerably severe tests. Several speakers plainly intimated their belief that both Cloquet and Oudet had been deceived by their patients. Just as the one side was obsessed by the idea of Magnetism, so the medical world was obsessed by the idea of fraud. For the most part fraud was imputed to the subjects only. But Burdin and Dubois do not hesitate to explain the alleged induction of somnambulism at a distance, of which two or three cases were recorded in Husson's Report, by collusion between the subject and the operator. The operator was M. Foissac, a member of their own profession.[1]

With subjects who were for the most part poor, uneducated, and liable to all the infirmities and perversions which accompany the hysterical temperament, there was, no doubt, good reason for suspecting fraud as the true cause of the marvels recounted by the magnetiser. Mdlle. Céline and her tribe, as we have seen in recent times at the Charité under the late Dr. Luys, will always find ways and means of fulfilling what is expected of them. But the case of Madame Plantin was not that of an hysterical girl, willing at no cost to herself to humour the fancies of her magnetiser by going into pretended convulsions, or surreptitiously glancing under closed eyelids. Madame Plantin was an old woman, about to submit herself to a serious and, as it proved, fatal operation. Nor was it here simply a question of a firm will. Either Madame Plantin was in a somnambulic trance, and insensible to pain, or else she deliberately feigned to be so, and feigned also the vivid emotion with which, on waking from her simulated trance, she received the congratulations of her children. What conceivable motive could have induced an elderly woman, on the threshold of death, to undertake and carry through a prolonged deception of this kind? But the last word of fanatic incredulity does not rest with the French physicians of 1837. It was reserved for an English surgeon ten years later to suggest that remorse for the part which she had played contributed to bring about poor Madame Plantin's death.[2]

[1] *Hist. acad.*, pp. 415, 416, *note*.   [2] See *Zoist*, vol. i. p. 209.

Possibly even the Academy felt that the hypothesis of deliberate fraud in such a case was beaten a little too thin, and that the subject could not be so summarily dismissed. At any rate, before the conclusion of the adjourned discussion on Oudet's case, a letter was received from a young physician, Berna, offering to demonstrate on some subjects of his own facts conclusive in favour of Magnetism. It was resolved to accept the invitation, and a committee of nine members, including Oudet himself and Dubois (of Amiens), part author of the *Histoire académique*, was appointed to meet M. Berna. The chief phenomena which M. Berna proposed to demonstrate to the Committee at the outset were the state of somnambulism, insensibility to pain, and the action of his unexpressed will on the somnambule, as shown by the loss or restoration of movement and sensation in any particular limb. The subject was a young woman of seventeen or eighteen years of age. Three sittings were devoted to experiments on the lines indicated above, but the results were quite inconclusive. The insensibility and the inability—real or alleged—to move the limbs failed to correspond with the intention of the magnetiser, dictated to him by the Committee. The Committee obviously suspected the young woman of deliberately feigning trance, insensibility, and immobility. In the light of fuller knowledge there seems no reason to doubt the genuineness of the exhibition ; but Berna was clearly mistaken in attributing the results to his unexpressed will. For when, under the stringent conditions enforced by the Committee, no indication of his intention was allowed to appear, the subject found herself at fault, and the results followed at random.

Failing to find any proof of Magnetism in these inconclusive results, the Committee asked Berna for a more decisive test. At the fourth and last sitting a new subject, a woman of thirty, attended for the purpose of demonstrating clairvoyance and transposition of sensation. Again, under the strict conditions imposed by the Committee, the marvel failed of demonstration. The subject's eyes were bandaged and cards or other objects were held behind her head or on

I

her forehead, Berna being in every case ignorant of the
object. Not only did the subject fail to describe what was
there, but she unfortunately essayed to describe what was
not there. The demonstration seemed to the Committee
conclusive of fraud. Berna was not prepared to offer any
more subjects for experiment; no other magnetiser responded
to the Committee's invitation, issued through advertisement
in the Press, to submit themselves and their patients to investigation; and the Committee on July 17, 1837, presented
to the Academy their Report. In summarising the results
they found that no proof had been afforded of the existence
of the alleged magnetic somnambulism, nor of the abolition
or restoration of sensibility, nor of induced paralysis, nor of
the influence of the unexpressed will of the operator, nor of
transposition of the senses, nor of clairvoyance. In connection with the last-named subject, they regarded the
attempts of the clairvoyant to describe things which were
not really there as specially significant. They concluded
that Berna had himself been deceived, and saw no reason
to doubt that all other magnetisers were in like case. "If
they have anything to show, they have not ventured to
produce it in the full light of day; they have not ventured to challenge the approval or condemnation of the
Academy." [1]

The reading of the Report elicited a vehement and not
altogether unreasonable protest from M. Husson. The
verdict, based upon a few hours' experiments with two
subjects, could at most be accepted as a verdict upon
M. Berna's pretensions; it was not a judgment passed
upon Animal Magnetism. But Husson found no supporters; the question was put to the vote, and the
conclusions of the Report adopted by a very large
majority.

But the verdict of the Academy of Medicine seemed likely
to have small immediate effect upon the future of Animal
Magnetism, which offered a lucrative and unlaborious liveli-
hood to so many medical clairvoyants and itinerant enter-

[1] *Hist. acad.*, p. 511.

tainers. In both cases the chief item in the programme was this very clairvoyance or transposition of vision. Again, from the scientific standpoint this alleged faculty was the only one of all the marvels vaunted by the magnetiser which could be readily tested. Somnambulism, insensibility to pain, paralysis, could all be feigned; the predictions of epileptic fits could be made to work out their own fulfilment; the description of diseased organs must wait for its verification until the death of the patient. But vision without eyes could be tested on the spot and without the possibility of error or deception. Moved by these considerations, a member of the Academy, M. Burdin, deposited with a notary the sum of three thousand francs as a prize for the person who should first prove his ability to read without the aid of eyes.[1] A committee was appointed to examine the claims of any candidates who should present themselves. The Committee met on January 2, 1838, to consider six letters from provincial doctors and others describing the clairvoyance of their subjects. M. Ricard, of Bordeaux, assured the Committee that there were more than a thousand magnetisers who could demonstrate clairvoyance in their subjects. Dr. Despines, of Aix, had witnessed transposition of sensation at least five hundred, probably a thousand, times. But none of the Committee's correspondents were ready to submit their subjects forthwith to examination. Some found a difficulty in conveying themselves and their clairvoyants to Paris; others required a longer time to enable their clairvoyants to develop their powers to perfection. In other cases the relatives refused their consent to a trial in public. In the event two magnetisers only presented themselves before the Committee; and only one somnambule was actually offered for examination. M. Pigeaire, a doctor from Montpelier, came to Paris in May, 1838, bringing with him his

---

[1] *Histoire académique*, p. 575. The original wording runs, "sans le secours des yeux et de la lumière." But the last four words were subsequently omitted on the representations of M. Pigeaire that his clairvoyant found it essential that the object should be strongly illuminated.

young daughter, who was alleged to be clairvoyant. After spending some weeks in giving demonstrations of his daughter's powers to various distinguished persons, he wrote to the Committee for an appointment, at the same time indicating the lines upon which he wished the experiment to proceed. The Committee naturally replied that it was for them to determine the conditions. The Committee had prepared a screen of black silk, so contrived as to be suspended by iron wires about six inches in front of the face. This, while effectually excluding all rays of light from the object to be described, would have enabled the Committee to watch the eyes of the subject. On the proposed screen being shown to M. Pigeaire, he objected that it was essential to exclude light from the subject's eyes ; and he proffered for use a bandage of black velvet, such as the clairvoyant was in the habit of using. M. Double, the president of the Committee, pointed out to M. Pigeaire that this bandage, which was only two or three inches broad, was scarcely large enough to form an effective safeguard. He intimated that it would be acceptable to the Committee if it were made somewhat larger, so as to cover part of the cheeks. M. Pigeaire replied that it was essential to the success of the experiment that the face should not be covered, on the ground, as he seems to have suggested, that vision was possibly effected by means of the fifth nerve which supplies the face. M. Double, who, like the rest of the Committee, had received accounts of Mdlle. Pigeaire's demonstrations and had grounds for something more than suspicion, pointed out that under such conditions, however carefully the eyes were plastered and the enveloping bandage applied, it was always possible for crevices to be left, or to develop subsequently, through which light might penetrate to the eyes. The Committee were willing, however, to accept M. Pigeaire's bandage, with all its imperfections, if he would consent that the book to be read should be held not, as was Mdlle. Pigeaire's custom, on her lap or on the table—that is, *below* the level of the eyes—but directly in front of the eyes, so that no ray of light could reach the eye except through the bandages. M. Pigeaire refused to accept these conditions, and Mdlle. Pigeaire did not pursue her candidature for the prize.[1]

The only somnambule whose claim appears to have been actually tested by the Committee, and that not until the offer of the prize had been specially prolonged for a twelvemonth beyond the original term of two years, was a subject magnetised by Dr. Teste, afterwards well known as a writer on the subject. Teste informed the Committee that he had two subjects who could read writing enclosed in cardboard or wooden boxes, the sole condition being that they should be informed of the direction of the lines of print or writing. The Committee accordingly prepared several boxes, each containing some printed or written characters. From these a small square cardboard box was chosen. The box was handed to the somnambule, who in handling and turning it round broke one of the paper bands which secured it. Finally, after the lapse of an hour, she announced that she could see two lines of print, and that she could read the two words "*nous sommes*." The box on being opened was found to contain *six* lines of poetry quoted from *La Guerre de Jugurtha*, by Leprevost. Neither of the two words given by the somnambule occurred in the quotation. With this, their first and last experiment, the labours of the Burdin Committee terminated. In reporting the results to the Academy M. Double

[1] M. Pigeaire's account of the interview with M. Double (*Puissance de l'Électricité animale*, Paris, 1839) does not differ materially from that given by the authors of the *Hist. acad.*, on which the account in the text is based. But the former quotes from the *Gazette Médicale* of July 28, 1838, a detailed report professing to give an account of an actual experiment made by the Commission on Mdlle. Pigeaire, in which the girl is reported to have contorted her face and her body, and thus displaced the bandages sufficiently to read. As no such experiment ever took place before the Commission, Pigeaire is naturally indignant. MM. Burdin and Dubois, in commenting on the matter, throw the whole blame on Pigeaire for accepting the report without verifying it from the archives of the Academy. But as both Pigeaire and the authors of the *Hist. acad.* are agreed that the report in the *Gazette Médicale* contained grave misstatements of fact, it was surely the duty of the Academy to have corrected it.

proposed that thereafter the Academy should cease to concern itself with the question of Animal Magnetism, and should refuse to accede to any further demand for investigation. " L'académie de Médecine a aussi ses questions de mouvement perpétuel et de quadrature du cercle dont elle doit désormais refuser de s'occuper." [1]

So far as the question of reading with the eyes bandaged was concerned the Committee's conclusion was, no doubt, justified. But their justification consisted, not in the single experiment cited, but in other contemporary facts which had come to their knowledge. Any one who cares to make the experiment by pricking a card with a pin will find that a very small hole suffices for distinct vision, provided that the conditions are favourable. Amongst these conditions are that the object to be seen should be clearly illuminated ; that the hole should be near the eye ; and that as far as possible all other light should be excluded from the eye, except that which proceeds from the object itself. Now these conditions were all fulfilled in such experiments as those conducted by Mdlle. Pigeaire. Pigeaire himself prevailed upon Burdin to modify his original offer, so as to permit of the object being illuminated ; the black velvet bandage effectually excluded from the eyes all light from general sources. It remains to prove the possibility of light from the object reaching the eye through a narrow channel or pinhole. Short of placing the object in a closed box the best methods of effectually excluding such a possibility are to hold a screen of suitable size in front of the eyes, or to allow the bandage to cover a great part of the face. It has been shown that Pigeaire absolutely refused to allow either of these methods to be adopted. But the crevices can be rendered useless if the object is held straight in front of the face, *i.e.*, approximately at right angles to any possible crevice. This precaution, again, Pigeaire refused to adopt. That Mdlle. Pigeaire did actually see cards and read books by means of such crevices in the bandaging is not merely matter of conjecture or suspicion. M. Burdin's Committee

[1] *Hist. acad.*, p. 630.

appear, indeed, neither collectively nor individually to have witnessed her performances. But another observer, Professor Gerdy—to whom the *Histoire académique* is dedicated —has left us a full account of what took place. The somnambule's eyes were covered by a band of calico, then by small pellets of cotton (? cotton-wool) ; the black velvet band already described was tied over all, and its lower edge attached to the cheek by small bands of gummed "taffetas." The bands were not continuous. At Gerdy's first sitting the girl complained of headache, moved her eyebrows a good deal and rubbed her forehead and eyes with her hand, and on her mother's bosom. After a full hour of this nothing had taken place, and Gerdy had to leave. On the second occasion Gerdy was requested himself to apply the bandages ; but it was Pigeaire who arranged the gummed slips of taffetas, and though Gerdy did his best, he found that some crevices remained between the gummed slips. The girl, who had been quite quiet until the bandage was put on, again began to complain and to fidget with the bandage. Some of the gummed slips partially detached themselves, and fresh crevices appeared between the velvet and the skin. Then the girl pushed her finger under the upper edge of the bandage and altered the position of the cotton. Finally, after a considerable interval, she played at cards, and read a book, placed in a position chosen by herself. She was unable to read when the book was placed directly in front of her eyes. When the experiment was concluded, Gerdy was allowed to remove the bandages. He did so from above, leaving the lower edge of the velvet intact. When he had taken out the calico and the cotton-wool he was able, by placing the girl's head in a suitable position, to see several small crevices between the bandage and the skin through which the daylight showed.

Gerdy was present at similar trials with two other somnambules, Callyste and Prudence, and in each case he made similar observations. Callyste disturbed the bandage by grimaces and movements of the facial muscles. It was replaced again and again in its former position ; and again and again Callyste repeated the manœuvre. The experiment failed. In Callyste's case the bandaging had consisted of cotton-wool and a handkerchief. In the case of Prudence the bandage consisted solely of slips of gummed taffetas crossing each other and fastened to the skin. Prudence did not complain of headache and made no grimaces. But her name was justified. For the taffetas, which had been moistened to admit of its being applied to the skin, naturally shrank somewhat in drying, and in a few minutes afforded all the crevices required. Gerdy demonstrated their exist-ence by slipping pieces of thick paper into them. Later, a friend of Gerdy's had himself bandaged by an enthusiastic magnetist in the same way as Mdlle. Prudence, and succeeded easily in seeing. The light, he found, came to him chiefly from below, and by the inner angle of the eye, *i.e.*, along the nose. Further, he found that the taffetas, which was saturated with fish-glue, became semi-transparent when moistened.[1]

Another experiment in clairvoyance which took place shortly after the report of the Burdin Committee is not less instructive. Hublier, a doctor of Provins, had written to the Academy in 1837 that he had an excellent clairvoyant, whom he was preparing for examination. But the somnambule was not forthcoming, and in September, 1840, Frappart, a doctor who, though not a member of the Burdin Committee, had taken a keen interest in the subject, wrote to Hublier to remind him that the term fixed for competing for the Burdin prize would expire in ten days. Hublier replied by sending his somnambule, Emélie, not to the Commission, but to Frappart. Emélie came to Frappart's house, and was sent into the somnambulic state by means of a ring magnetised by Hublier which she had brought with

[1] The Society for Psychical Research has conducted several experi-ments in " clairvoyance " with subjects whose eyes were bandaged. The results have always been the same. It is practically impossible to bandage the eyes so as to prevent the possibility of vision through crevices; but the interposition of a screen has always stopped the clairvoyance. See the *Journal* of the Society, vol. i. p. 84.

her. The first essay in clairvoyance proved unsuccessful.
Mdlle. Emélie professed to be embarrassed in the exercise
of her faculty by the number of books in Frappart's library.
Frappart suggested that the trial should take place in the
adjoining room, and that one book only should be placed
before her. Matters were arranged accordingly, and Frappart, having seen the somnambule pass into what was
apparently a magnetic trance, left her alone, and going
into the next room, applied his eye to a hole which he
had made in the partition dividing the two rooms. In a few
minutes he saw two hands stretched out, the book was
seized, and the somnambule diligently studied it for some
time. When Frappart returned the somnambule had no
difficulty in proving her clairvoyant powers. Frappart
summoned Hublier from the country, and the same comedy
was played a few days later before a large audience of
doctors.

The question of clairvoyance thus disposed of, the official
medical world in France, as we have seen, felt themselves
dispensed from any further obligations in regard to Animal
Magnetism. The study was still pursued, subterraneously,
so to speak, and we shall have occasion later to treat of some
of its non-scientific or mystical developments. It was not,
however, until the appearance of Liébeault's book, *Du
Sommeil et des états analogues*, in 1866, nearly thirty years
after the date of the Burdin Committee, that the importance
of the subject for therapeutics and psychology began to be
recognised.

CHAPTER VII

MESMERISM IN ENGLAND

Professor Bell, de Mainauduc, and others—Demonstrations by
Chenevix in 1829 : Chenevix a believer in suggestion—Elliotson's
demonstrations in 1838 at University College on the Okey girls—
Suspicions of fraud—The case of Anne Ross and others—Wakley's
counter-experiments with the Okeys—Elliotson resigns from University College—Induced anæsthesia and the incredulity of the medical
profession : the case of Wombell and the Medico-Chirurgical Society :
Esdaile's painless surgery in India : Lord Ducie and the *Medical
Gazette*—Braid's view : his hypothesis of suggestion, and his counter-
experiments—Discovery of chloroform, growth of modern Spiritualism
and concurrent decay of interest in Mesmerism.

IN the discussion which preceded the appointment of the
second French Commission the land of the immortal
Newton, as we have seen, was held up to honour
because above almost every civilised nation it had steadily
pursued the exact sciences, and disdained the moonshine and
mysticism of Animal Magnetism. On the whole the eulogy
was not undeserved. But some echoes of the marvellous
doings of Mesmer and his followers had nevertheless from
time to time reached the shores of these islands. So early as
1785 one Dr. Bell, member of the Philosophical Harmonic
Society of Paris, and fellow correspondent of Court de
Gébelin's Museum, came to England and lectured throughout the country—at London, Dublin, Bristol, Cheltenham,
Gloucester, Worcester, Wolverhampton, and elsewhere. He
brought with him credentials signed by Despremenil, Bergasse, Puységur, and other well-known practitioners in Paris.
Bell is the first of that tribe of itinerant professors who have

for more than a century exploited the art for commercial purposes. There is a curious remark in one of his lectures which betrays his attitude, and marks him off from generous enthusiasts, such as were Puységur and many of the early French magnetisers. He recommends his disciples to have as little to do as possible with scrofula, cutaneous eruptions, and consumption; such diseases were very dangerous to treat. In the first two cases the magnetiser may contract the disease, in the last he may impart too much of his own vital force to the sufferer. For the rest his lectures faithfully reflect the ideas of the time. He employed a Baquet and gave his pupils detailed instructions for its construction. In treating the sick he places the patient with his back to the north, he makes free use of mineral magnets and of magnetised water, he gives instructions also for magnetising coins, trees, rivers, and other objects. He describes the aura which streams from the magnetiser and can be seen by sensitive patients as a soft radiance. "A celebrated monk," who took off part of his clothing in a dark room, was told by his patient that he shone like the sun.[1]

Bell was followed in 1788 by de Mainauduc, a pupil of Deslon. A few years later several native professors of the art came into prominence, amongst whom the best known is Loutherbourg, the artist. It is reported that on one occasion three thousand persons endeavoured to get admission to his lectures in Hammersmith. Most of the practitioners in England at this time appear to have been without medical training, and apparently their chief concern in the matter was their pecuniary advantage. De Mainauduc charged twenty-five guineas for a course of lectures. Holloway's fee was five guineas, whilst tickets for Loutherbourg's lectures are said to have been sold for a guinea apiece.[2] But a physician at Bristol, George Winter, who is our authority for the details given in the preceding paragraph, appears to have used it

---

[1] *The General and Particular Principles of Animal Electricity and Magnetism,* &c., by Monsieur le Docteur Bell, 1792. Entered in Stationers' Hall.

[2] *Animal Magnetism,* &c., by George Winter, M.D., Bristol, 1801.

with success in his private practice for some years, and there were doubtless others. In 1798, however, Perkins appeared on the scene with his Metallic Tractors, and after Dr. Haygarth had demonstrated that tractors of wood painted to resemble iron were equally efficacious in the cure of rheumatism and gout, the popular craze for marvellous remedies seems to have died down. It is probable that Animal Magnetism did not at this time produce any effect on scientific opinion in this country.

Even after the revival of interest on the Continent at the close of the Napoleonic wars, Animal Magnetism attracted little attention in England. We hear little more of it, indeed, until 1829. In that year the subject was brought forward by Richard Chenevix, F.R.S., a well-known chemist and mineralogist. Chenevix had been resident for many years in Paris, and had there learnt how to magnetise from the Abbé Faria. He began by treating the children of some Irish peasants who were brought to him to be cured of epilepsy and other complaints. Before his departure from Ireland he taught the parents to treat the children themselves, holding that Mesmerism was an art that could be practised by all. At the time when he wrote his account of his experiments he had eleven patients under treatment by relatives and friends whom he had taught to practise Mesmerism. It is noteworthy that Chenevix held the view, prevalent amongst Mesmer's early followers, that the susceptibility to the influence was in itself a symptom of disease. When one of his patients came to thank him for her cure, he tells us that, to prove the reality of the cure to himself, he mesmerised her for thirty minutes without effect, and a similar attempt on the following day was equally unsuccessful.

In London he was given opportunities for practising in a military hospital, under the direction of Surgeon-Major Whymper of the Coldstreams, also at St. George's Hospital and elsewhere. In addition to alleviating disease he essayed to give demonstrations of the effect of his unexpressed will. As a disciple of Faria he recognised that the physical sensations experienced by the patient were illusory—his article is headed "Mesmerism, Improperly Denominated Animal Magnetism." He conceived that these sensations were produced by the will of the operator acting directly upon the nervous system of the patient. Thus in the presence of Dr. Whymper, who attests the facts, he experimented upon a soldier. He told Whymper out of the patient's hearing that he would produce in the hand sensations of heat and cold at will. Six times in succession he touched the hand with his silver pencil-case, and each time the predetermined effect followed. After that the effects became more uncertain—a result, as Chenevix himself points out, which generally follows if experiments of the kind are continued to the point of fatigue. On another occasion he claims to have sent a patient into the trance by operating through a closed door at a distance of fifteen feet. Dr. Elliotson came on two or three occasions to see the treatment, and, as he tells us, was much impressed by seeing Chenevix paralyse an arm or a leg, and give or take away pain in any limb, without saying anything to the patient, his intention being announced beforehand to Elliotson in French, a language of which the patient was ignorant.

Amongst those who witnessed Chenevix's performances were Sir B. Brodie, Drs. Prout and Holland, Professor Faraday, and Lord Lansdowne. Some thought that the sleep was feigned, others that it was simply due to giddiness, or that it resembled the sleep induced by rocking a cradle. Elliotson alone seems to have been seriously impressed by what he saw. Unfortunately, Chenevix died in the following year, and the subject fell again into oblivion. Thus, for the second time in the history of the science, the spread of rational views on the subject was hindered by an untimely death.[1] Three years later J. C. Colquhoun complains in *Isis*

---

[1] See the articles in the *London Medical and Physical Journal* for 1829, vol. 61, p. 219, vol. 62, pp. 119, 315, "On Mesmerism, Improperly Denominated Animal Magnetism." See also *London Medical and Surgical Journal*, July and December, 1829, p. 484, for an expression of the hostile medical view.

Revelata[1] that "of late our medical men seem liable to the reproach of having almost entirely neglected the most important labours of their professional brethren upon the Continent," *i.e.*, in connection with Mesmerism.

In 1837 du Potet, who had assisted the second French Commission in their inquiry, came to London, and was admitted by Elliotson, at that time Senior Physician to University College Hospital, to practise upon some patients in the hospital. Later Elliotson undertook to practise Mesmerism himself, and soon succeeded in producing the somnambulic state.

Elliotson at this time occupied a considerable position in the medical world. From its foundation he had devoted himself enthusiastically to University College, and had done much to assure its progress in its early years. He was the founder of the Phrenological Society—then a more respectable study than now—had been President of the Medico-Chirurgical Society, Censor and Lecturer to the Royal College of Physicians. He had, besides, an enormous private practice. He is described by a writer in the *Medical Times*[2] as vigorous, unconventional, self-willed, and impetuous, with the hand, and something of the disposition, of a pugilist. His attitude towards his own profession had never been conciliatory; he had already made himself conspicuous by his impetuous and hitherto successful patronage of new inventions. He had been the first to use the stethoscope in England, and he had forced upon the profession many important additions to the *materia medica*. Such was the man who in the spring and summer of 1838 gave public demonstrations of Mesmerism in the theatre of University College Hospital. His colleagues on the staff held aloof from the spectacle, but the theatre was thronged by a number of distinguished persons from outside. The principal subjects at these public demonstrations were two young girls, Jane and Elizabeth Okey, sixteen and seventeen years old respectively, of

---

[1] *Isis Revelata: an Inquiry into the Origin, Progress, and Present State of Animal Magnetism* (Edinburgh, 1833).

[2] Vol. xi., February 1, 1845.

diminutive stature and childish features. The sisters, as we gather from the report of a physician who had attended them before their admission to University College Hospital,[1] were well-marked examples of a type of nervous instability much less common then and now in England than in France, where its characteristic manifestations have been carefully investigated at the Salpêtrière and elsewhere. Both sisters were epileptic, and so abnormally sensitive to shock that a loud knock at the door would sometimes have the effect of bringing on an attack. The younger, Jane, had experienced accesses of spontaneous delirium before Animal Magnetism had been used upon her; she had also fallen occasionally into a state of spontaneous catalepsy, in which her senses were in abeyance. One of the sisters, as we learn from an editorial in the *Lancet*, had gone to a meeting at Irving's Chapel, and had proceeded to "speak with tongues" until she was turned out.

Under the influence of Animal Magnetism, or "Mesmerism," as it was now commonly styled in this country, the sisters exhibited various stages of dissociation of consciousness, all of them marked by apparent oblivion on waking. In the most alert state they showed themselves extremely lively and talkative, not seldom witty, and their behaviour to all around, but especially to Elliotson and his clinical clerk, Wood, was marked by impudent familiarity. Thus at one demonstration the first object which caught Elizabeth's attention when thrown into the alert state was the white trousers worn by Lord Anglesey, who occupied a seat in the front row. She immediately went up to him and commented on them—"Dear, you do look so tidy, you do. What nice things! You are a nice man." She then attempted to snatch the hat of a doctor who sat near. When Elliotson frustrated the attempt she made saucy remarks and used silly terms of endearment to him. Jane's conduct was fashioned on the same model. She shocked the clergy who were present by constantly appealing to the devil; she twisted a handkerchief up in imitation of a clergyman

[1] *Lancet* for May, 1838, p. 379.

preaching; she tried to tell funny stories of such a nature that Elliotson at an early stage found it necessary to cut them short.

Notwithstanding his familiarity with the views held and demonstrated by Chenevix, Elliotson from the first appears to have been convinced of the fluidic nature of the influence, and the phenomena shown were interpreted in accordance with this preconception. The patient was put into the trance by drinking mesmerised water, by contact with mesmerised metals, by passes made from behind a screen, which were presumed to be made without her knowledge. A pile of mesmerised sovereigns would send her to sleep, but the sleep would deepen if the same sovereigns were presented to her flat, so as to increase the acting surface. In the trance she would imitate movements of head, hand, and mouth made by Elliotson or Wood behind her back. She would show herself indifferent to pinches and pricks bestowed on her by the spectators. On one occasion a needle was found imbedded in Elizabeth's arm, and a small operation was necessary for its extraction. She showed no pain at the time, and on being awakened professed ignorance of what had occurred, and tore off the bandage to see what they had been doing to her. On another occasion, her arm having been carefully bound in a splint to prevent possible injury to the wrist, she lifted a weight of seventy pounds to a height of four inches from the floor. It was found that, when hungry, she could detect bread—" see it," as she said— with the back of her left hand. Repeated trials were made with her eyes bandaged and a cardboard screen held in front of her in such a manner as to make vision impossible. She never failed to detect the bread when held within two inches of the hand, nor ever mistook any other substance for bread. This result can perhaps be attributed to hyperæsthesia of the skin. She predicted that a pinch of tea in her hand would send her into a sleep from which she could not be wakened; she predicted the occurrence of headaches; when asked questions which she was unable to answer she would refer them to her " negro," and would report his answers. In his hospital practice Elliotson employed Elizabeth's clairvoyant powers on his other patients; he even on one occasion took her into the men's ward, for the purpose of testing her powers of prediction on the sick. On one bed she saw "Great Jackey" sitting, and said that the man would not recover. In fact, he died very shortly afterwards. But the girl's prophecy had been overheard by the man in the next bed, if not by the patient himself.

Elliotson's high standing in the profession had sufficed in the first instance to ensure a respectful hearing for his theories. But from the outset some appear to have regarded the Okey girls as simply impostors. At a meeting of the Medical Society of London this opinion was freely expressed; but Dr. Hughes Bennett, on the other side, pointed out that the pulse and the temperature of the skin were altered in the trance. The suspicion of fraud had, however, affected Elliotson's students; tests were applied, and several "exposures" followed, the results of which were communicated by Elliotson to the Lancet.[1]

In judging of these cases it is necessary to bear in mind that Elliotson conceived the trance and its accompanying manifestations as definite physiological effects produced in the organism, independently of the patient's imagination, by a specific external agent. Obviously the trance itself and most, if not all, of the manifestations could be feigned; the proof of their genuineness lay in their correspondence to certain physical reagents. From this standpoint the demonstration of deception in the cases cited by Elliotson no doubt seemed complete. The first case was that of a girl of twelve who was under treatment for debility of the spine. Elliotson's account merely states that tests were applied and the girl's sleep was found to be feigned. The nature of these tests we learn from an anonymous article in the Lancet. It appears that Elizabeth Okey had from the first taken a strong dislike to the little patient Charlotte Bentley. She charged her with being an impostor, bullied and threatened her, and finally made her drink "mesmerised"

[1] July, 1838, p. 634.

K

and unmesmerised water in turn. Both drinks produced the mesmeric sleep, and Elizabeth triumphantly proclaimed the girl's imposture. Elliotson appears to have accepted the test and to have regarded the girl's deception as proved. By an ironical fate Elizabeth herself was to be tried by the same test a few weeks later, and Elliotson was to set aside the verdict.

The case of Anne Ross is even more dubious. She was an epileptic, twenty-three years of age. Under mesmeric treatment her fits were reduced in severity, and the premonitory convulsive movements of arms and legs, which had previously come on several days before each fit, lasting for two or three hours a day, almost disappeared. In the trance she announced that an angel had appeared to her and prescribed the removal of two teeth. The teeth were taken out, on two separate occasions, without any sign of pain on the part of the patient. Nevertheless, some of the students—on what grounds does not appear—suspected imposture, and devised what seemed to them a conclusive test. Within hearing of the entranced patient they mentioned that some somnambules would awake when the index finger was pricked. They then tried the experiment on Anne Ross, and she awoke immediately. On the following day the students announced in her hearing that Elizabeth Okey had predicted that Anne Ross would roll her head from side to side for half a minute ; that she would feel no pain on one side of the body for a time, that subsequently sensibility would be restored ; that she would waken when her nose was pinched and say, " God bless my soul ! " and so on. All these suggestions were punctually fulfilled. Again, this time in Elliotson's presence, the patient, at the suggestion of the students, assumed delirium—and Elliotson said that he had never seen worse acting.

On this evidence Elliotson and his pupils regarded the girl's imposture as proved, and under pressure she was induced to admit that she had never felt more than a certain degree of drowsiness under Mesmerism, and that all else was feigned.

For the modern student of hypnotism, it need scarcely be said, there is nothing in the results recorded inconsistent with good faith on the part of the patient. That a hypnotic patient should act promptly on suggestions made in her hearing is what experience has led us to expect. Her very "confession" was, in fact, probably suggested to her by Elliotson. The facts that, as expressly stated by him, there had been marked improvement in her malady under mesmeric treatment, and that she had given no signs of pain when her teeth were extracted, furnish some positive evidence that her state was not feigned. Two other epileptics at the same time were suspected of trickery, on what grounds is not stated, and were discharged.[1]

But an exposure of a more disastrous nature was to follow. Elliotson had made numerous experiments purporting to illustrate the physical nature of the mesmeric effluence. Gold, silver, platinum, water, and the moisture of the skin were found to transmit it ; copper, zinc, tin, pewter, &c., unless wet, were non-conductors. Of the conductors, nickel and gold were said to be the best ; but the mesmeric influence as transmitted by nickel was of an extremely violent and even dangerous character. Some of the most striking effects were produced by gold : thus, if a sovereign, mesmerised by being retained in the operator's hand, were placed in the hand of one of the Okeys, it would cause cramp, either local or general, trance, or coma, the effect being, it was alleged, strictly proportioned to the strength of the original dose of mesmeric fluid communicated to the metal. Analogous effects were observed if a sovereign was placed successively in the hands of several hospital patients and thence transferred to the hand of the sensitive, the effect produced in the latter varying in strength with the state of the patient's vitality. If mesmerised sovereigns were placed in a pewter vessel, the influence would be gradually transmitted to the sensitive's hand. In stooping to pick up a mesmerised sovereign from the floor, the Okeys would suddenly become cataleptic, as their hands approached the

[1] *Lancet*, 1838, pp. 546 and 634.

metal, and remain fixed in a stooping position. Dr. Herbert Mayo, Professor of Anatomy and Physiology at King's College, who had contributed reports of Elliotson's demonstrations to the pages of the *Lancet*, records[1] a still more striking experiment. It sufficed for the mesmerist to gaze intently at a stone mantelpiece, and to place a sovereign on the spot where his gaze had fallen, for the metal to become imbued with the mesmeric virtue, and to produce the characteristic reactions with a sensitive subject.

Again, Elliotson claimed to have succeeded in mesmerising a patient by making passes over her image reflected in a mirror. A surgeon at Windsor improved on this experiment. He placed his patient in his study, within the focus of a telescopic lens inserted in the closed door. At the opposite focus a mirror was placed, and by means of a second mirror the rays were reflected to where the surgeon stood, forty-six feet from his patient. Nevertheless, the mesmeric passes proved effective.[2]

Further, as shown in the experiments with the Okeys already mentioned, clairvoyance, prevision, and transposition of sensation were said to have been observed in certain cases. Thomas Wakley, editor of the *Lancet*, had at first, as we have seen, opened his columns to the recital of these "beautiful phenomena," as Elliotson was wont to call them. But in the month of August, 1838, he determined to test them for himself. Elliotson brought the two Okeys to Wakley's house, and there, in the presence of several medical men, experiments were made under Wakley's sole direction. On the first day the violent contortions and muscular cramp, which were the characteristic results of contact with mesmerised nickel, were produced when the nickel—unknown to Elliotson and most of the company— was safe in the waistcoat pocket of one of the spectators. It was shown in a further series of experiments that unmesmerised water could produce sleep, whilst water which had been carefully mesmerised had no effect; and that

[1] *Lancet*, September 1, 1838.
[2] Letter in the *Lancet*, June, 1838, p. 454.

whilst three or four mesmerised sovereigns could be handled with impunity, well-marked catalepsy was produced when Jane Okey stooped to pick up a sovereign which had merely been warmed in hot water, without human contact at all.[1] Wakley reported these experiments as a conclusive exposure of the pretensions of the Mesmerists. "The science of Mesmerism," he writes, "like the science of fortune-telling, will always flourish where there are clever girls, philosophic Bohemians, weak women, and weaker men."[2] All his subsequent utterances betray an almost personal animus against the Mesmerists, no doubt partly due to the fact that he had allowed his own journal for some months to be their chief medium of communication with the world.

But Wakley's experiments, of course, however conclusive against Elliotson's conception of a physical agent, did not, in fact, prove either imposture on the part of the Okeys or the unreality of the induced trance and its accompanying psychological phenomena.

Meantime Elliotson had become involved in a personal dispute with the authorities of University College Hospital. After the exhibition of the Okeys in the hospital theatre, in June, 1838, the Committee had requested Elliotson to refrain from giving further demonstrations of Mesmerism. He still, however, continued the practice of Mesmerism in the wards. In October, the question of retaining Elizabeth Okey as a patient came, in the ordinary course, before the Committee. Elliotson represented that she was too ill to be discharged. In the case of an ordinary patient such an expression of opinion from the senior physician would, of course, have settled the matter. But a nurse reported to the Committee the visit of Elizabeth to the men's ward, her vision of "Great Jackey," and the subsequent death of the patient. The matter was referred to the General Council, who issued instructions that Elizabeth Okey was to be discharged, and that the practice of Mesmerism within the hospital wards should be discontinued altogether. On the resolution being communicated to Elliotson he sent in his resignation.

[1] *Lancet*, September, 1838.   [2] *Ibid.*, September 15, 1838.

The mixed feelings with which the incident was regarded are reflected in the attitude of the students at a crowded meeting held to consider the question. Elliotson was very popular with the students on personal grounds. He was a man of conspicuous ability and originality, an admirable lecturer and teacher. The resignation of such a man would be a serious loss to the staff: at the same time, it was generally felt that by his imprudence and extravagance he had brought discredit upon the hospital. In the event a resolution was passed praying the Council to take steps to secure the withdrawal of the resignation. But the resolution came too late. Some weeks later Elliotson sent to Hoffmeister, one of his old students, a letter of thirty-six pages, asking him to communicate it to his former class, as his farewell. Hoffmeister felt compelled to refuse, on the ground, as he explained to his fellow-students, that the letter contained so many reflections on the character and conduct of Elliotson's late colleagues.

Elliotson's impulsive conduct appears to have seriously injured his private fortunes. His practice fell off considerably during the next few years. Bnt his ill-considered experiments and extravagant theories had a still more prejudicial effect upon the progress of Mesmerism. Wakley's views appear to have found acceptance with the profession generally. His article is commonly referred to by contemporary writers as the exposure at once of the Okeys and of the pretensions of the Mesmerists ; and the columns of the *Lancet* and other medical journals were closed for some time to come against the partisans of the new science. Elliotson's name was rarely mentioned without a sneer ; and when, in 1846, it came to his turn to deliver the Harveian Oration, some of the medical journals expressed regret that the Council had not the courage to pass him over, or Elliotson himself the discretion and good taste to refuse the proffered honour.[1]

The intolerance of the medical profession from 1839 onwards to Mesmerism, and especially its obstinate rejection of the cumulative evidence of the relief from pain occasionally

See the *London Medical Gazette,* June 19th, and *Lancet,* July 4, 1846.

afforded by its means in surgical operations, is one of the most noteworthy episodes in the history of medical science. Wakley cited Anne Ross as an example of insensibility to pain deliberately feigned ; in this case Elliotson, as we have seen, agreed with him. The case of Madame Plantin has been described in a previous chapter,[1] and there were English surgeons at this date who did not scruple to say that the strenuous efforts which she made to conceal the pain of the operation and her subsequent remorse for the deception had hastened her death. The first considerable operation performed in England in the mesmeric trance took place in 1842 at Wellow, in Nottinghamshire, the patient being one James Wombell, whose leg was amputated above the knee. W. Topham, a London barrister, was the mesmerist, and the operation was performed by Squire Ward, M.R.C.S. The patient lay motionless, except for a low moaning as if in a troubled dream ; the operator even touched the severed end of the sciatic nerve without giving rise to any movement or any increase in the low moaning. An account of the case was read before the London Medico-Chirurgical Society at their meeting on November 22, 1842. The paper was received with much disfavour, many of the medical men present expressing their opinion that the alleged insensibility was simulated, and that Wombell had been trained to bear pain without betraying any signs of it. Dr. Marshall Hall, a noted authority on the nervous system, maintained that the motionless attitude of the patient proved too much ; if he had been simply unconscious, there would have been convulsive reflex movements. The trial, therefore, proved, not coma, but voluntary repression of the signs of pain.[2] In the interval before the next meeting the authors published the paper on their own account,[3] and the Society gladly took advantage of this breach of etiquette to expunge all notice of the discreditable transaction from their Minutes. But this

---

[1] See above, p. 110.

[2] *Medico-Chirurgical Review*, January 1, 1843.

[3] *Account of a Case of Successful Amputation of the Thigh during the Mesmeric State* (London, 1843).

was not enough for the opponents of Mesmerism. It was freely stated by medical men in the public Press and elsewhere, whenever the subject of Mesmerism was under discussion, that James Wombell had subsequently confessed to a wicked deception ; that he had, in fact, felt the whole pain of the operation, but to gain his private ends had successfully concealed his feelings at the time. Elliotson took the trouble in 1843 to get a statement signed by the man himself and witnessed by the clergyman of the parish, giving the lie to the slander.[1] Eight years later it was revived. At a meeting of the same Society on December 10, 1850, Dr. Marshall Hall " begged leave to communicate a fact of some interest to the Society. . . . He understood that this man (Wombell) had since confessed that he had acted the part of an impostor." Mr. Topham wrote to ask Dr. Hall for his authority. Dr. Hall replied, " The fact . . . was communicated to me by a gentleman whom I have known for the third part of a century, and whom I regard as among the most honourable and truthful of men." Dr. Hall refused to give up the name of his informant " without reserve," and he concluded his letter by calling upon Mr. Topham to take note— .

"That I shall never cease to raise my voice against everything derogatory to my profession, whether originating unhappily within its ranks, or coming intrusively from without. That I am of opinion that, in these days of multifarious folly and quackery, every member of my profession is called upon in honour to do the same.

"That you will be pleased to consider this as a final communication."

Dr. Hall, however, wrote to his informant, asking him upon what evidence he had made the statement, and published in the *Lancet*, together with a copy of the above-cited letter to Mr. Topham, the following extract from his still unnamed correspondent's reply—

"The confession of the man was distinctly and deliberately stated to me by a person in whom I have full confidence. It was in Nottinghamshire that I was told the fact, last August, and I fully believe it."

[1] *Zoist*, vol. i. p. 210.

Dr. Marshall Hall had, perhaps, heard in his youth that a statement could be established in the mouths of two or three witnesses, and may have thought that he was fulfilling the Scripture by multiplying the links in his chain of anonymous tradition. The evidence, in fact, seems to have been good enough for the Medico-Chirurgical Society, for at a later meeting the president refused to hear Dr. Ashburner and Dr. Cohen when they rose to refute the slander ; and the *Lancet* and other papers, in reporting the incident, expressed approval of the chairman's firmness and impartiality.[1]

Two years later, in August, 1844, another amputation of the leg was performed in the mesmeric trance. The patient this time was a young woman, the complaint fungus hematodes of the knee. The patient professed, when awakened after the operation, to have felt no pain. A doctor had been specially delegated to note the patient's movements and other symptoms. He records " low moaning, slight movements of sound leg and toes ; leg once contracted ; movements of limbs and eyelids (quivering)." In this case, it will be seen, Dr. Marshall Hall's requirements were fulfilled—there were reflex movements. But one or two of the surgeons present refused to believe in the patient's insensibility precisely because of these slight movements.[2]

The attempt, however, to produce suggestional anæsthesia sufficiently deep and prolonged for such severe operations appears to have been rarely successful in England. Braid could not point to a single case in his own practice, though he would, no doubt, have employed it in some cases if he could have done so. A demonstration on a large scale was, however, shortly afforded in India. James Esdaile was a young surgeon who, in 1845, was in charge of a hospital for poor persons and criminals at Hooghly. In April of that year he began to make experiments on the natives under his charge, and soon found himself able to induce coma so profound that in some cases the pupils failed to contract when

---

[1] *Lancet*, December 28, 1850, and March 1, 1851. See also *Zoist*, vol. ix. pp. 88, 106, where a full account of the incident is given.

[2] *Medical Times*, vol. x. pp. 491, 510, September, 1844.

exposed to the light of an Indian sun at noonday. Esdaile, like Elliotson, was prepossessed with the conception of a physical effluence, and remained under the domination of this idea until the end of his life ; and his demonstrations, like Elliotson's, were devised to illustrate the workings of this subtle agency. He invited Finch, the editor of the *India Journal of Medical Science,* and two other doctors to experiment for themselves on some of his patients. Esdaile suggested the use of mesmerised water, passes through a stone wall, and so on. The visitors accepted his suggestions, but substituted plain water and refrained from making any passes at all. The predicted results nevertheless followed, and Finch, at any rate, was convinced that the whole question was one of "incredible credulity" on the one side, "gross imposture" on the other. Esdaile, however, continued to practise Mesmerism for curative purposes and performed under its influence numerous severe operations. Some of the visitors who were allowed to witness these operations thought there might be something in it, and the Government of Bengal in 1846 appointed a committee, consisting of the Inspector-General of Hospitals, three other medical men, and three civilians, to inquire into the matter. Six patients were finally selected, on whom Esdaile performed severe operations (extirpation of huge tumours, hydrocele, &c.) in what purported to be a state of mesmeric coma. The patients all asserted that they had felt no pain under operations which certainly in the normal state would have involved severe suffering. The Committee reported that three showed no signs of pain during the operation, and made no movements of any kind. In the other three cases, convulsive movements of the arms were observed, writhing of the body, and distortion of the features, giving the face a hideous expression of suppressed agony—all the signs, in fact, of intense pain. The report was entirely non-committal. The Committee contented themselves with contrasting the signs of pain in three of the cases with the positive statements of the patients that they felt no pain. But they expressed the opinion that, owing to the length of time required to produce a coma of sufficient intensity, and the uncertainty of success, Mesmerism would in any event prove of little practical utility.

It is significant that the Committee made no comment on the very remarkable pulse-records of the six patients. The table given in the Report is as follows :—

	Immediately before Operation.	During Operation.	Immediately after Operation.
1	72	72	Natural.
2	60	60	,,
3	68	68	,,
4	84	124	,,
5	108	112	100
6	68	108	72

The three patients in whom the pulse remained wholly unaffected were the three who betrayed all the signs of severe pain ; in the three men who remained absolutely motionless the pulse rose, in two cases to an enormous extent. The Committee were apparently unable to explain this curious difference, but Braid, who comments on the report in the *Medical Times*,[1] was able from his own experience to supply the explanation. There is no proof, he points out, that either set of patients felt any pain. In the first three cases the convulsive movements were the reflex actions which would, as Marshall Hall had already pointed out, naturally be expected to occur. The pulse remained normal because there was nothing to disturb it. In the other three cases all reflex action was inhibited, because the whole body was in a state of rigid catalepsy. The same condition, by increasing the resistance, would account for the acceleration in the pulse-beat.

The Governor of Bengal did not, however, adopt the Committee's sceptical attitude. In acknowledging the receipt of the report his secretary wrote that "the possibility of making the most severe surgical operations painless to the subject of them is in his Honour's opinion established." Esdaile was forthwith appointed to a small hospital in Calcutta. The hospital was to be under his exclusive control for a year, and he was to make what experiments he would.

[1] Vol. xv. February 13, 1847, p. 381 ; vol. xvi. p. 10.

Medical men appointed by the Government would visit and inspect his operations.

At the end of the experimental year Lord Dalhousie appointed Esdaile a Presidency surgeon, and he continued his practice for eighteen months longer in a Mesmeric Hospital opened by public subscription.

During Esdaile's six years' practice in India he performed, on patients rendered insensible by the operation of Mesmerism, no fewer than 261 serious operations, besides a large number of minor cases. Of the serious operations two hundred consisted in the removal of scrotal tumours varying from 10 lbs. to 103 lbs. in weight. In these two hundred cases there were only sixteen deaths, though the mortality from the removal of similar tumours had previously been 40 or 50 per cent. There were besides several cases of amputations, removal of cancerous and other tumours, &c.

Esdaile was a man of private means. It need scarcely be said that he added little to his fortune by devoting himself to curing the ailments of native criminals and paupers. To the unprofessional mind it would seem that such a man merited at least the thanks of his profession for good work done. What reward he received is foreshadowed by a remark of Dr. Duncan Stewart, one of the official visitors to the Mesmeric Hospital. Commenting on the recent discovery of anæsthetic drugs, he exclaimed: " It is time to throw away mummery and work above-board, now that we have got ether." In fact, the medical Press in India severely boycotted Esdaile and his operations, and to the last persisted in regarding all his patients as deliberate impostors. Nor was he more successful in obtaining a hearing on his return to his native country. He tells us that, being invited by Professor Simpson of Edinburgh to contribute some account of his experiences to an English medical journal, he prepared two separate papers, and that the editor made excuses for not publishing either.[1]

[1] *Introduction of Mesmerism into India* (Preface). In this pamphlet Esdaile gives a number of curious examples of the abuse lavished on Mesmerism and its practitioners by the medical Press of the day.

In 1849 the Earl of Ducie, a Lord-in-Waiting to her Majesty and a strict Presbyterian, had taken the chair at the opening meeting of the Bristol Mesmeric Institute, and had publicly testified to the beneficial effects of Mesmerism. He had himself, he said, been treated for an attack of gout by its means, and had "experienced very great relief"; further, he had seen many extraordinary cures and a number of cases in which persons were readily relieved of intense pain and suffering.[1]

The *Medical Gazette* of July 6, 1849, in an editorial commenting on the report, wrote : " We are inclined to think that the affair is a hoax from beginning to end, and that the concoctor of the so-called report has been guilty of a species of ' mental travelling,' by no means uncommon amongst enthusiastic advocates of particular doctrines." The *Gazette* went on to point out that Lord Ducie, since his asserted cure by Mesmerism two years previously, had consulted orthodox physicians, "and that this statement of the cure of gout by Mesmerism, which has been falsely attributed to him, reflects undeservedly upon the non-mesmeric portion of the medical profession," and also upon Lord Ducie's own reputation for common-sense.

The article was obviously written by a man too well assured beforehand of the sympathies of his readers to be careful to regard the decencies of controversy, or even to observe common honesty. The writer admits that he had seen two reports, in one of which it was stated that Lord Ducie had " experienced very great relief," in the other that he had been " cured." The statement in the first report, that he had experienced relief, was of course not inconsistent with Lord Ducie's subsequent resort to orthodox practitioners for further treatment of an obstinate complaint, and would have afforded no basis for the outrageous insinuations made by the editor of the *Gazette*. Now, the first report, which originally appeared in the *Bristol Mercury*, and was quoted at full length in the *Zoist*, was practically *verbatim*. But the writer in the *Gazette* chose deliberately, or perhaps rather blindly, a

[1] *Zoist*, vol. vii. 153.

greatly abbreviated report which was on the face of it therefore likely to be less correct, in order that he might gratify the
odium medicum. By assuming the correctness of the abbreviated
report he was able safely to make offensive reflections not
only on the humbler persons concerned, but upon Lord Ducie
himself, whom he would not have ventured to attack directly.

In the following number there appeared a letter from Lord
Ducie affirming the accuracy of the report that he had
experienced very great relief.

The editor prints this letter without apology of any kind.
In fact, he makes his original offence worse than before by a
bitter and unscrupulous attack upon other speakers at the
meeting, comparing their remarks about clairvoyance and
prevision to the ravings of an unhappy religious maniac
whose case had lately been decided by the courts.

But the editorial conduct appears to have commended
itself to at least one other member of the profession. For an
anonymous physician sent the whole correspondence to the
Morning Post, asking that paper, "for the credit of the orthodox profession, to make the case known." The *Morning Post*,
however, in printing the physician's letter, took the view that
the whole affair was by no means "to the credit of the orthodox profession." The editor of the *Gazette* had made a misstatement; when the misstatement was pointed out to him
"he refuses to retract or apologise, but endeavours to justify
a line of conduct which is obviously unjustifiable. We deeply
lament the spirit in which such disputes are conducted." [1]

It is not necessary to multiply instances. The above
examples may be taken as typical of the sentiments, so far as
they were articulate, of the bulk of the profession towards
Mesmerism in the decade 1840–50. After Elliotson's resignation in 1838, indeed, there seemed some danger of the interest
in the subject dying out altogether. It was revived in 1841
by the visit of another Frenchman, La Fontaine, who came to
this country on a lecturing tour. It is to his lectures and
demonstrations that many of the writers on Mesmerism at
this time, including Braid himself, owed their impulse to

[1] *Morning Post*, August 8, 1849.

investigate. In 1843 there appeared the first number of the *Zoist*, a quarterly periodical which continued under Elliotson's direction until 1856. The *Zoist* was the organ of the medical Mesmerists. In the same year there appeared another periodical, the *Phreno-Magnet*, edited by Spencer T. Hall, which represented the popular side of the movement. Neither Hall nor his contributors had serious claims to scientific knowledge, and the *Phreno-Magnet* gave hospitality to many facts and speculations, emanating chiefly from America, even more extravagant and astounding than those for which Elliotson and his colleagues were responsible.

Again in the same year appeared Braid's *Neurypnology*. Braid was a Manchester surgeon, who, having tried mesmeric treatment on his own patients, satisfied himself that the observed phenomena were in all cases subjective, due to an influence exerted by the nervous system of the patient on his own organism. He pointed out that the sleep or trance into which the "mesmerised" subject fell, though it had some analogy with ordinary sleep, differed from it by the nature of its reaction to external stimuli. For this peculiar psychological condition he proposed the name Neuro-Hypnotism, later altered into Hypnotism, the name now generally adopted.

Such were the different mental forces at work upon the subject in the decade under consideration. If we consider more closely the nature of the phenomena alleged to occur, we shall be in a position to understand the sharp contrast between the three attitudes—that of contemptuous rejection, of implicit belief, and of discriminating acceptance, typified by the *Lancet*, by Elliotson, and by Braid respectively. In the first place the bulk of the medical profession, so far at least as they gave public expression to their views, were obsessed by the idea of fraud as the explanation of the phenomena. The Mesmerists and their subjects are alike referred to as impostors in the current medical literature.[1]

---

[1] "We cannot publish any more papers on the subject of such an odious fraud as Mesmerism." *Lancet*, 1848, quoted by Esdaile (*Introduction of Mesmerism into India*). Or again :—

"Dr. F—— need be under no apprehension of an attack in the

In explanation of this attitude it should be pointed out, in the first place, that of the characteristic features ordinarily presented in the induced trance there is none which it is not within the power of the subject to produce deliberately. It is true that in certain cases there are alterations in the pulse rate such as are beyond the conscious control of the subject ; or, again, reflex action may be inhibited. But phenomena of this kind are not reproducible in every case, and cannot be relied upon as tests. Esdaile, though he assures us that he witnessed instances of the insensibility of the pupils to a strong light in some of his earliest patients, was not able to exhibit any case before Dr. Finch and his colleagues in 1845. Insensibility to pain, within certain limits, can, no doubt, be feigned, and it is to be observed that in England cases of extreme insensibility were apparently of quite rare occurrence. The psychological phenomena in such a case as that of the Okeys would almost inevitably suggest imposture. Indeed, in hysterical cases it is even now almost impossible to distinguish between the effects of deliberate simulation and those of unconscious suggestion. For " both in spontaneous and artificially induced hysteria and somnambulism there is frequently *a super-added deceit*—which is a moral symptom of the disease itself, and not an indication that all is imposture.[1]

For proof of the reality of the mesmeric influence Elliotson and his colleagues relied partly on the beneficial effect of the treatment in cases of disease. But, as we have seen in the case of the Commission of 1784, such a test is difficult of application and little calculated to convince. The partisan of 1840 was ultimately driven back, like his predecessors sixty years before, on the asserted physical effects as the supreme test of the reality of the influence. The whole subject of Reichenbach's phenomena and of influence at a distance will

Mesmeric Magazine affecting him in the opinion of the profession. That journal only finds circulation among the class of impostors who record their doings in it" (*London Medical Gazette,* April 12, 1845).

[1] *British and Foreign Medical Review,* April, 1845, article on Mesmerism.

be dealt with in a later chapter. For our present purpose it is enough to point out that, whatever the explanation of the matter, it is certain that the sensations described by the sensitives which were held to attest the influence of the fluid could be produced in the absence of the supposed material cause by merely exciting the imagination, and frequently failed to appear when the material cause was actually present unknown to the sensitive.

To the dubious physical effects of the hypothetical fluid the Mesmerists generally added the not less dubious "higher phenomena"—community of sensation, clairvoyance of the human body, prevision, vision with closed eyes, travelling clairvoyance. Elliotson, indeed, exercised a certain reserve in his utterances on these subjects ; it was not until 1844 that he admitted himself satisfied of the truth of travelling clairvoyance ; even after this date he seems to have been more alive than most of his colleagues and disciples to the possibilities of deception.[1]

But most of the writers on Mesmerism at this date seem to have accepted the higher phenomena unreservedly. A conspicuous demonstration both of vision with closed eyes and of clairvoyance at a distance was afforded in the years 1844 and 1845 by two young Frenchmen, Alexis and Adolphe Didier. The performances of the former, in particular, reached the height of achievement in this direction and excited extraordinary interest, chiefly in fashionable circles. Some account of the wonders described will be given in Chapter IX. below.

Of the nature of the phenomena of "prevision" and "introvision" enough has already been said. The exhibitions of vision with closed eyes by Alexis Didier and other performers in no case furnish clear evidence of a new faculty. Cases of "travelling clairvoyance" were almost always open to suspicion ; moreover, they were of comparatively rare occurrence, and the difficulties in the way of testing them were almost insuperable. Weighted as it was by these dubious phenomena and extravagant theories, it is not

[1] See the Valedictory Address in the *Zoist*, vol. xiii. p. 443.

altogether surprising that Mesmerism found small acceptance in medical circles at this period. Elliotson to the last remained an Ishmael in his profession. His combative nature would not admit of compromise or condescend to any methods of conciliation. The abuse and contempt with which his doctrines were treated by the medical Press in general he repaid in kind. His hostile critics were assailed in the *Zoist* with such phrases as "laughable folly," "discreditable conduct," "untruthfulness," "stupid obstinacy," "slobbering childishness."

Braid, as already said, whilst imputing all the alleged physical effects of the fluid to imagination, and disregarding or explaining away the "higher phenomena," attached considerable importance to the psychological condition revealed by the mesmeric procedure—a condition hitherto scarcely recognised by the profession. From 1842 onwards he employed Mesmerism, or, as he preferred to name it, "Hypnotism," in his own practice with beneficial results. He found it invaluable in procuring sleep, in beneficially stimulating the organic functions, and in relieving pain. Among the more striking cases which he enumerates in his *Neurypnology* are the cure or marked alleviation of long-standing nervous headaches, neuralgia, tic doloureux, functional paralyses of various kinds, weakness of spine and impaired sensibility, rheumatism, epilepsy, palpitation of the heart, cases of tonic muscular spasm, improvement of sight, so that persons who had worn spectacles for years were able to do without them, the absorption in one case of opacity of the cornea, the improvement of hearing so that deaf-mutes were in some cases able to hear words addressed to them, restoration of the sense of smell, the cure of skin diseases such as eczema and impetigo, and many minor ailments.

The columns of the *Lancet* were closed to Braid equally with Elliotson. But he found ready hospitality in the *Medical Times*—the *Lancet's* chief rival. The sobriety of his views, his clear and convincing expositions, gradually won some measure of recognition in the scientific press. The first and only edition of his book *Neurypnology* was soon exhausted ; his later writings appear to have met with some success ; his work is referred to with respect by such men as Carpenter, Hughes Bennett, Holland, and Brewster.

In contrast it is curious to note that Elliotson showed himself as bitterly hostile to Braid as to those of his critics who rejected the mesmeric treatment altogether. Elliotson's nature was intolerant of any difference of opinion. He deeply resented Braid's criticism of the mesmeric theory, and his demonstrations of the subjective nature of many mesmeric phenomena. Braid's writings are almost completely ignored in the *Zoist*. In the whole thirteen volumes his name is mentioned only two or three times, and then only to compare his " coarse method " with the old-established methods of Mesmerism, or to claim credit for the mesmeric cure of a case in which hypnotism was asserted to have failed.[1]

The period which we are now considering was, it must be admitted, peculiarly unfavourable for the introduction of Mesmerism and its phenomena. In India, notwithstanding the bitter incredulity of the profession generally, it can scarcely be doubted that Esdaile's brilliant demonstrations of painless surgery, if only on native patients, must ultimately, if an untoward fate had not intervened, have compelled recognition. It happened, however, at the very time when Esdaile was conducting his Mesmeric Hospital under Government auspices, that the use of ether and chloroform was rapidly spreading amongst the profession. Whatever advantages Esdaile's method possessed, in its safety and freedom from unfavourable after-symptoms, were in actual practice outweighed by the convenience and certainty of the results obtained by the use of anæsthetic drugs. To produce anæsthesia sufficiently deep for the performance of a capital

---

[1] *Zoist*, vol. iii. p. 345. See also Braid's reply in the *Medical Times*, vol. xi. p. 99, October, 1845. Other incidental references to Braid in the *Zoist* will be found in vol. ix. p. 316 and vol. xi. pp. 391, 395. In the former reference a pamphlet of Braid's is cited with other titles of books at the head of a review, but the reviewer cannot bring himself to mention Braid's name in the course of the article.

operation the patient under Esdaile's system required to be treated for several days in succession, and even then a cough or any nervous idiosyncrasy of the patient might interfere with success. The most striking test of the genuineness of the mesmeric state was, therefore, not disproved but robbed of its interest and practical value by a purely extraneous circumstance.

In England there was a growing feeling amongst the more open-minded of the profession that Mesmerism had not had a fair trial. This feeling found expression, as we have already seen, in Braid's work, and in the attitude of many who followed Braid's demonstrations with an interest which was not, however, sufficiently energetic to induce them to follow his example by employing the new method in their practice. So early as 1845 the *British and Foreign Medical Review* expressed the opinion that the subject " had hardly received fair play at the hands of many of our professional brethren." In particular the reviewer deprecated the rancorous incredulity with which the demonstrations of mesmeric anæsthesia had been received. It was much easier, he pointed out, in such cases to believe in the reality of the patient's insensibility than to suppose that men of honourable standing in their profession, with every motive for closely guarding their own reputations, should again and again have been deceived. In 1851 the Mesmerists found some new allies. There came to England in that year from America a number of lecturers who gave platform demonstrations of the new science of Electro-biology. Electro-biology was Mesmerism under another name. The subject was thrown into the hypnotic state, generally by gazing at a disk, and was then made to carry out suggestions of the operator of the kind with which popular lecturers on Mesmerism have in recent years made us familiar. When the subjects drank salt water in the belief that it was champagne, dandled a baby extemporised out of a handkerchief, and otherwise made fools of themselves before an audience composed of their fellow-townsfolk, it was obvious to all that the results were due, not to a thaumaturgic fluid, but to the operation of the subject's own imagination. It was also obvious to unprejudiced observers that the feats were genuine, in the sense that the actions of the "electro-biologised" persons were for the time beyond their voluntary control.[1]

These platform performances drew renewed attention to the subject. Hughes Bennett,[2] Carpenter,[3] Sir David Brewster,[4] and others wrote or lectured on the demonstration of the power of the mind over the body, and there seemed some chance that the importance of the induced trance and the suggestion phenomena, alike to psychology and to therapeutics, might at length be recognised. But the influence of some evil star—the metaphor seems inevitable in treating of Mesmer's cosmic conception—again prevailed. The doctrine and practices of the Mesmerists had originally suffered some prejudice because of Elliotson's personal opinions. Apart from his intemperate methods of advocacy, he was known as a free-spoken and intolerant opponent of all religious beliefs. The dubious science of phrenology, with which his name was prominently associated before he began to champion Mesmerism, connoted with him a rather crude materialism. All mental phenomena were in his view "produced" by the brain, much as bile is produced by the liver ; he was constantly deprecating the useless belief in the immortality "of a certain thing called soul and immaterial."[5] Other men of the same way of thinking, such as H. G. Atkinson, the "Mentor" of Miss Martineau, found in Mesmerism and its parasitic science of Mesmero-phrenology fresh weapons with

---

[1] Not all were willing, however, to admit so much. See the grotesque address on *Darlingism misnamed Electro-biology* (Dr. Darling was one of the chief lecturers on the subject) delivered before the Medico-Chirurgical Society of Glasgow by Dr. Buchanan in 1851. Dr. Buchanan attributed the results presented partly to want of moral principle, partly to weakness of intellect on the part of the subjects.

[2] *The Mesmeric Mania of* 1851, a lecture by J. Hughes Bennett.

[3] *Mental Physiology.*

[4] *Lecture before the Philosophical Institution of Edinburgh,* 1851. See also the *British and Foreign Medico-Chirurgical Review,* October, 1851, p. 431 : "The phenomena are destined to lay the foundations for a complete revolution in metaphysics and mental philosophy."

[5] *Zoist,* vol. iii. pp. 423, 424.

which to do battle for their views. But from 1853 onwards Mesmerism was menaced by a danger of an opposite kind. When table-turning and spirit-rapping were introduced into this country from America, the Mesmerists soon identified the mysterious force which caused the phenomena with the mesmeric or neuro-vital fluid.[1] A little later, when the trance and its manifestations were exploited in the interests of the new gospel of Spiritualism, many of the English Mesmerists, who had been prepared by the utterances of their own clairvoyants for some such development, proclaimed themselves adherents of the new faith. Elliotson himself before his death became a convert to Spiritualism.[2] The Mesmerists generally found the marvels of the magnetic fluid insignificant in face of the new revelation. Mesmeric operators became spiritual healers, and their subjects trance mediums; the spiritualist platforms were thronged with magnetic clairvoyants who had developed into "inspirational" speakers. The two movements naturally became identified in the minds of the public, and shared in a common condemnation. No physician who valued his professional reputation could afford to meddle with the subject, and the study of the induced trance and its attendant phenomena was relegated to oblivion, in these islands at any rate, for more than a generation.

[1] See the articles on the subject in the *Zoist*, especially vols. xi. and xii.

[2] The process of conversion in his case did not stop at this point. He died a Christian. See his obituary notice in the *Morning Post*, August 3, 1868.

CHAPTER VIII

THE FLUIDIC THEORY

Fluid or fraud : no room found for the intermediate views of Bertrand and Braid—Alleged proofs of Magnetic fluid—Reichenbach's experiments : his unscientific temper : his subjects probably unconsciously "educated"—Braid's counter-experiments—His demonstrations completely ignored by Reichenbach and the Mesmerists—Braid's own demonstrations in Phreno-mesmerism possibly due to thought-transference—Thought-transference a possible explanation of induction of trance or sleep at a distance : experiments by Townshend, and later experiments by Janet and Gibert.

OUR survey of the history of Animal Magnetism, or, as its later disciples in this country preferred to style it, Mesmerism, is now complete. After 1850 the movement gradually disappears from view. But Mesmerism died, so to speak, only to become the fruitful mother of children, some of them more vigorous and likely to be more long-lived than their parent. For the best part of a generation, indeed, we hear little more of its employment in therapeutics.[1] Treatment on the lines laid down by Braid had, however, been pursued at Nancy by Liébeault since 1860, and in the early eighties, as a result largely of his example, we find it employed in the Civil Hospital at Nancy by Bernheim, at the Salpêtrière under Charcot, and at different centres in Germany and the Scandinavian countries. In this country it first received official recognition in 1893 from a committee of the British Medical Association, which reported

---

[1] The *Zoist* continued until the end of 1856. But the interest in the subject in England was waning, and, as already indicated, many champions of Mesmerism had become Spiritualists.

that they had satisfied themselves of the genuineness of the hypnotic state and of the value of hypnotism, within limits, in relieving pain and alleviating functional ailments. The subject has now, under the name of Hypnotism or Suggestion, obtained a definite, if still somewhat precarious, foothold in the medical practice of every civilised country, and is recognised as an indispensable auxiliary in the new science of experimental psychology.

But Hypnotism is only the youngest and at present by no means the most prominent of the progeny of Mesmer. All the mysticisms and pseudo-sciences of the present day, no doubt, owe something to the Viennese doctor. There are, however, three distinct schools of thought, each claiming a scientific foundation, whose descent may be traced directly back to that universal system of knowledge whose boast it was to unite two well-known sciences—Astronomy and Medicine. The three faiths in question are the fluidic theory, which finds its headquarters, appropriately enough, in modern Paris ; the religion of modern Spiritualism ; and the movement of Mental Healing, of which the sect known as Christian Scientists are the most prominent representatives.

The remaining chapters of this book will be devoted to tracing the connection between these modern phases of thought and the movement whose rise and culmination have been already sketched. In the evolution of life on this planet there has been, we are told, a constant tendency to the extermination of intermediate types. Woe to the unhappy animal or vegetable which attempts to occupy the vacant space between opposing armies ! In the battle of life there is no mercy for the Laodicean. A like tendency is manifest in the evolution of opinion. Even the progress of science is frequently attained by a kind of dichotomy ; any novel current of opinion appears by a kind of psychological induction to create a current of at least equal intensity in the reverse direction. We may trace this tendency in the history of most recent sciences. In geology, for instance, we have witnessed successively the vulcanists and the neptunists, the catastrophists and uniformitarians, each party seeing one aspect of the truth, and ignoring that seen by its opponents. This extinction of intermediate types is clearly seen in our own political history. Where is now the Fourth Party? Where in a few months or years will be the Liberal Unionists? Does not Nature itself abhor a Mugwump?

The history of Mesmerism well illustrates this law of evolution. On the one side, alike in France and in England, generation after generation, stood those who had seen things new and marvellous, and believed ; on the other stood those who, for the most part not having seen, disbelieved. The one party talked only of fraud, the other only of fluids. In each case the opinion was held in face of reason and facts until it became a veritable obsession. Between the two opposing camps stood in France Alexander Bertrand, in England James Braid. Their fates, as we have seen, ran parallel up to a certain point. Neither stirred enthusiasm, neither found followers nor created a school ; neither, indeed, appears to have exercised much influence on his contemporaries, or to have had any effect at all on the extremists on either side. But Braid enjoyed a longer life than the young Parisian : his books, even in his lifetime, found a select public, and it is matter of history that the revival of interest in the subject on the Continent some years after his death was stimulated by his writings.

It is tempting to speculate on what might have happened in this country if, say, Elliotson on the one side and Wakley on the other had condescended to learn from Braid. However mischievous at the time the credulity and extravagance of the Mesmerists must have appeared, in the light of subsequent happenings the persistent and unreasonable imputation of imposture must seem now more mischievous still. Viewed as a reaction from the other side, the attitude of'the medical world was not, perhaps, altogether unreasonable. Elliotson, in the intemperance of his language and the extravagance of his conduct, was like a man intoxicated. His co-disciples joined with him in rejecting or ignoring the plainest proofs, not necessarily of imposture, but certainly of mistake, and the whole subject was redolent of delusion and hysteria. Fraud, no doubt, played a part, it may be a considerable part, in the business. But the fraud was itself a factor in the problem to be investigated. Some of the cures were attested by men of established reputation. The parrot cry of imposture was scarcely convincing in the case of the Okeys and Anne Ross ; it is difficult to say whether it becomes more ludicrous when applied to M. Cloquet's patient, to poor Wombell, to the hundreds of Indians who bore without complaining prolonged and severe operations at the hands of Esdaile, or to the men and women of good education and social position who, as in the case of many of Reichenbach's sensitives, testified to the phenomena in their own persons.

The deliberate negligence of the scientific world left the whole field to be cultivated by the visionary and the charlatan. The abundant crop of false beliefs and extravagant systems which flourish at the present time is the direct result of the apathy or obstinate incredulity shown by the physicians of two generations ago. The positive loss to psychology and to medical science itself in all the intervening years is probably greater still. But all this was, no doubt, inevitable, partly because of the personality of the protagonists, but mainly from the general circumstances of the time.

Of the three derivative systems above referred to, the persistent belief in fluidic emanations from the human body, magnets, metals, drugs, and other substances, though the least important in its range and immediate influence, is not the least interesting, nor likely, perhaps, to be the least enduring. At the period which we are now considering, the decade from 1840 to 1850, the belief rested mainly on three classes of facts—what may be roughly classed as "Reichenbach phenomena," the manifestations of phreno-mesmerism, and the alleged action at a distance of one human body on another, chiefly demonstrated in the provocation of sleep without the knowledge of the subject.

Many illustrations have been given in the preceding pages of results supposed to attest the operation of a physical effluence from the mesmerist. Wakley's experiments were sufficient to show that the physiological phenomena manifested by the sensitive had no objective validity. Since the alleged sensations, sleep, &c., occurred indifferently when the hypothetical cause was actually present, and when it was only supposed by the sensitive to be present, it seems clear that they were not due to any uniform external cause, but were self-engendered. Wakley's conclusion, however, that the results were due to deliberate fraud, was scarcely more justifiable than Elliotson's, that they testified to a physical effluence. In most cases there is no doubt that the operator unwittingly by his manner and gesture gave sufficient indication to the abnormally susceptible subject of the result expected. There are, indeed, a few cases recorded in which the experiment was so devised that the operator was as ignorant as the patient. One out of several glasses of water would be mesmerised whilst he was out of the room, or a marked sovereign after being mesmerised would be thrown into a hat and shaken up with several others.[1] When the experiment succeeded under these conditions the simplest explanation is to suppose that the subject detected the mesmerised object, in the case of the metal by means of the difference in temperature, in the case of the water by the smell. Braid states that he had satisfied himself that some hypnotics could detect by this means a glass of "mesmerised" water—i.e, a glass of water over which passes had been made ; and we have seen already, in the case of the Okeys, that the back of the hand was apparently sufficiently sensitive to differences in temperature to detect the presence of a piece of bread two inches off. We know that certain hypnotic or hystero-epileptic subjects manifest extraordinary acuteness of the special senses ; and we have not yet learnt the limits of hyperæsthesia.

Another marvel recorded frequently by the Mesmerists of this date is perhaps susceptible of a similar explanation—the *fixation* of a subject by mesmerising his seat or a part of the floor over which he must pass. Mr. Parsons, of Brighton, mesmerised the sill of the doorway leading to the cellar, and thus prevented his sensitive from going downstairs and raiding the larder.[2] Esdaile made similar experiments on his patients

[1] See, *e.g., Zoist,* vol. iv. p. 109, v. p. 127.   [2] *Ibid.,* vol. vi. pp. 335, 359.

in Calcutta. His first experiment of the kind was as follows: Seating himself in an armchair, he placed his hands on the end of the arms and breathed on them. He then sent for a patient from the hospital, who was placed in the same chair, and questioned by some of the medical visitors on a recent operation. On being bidden to depart, he placed his hands on the knobs at the ends of the arms to assist him to rise, and found himself unable to remove them. His hands and both arms up to the shoulder were in a state of rigid catalepsy. Esdaile released him by upward passes and then, leaving the room, made passes on the floor just outside the door. When the man crossed the spot he became violently convulsed, and called on Esdaile for help.[1]

In the second trial it is not difficult to suppose that the man's sharpened sense was subconsciously aware of Esdaile's movements in the passage. The startling success of the first trial, with the chair, is, no doubt, not so easy to explain. But it seems practically impossible in an experiment of this kind, where some of those present are hoping, or at least anticipating, a particular movement on the part of the subject, to be satisfied that no hint of the result expected could be conveyed, by look, gesture, tone of voice, or even change of breathing, to the abnormally acute senses of the patient. Sixty years ago neither party was sufficiently alive to the importance of these subconscious indications.

In 1845 the theory of a physical effluence received strong confirmation from the classical researches of Baron von Reichenbach—a man of some scientific attainments, a chemist and metallurgist of repute, and the first living authority on meteorites.[2] Reichenbach conducted elaborate experiments, extending over several years, with a very large number of persons. His first subjects were young women of the class

---

[1] *Natural and Mesmeric Clairvoyance*, pp. 126, 127.
[2] An abstract of Reichenbach's researches was published in this country in 1846 by William Gregory, Professor of Chemistry in the University of Edinburgh. In 1850 Gregory published a full translation of the work, under the title *Researches on Magnetism, Electricity* . . . *in their Relations to the Vital Force.*

of spontaneous cataleptics and somnambulists. Afterwards he found sensitive persons amongst the ranks of his own acquaintance and many other persons, both men and women, of good social position and apparently sound health. To give a full account of the extraordinary phenomena attested by these persons would not be worth the labour. Briefly, flames of different colours were seen to issue from magnets, crystals, and the human body. Metals and other chemical substances shone to the eyes of the sensitive with a dull glow, each having its appropriate colour. Copper showed a red glow, with a green flame playing on it; silver a white glow; lead and cobalt gleamed blue; rhodium, osmium, and mercury red; chromium green; and sulphur blue. Further, from magnets, metals, crystals, from the planets and the fixed stars, proceeded emanations which produced on the sensitive feelings of heat or cold, sensations pleasurable or disagreeable. Different persons showed different degrees of susceptibility to these emanations; but it was claimed that, apart from the discrepancies due to this cause, the results were practically uniform. The new force, for which Reichenbach proposed the name Od, produced no chemical, thermal, electric, or magnetic effect on any of the materials employed to test it. The magnet had so strong an attraction on the hand of the sensitive that the hand would follow its movements, and adhere to it as firmly as a piece of iron would have done. But the same hand exercised no effect whatever upon the magnetic needle, and when a large horseshoe magnet was placed in a balance, though the patient's hand was attracted as strongly as ever, the balance remained unaffected. It is clear that the effect produced in this case was not therefore physical, but psychological.[1] The control experiments which Reichenbach records are vitiated by the fact that he knew the position and nature of the object

[1] Reichenbach claimed, indeed, that the magnet influenced the photographic plate, but the claim was made on the strength of two experiments only, which he appears never to have repeated. In view of the numerous sources of error in such experiments the results, it is hardly necessary to point out, are not conclusive.

to be tested, and that he himself questioned the sensitive.[1]

In short, the only proof of the existence of the hypothetical fluid lay in the concordant testimony of so many witnesses of repute. But by reading between the lines we can see how the marvellous agreement between the different sensitives, upon which Reichenbach lays so much stress, gradually came to be. In the first instance, in the absence of a clear lead, the sensations described are ambiguous and indeterminate. The earliest sensitives saw the magnetic light as a white flame, with occasional flashes of colour. Gradually the flames at the several poles became differentiated, as the subjects learnt how to see. So the sensations first experienced from metals or salts held in the hand are described as warmth, with a cool aura. " The less sensitive persons," remarks Reichenbach, " are at first more or less uncertain in their statements " (p. 170). Mdlle. Sturmann was " not always clear in her distinction between tepid and cool sensations " (p. 50). When blindfolded the subject was always liable to give uncertain answers (p. 40). In fact, the subjects had to be gradually educated into uniformity. There is no reason to think that this process of education was deliberate on either side ; it is precisely in that circumstance that the chief fallacy lies. The sensitive unconsciously took the hints, which Reichenbach unconsciously gave by leading questions, by the tone of his voice, and so on. Occasionally he indicates how apparent discrepancies in the statements of his sensitives could be explained away. He warns experimenters who wish to repeat the tests with chemical substances that they should be reduced to powder ; but the powder must not be used for some hours—lest the influence of the pestle and mortar should persist, or the electricity generated by the friction should mask the results. The temperature of all substances compared must be uniform ; the substance must not have been in the neighbourhood of other powerful

---

[1] There is one exception, on pp. 17, 18 of Gregory's translation, where the lens was shifted by Reichenbach's assistant. But the results are only given in general terms.

chemicals, nor have been exposed to sunshine or moonlight, or held long in the hand.[1] If all these rules were followed, and the results were still not in accordance with expectation, it was always open to suppose that the sensitiveness of the percipient, owing to some variation in health, had for the moment deserted her. With so many plausible reasons to account for failure, it seems hardly possible not to achieve uniformity.[2]

In 1846, on the appearance of Gregory's condensed translation of the first part of Reichenbach's researches, Braid instituted some counter experiments of his own,[3] showing that the imagination, even in a healthy person, was quite competent under suitable guidance to produce all the results attested by the Austrian savant. Thus Braid operated on a young man by drawing his gold pencil-case along the palm

[1] P. 181.

[2] It becomes clear, on a careful analysis of his work, that, notwithstanding his familiarity with the materials of chemistry and electricity, and the ostentation of scientific accuracy shown in his list of chemical substances, and his tables of the diurnal variations of the odylic force in the human body, and all the rest of his elaborate data, Reichenbach was not of a scientific habit of mind; he was willing to slur over discrepancies; he did not realise the fallacies implied in his methods; he was unable to appreciate the real bearing of some of the results which he records. Above all, he did not possess that rare, but to a student of science indispensable, quality, the intellectual candour which would have enabled him to profit by the criticism of others. It is probable that he started with an open mind, but soon became intoxicated with his own success as a pioneer in a new field of scientific discovery; he was hardened and confirmed in this attitude by the rancorous abuse which his original publications met with in the German-speaking countries, and by the gratuitous insults offered to the character of his subjects. He ended as a blind partisan—a partisan so blind and so perverse that, though four years had elapsed since the publication of Braid's courteous and temperate criticisms, Reichenbach in the later edition of his work makes no mention of Braid's name or his theories, and has not even devised a single counter experiment. It is this wilful ignorance on his own part, not the spiteful abuse of German critics, which discredits Reichenbach's researches and damns his reputation.

[3] His account of these experiments originally appeared in the *Medical Times*, vol. xiv., and was afterwards republished as a separate pamphlet, under the title *The Power of the Mind over the Body* (London, 1846).

of the hand. The subject experienced a sensation of pricking and a distinct aura, just as any of Reichenbach's sensitives would have done. On reversing the direction of the
pencil the aura and the other sensations were changed in
character. Braid then asked the patient to turn his head
aside during the further progress of the experiment. He did
so, and again felt the aura and the pricking sensation. But
Braid this time had done nothing; the gold pencil-case
remained in his waistcoat pocket. Braid then explained
to his subject the nature of the experiment, and told him
that he could himself provoke similar sensations in the upper
part of his foot, by merely concentrating attention on that
part. The patient obeyed, and to his astonishment succeeded, though at the cost of a severe headache. Braid
made other patients, men and women, experience sensations
of cold, attraction, and muscular cramp from the passes of a
magnet, and found precisely similar results to follow when
the magnet was present only to their imagination. His subjects saw flames issuing from a magnet in the dark, and
continued to see them when the magnet was no longer
there ; others, when told what to expect, saw flames of
varying colour issuing from the bare walls of a dark closet.

An " eminent physician " and mesmerist demonstrated to
Braid the wonderful power of a magnet in inducing catalepsy
in an entranced patient by mere contact with the surface of
the skin. Braid replied that he had in his possession an
instrument endowed with still more marvellous powers. He
placed this instrument in the patient's hand, and it produced
catalepsy of both hands and arms; he reversed the position
of the instrument, and the patient's hand opened. A single
touch of the instrument caused any of the subject's limbs to
rise and become stiffened; a second touch caused it to lose
its rigidity and fall. Placed on the third finger of the left
hand, it produced sleep. Removed and placed on the second
finger of the same hand, it rendered the patient proof against
all the mesmerist's endeavours to send her to sleep. Each
of these results had been predicted by Braid within the
hearing of the patient ; the instrument by which this modern

magician secured obedience to his commands was nothing more than his portmanteau key and the ring on which it was suspended.

Braid's main conclusion, that the phenomena described by Reichenbach were subjective—*i.e.*, that they were of the nature not of authentic sense-perceptions, but of hallucinations— would probably not be disputed by any competent inquirer. His further conclusion, that they were dependent solely on the imagination of the percipient, guided by suggestions given unconsciously by the experimenter, however probable in itself, does, no doubt, go beyond the warrant of the facts. So it appeared, in 1851, to a writer in the *North British Review*. Braid's experiments, he points out, are no doubt sound and relevant; but they do not for all that necessarily overthrow Reichenbach's main thesis.

The reviewer suggests that there are forces, of which the magnetic force is the best known, which, though they produce no appreciable effect on ordinary men or women, can influence the nervous system of exceptionally sensitive persons.

"The wondrous and incalculable inward stir that is ceaselessly going on within the body of the so-called animal magnet excites an inward stir within the substance of the exceptional nerve, and that stir bodies itself forth through the said exceptional nerve to the percipient owner as a cool aura, a warm breeze, a luminous flame, a thread of light or phosphorescent vapour or what not."

In short, odyle is "a nerve-stirring resultant of the general cosmical powers of nature," and Reichenbach has established the proposition "that the whole of Nature is reactive on the nervous system of man, on a breadth of basis which cannot be shaken."

The reviewer's conjecture was of course opposed to the better opinion in science sixty years ago, and the progress of research has confirmed the verdict of the majority. Endeavours have from time to time been made to substantiate the phenomena alleged by Reichenbach, but the results have been invariably negative or inconclusive. It is, no doubt,

M

wonderful, as Lord Kelvin has said,[1] that the magnetic force which acts so powerfully on many other substances should have absolutely no perceptible effect upon the human body ; but such appears to be the case. The ordinary man is not conscious of any unusual sensation when his head is placed between the poles of the most powerful electro-magnet, and it still remains to be proved that any rays proceed from it visible in the most profound darkness to the most sensitive eyes.[2]

But the demonstrations of Wakley and Braid had no effect upon the Fluidists of their day. Braid's criticism of Reichenbach's results, with an account of his counter experiments, appeared in 1846 in a series of articles in the *Medical Times*, afterwards reprinted in a small volume, *The Power of the Mind over the Body*. It is inconceivable that Gregory can have been ignorant of the existence of this work. Yet in his Preface to the translation of 1850 he writes: " Up to this time I have not become acquainted with any scientific criticism, published in this country, on the author's researches, which requires any notice from me in this place "; and in dealing at some length with objectors and objections he does not refer either to Braid or to his theory that the results were due to suggestion and expectant attention. Reichenbach himself, as we have seen, completely ignored Braid's criticisms.

Again, writing as late as 1856, Esdaile stated :—

" I am convinced that Mesmerism as practised by me is a physical power exerted by one animal on another . . . and I should as soon

---

[1] See his address on the *Six Gateways of Knowledge*, in *Nature*, March 6, 1884.

[2] For some recent experiments to test Reichenbach's phenomena see *Proc. S.P.R.*, vol. i. p. 230, and vol. ii. p. 56, and *Proc. American S.P.R.*, p. 116. The results were in all cases negative or inconclusive. Some experiments have recently been conducted in Amsterdam, for which positive results are claimed ; but until full details are published it is impossible to estimate the significance of the results (see *Dreimonatlicher Bericht des Psycho-physischen Laboratoriums zu Amsterdam*, 1907, No. 3).

adopt the diabolical theory as a satisfactory solution of the problem, as attempt to account for what I have seen and done by the action of the imagination alone." [1]

That the repetition *ad nauseam* of demonstrations similar to those of Braid still leaves it possible for men of scientific training at the present day to believe in the action at a distance of drugs and magnets upon the human body, in nerve atmospheres, in radiant emanations which can be seen only by persons of Gallic or Celtic blood,[2] and the like, is in itself a phenomenon which calls for consideration.

That the phenomena are only perceptible to certain persons is admitted. Neither by Reichenbach nor by any subsequent experimenter has satisfactory proof ever been adduced of the power of the alleged emanations to affect a galvanometer or a photographic plate or to produce any other objective result. No adequate control experiments to prove that the phenomena are independent of the percipient's imagination have ever been published. And yet the belief persists even in some scientific circles, and from time to time breaks out in new directions.

The strange vitality of the belief would be explained if we could suppose that, to adopt the phraseology of the Scottish reviewer, there is in certain cases "an inward stir within the substance of the exceptional nerve," and that this stir corresponds not to the supposed vibrations from crystal or magnet, but to the far subtler and more elusive molecular disturbance in the nervous system of the experimenter. Of course, if the demonstrations had been conducted under rigid test conditions, and if adequate control experiments had ever been instituted, it would be an easy matter to test this hypothesis. In the absence of such control experiments the suggested action of thought-transference must remain purely conjectural.

[1] *Introduction of Mesmerism into India* (edition of 1856).
[2] A concise history of the alleged discovery of the *n* rays will be found in Mrs. Sidgwick's Presidential Address to the Society for Psychical Research (*Proc.*, xxii. p. 12). The belief in *n* rays has now apparently suffered euthanasia.

But there are other experiments recorded in the decade 1840–1850 which seem more obviously to call for some such explanation. The stimulation of the alleged phrenological organs by the mesmeric fluid was a favourite demonstration. Braid repeatedly tested the reaction on private persons amongst his acquaintance, who had never witnessed any demonstration of phrenology, and who knew nothing of the alleged positions of the organs. He was of course alive to the risk of suggestion, and was careful to guard against any hint of the desired result reaching the patient either from himself or from the spectators. The demonstrations were of a most surprising kind, and sufficient at the time to convince Braid that there was some physiological connection between the part of the scalp affected and the resulting emotional reaction. Modern physiologists would probably find it easier to reject Braid's facts than to accept the explanation which he proffers. If we can place confidence in Braid's account of the manifestations observed by him, and can share his conviction that the sensitive could have received no hint of the results to be expected, we must recognise that an explanation in physiological terms is not yet forthcoming.[1]

But thought-transference, through the operation of one nervous system upon another, is more directly suggested by some other experiments of this date.

Jussieu, it will be remembered, in his separate report of 1784, recorded some observations which seemed to indicate

---

[1] *Neurypnology*, in which Braid's experiments in phreno-mesmerism were recorded, was published in 1843. The experiments recounted in the *Medical Times* of November, 1845, show that Braid had already begun to feel dubious about the records given in the earlier work. In reviewing some years later the whole subject of hypnotism (*Magic, Witchcraft*, &c., third edition, 1852) he makes, so far as I can discover, no explicit reference to Phreno-hypnotism—an omission the more significant in view of the large space devoted to the subject in his *Neurypnology*. From a passage on p. 71, however, it may perhaps be inferred that, in looking back on the matter, he was not quite satisfied that he had correctly represented the conditions under which his recorded results were obtained. Possibly more than he realised at the time may have been due to previous training of a subconscious kind, or to inadvertent suggestion on his own part.

that the magnetic influence could be conveyed from a distance without the knowledge of the patient. The belief in such action at a distance was universal amongst the early Magnetists; but it was rarely put to the test. The experiments made by the second French Commission, as already indicated, were inconclusive. At the epoch we are now considering there were many demonstrations of this alleged influence at a distance, in inducing temporary catalepsy, hypnotic sleep, or irresistible attraction to the operator. Esdaile claims to have entranced a blind man at a distance of some paces, and to have thrown into the cataleptic state in a Court of Justice three persons successively, each of whom was unaware of his intention to mesmerise them.[1] An amateur mesmerist, W. H. Stafford Thompson, claimed on many occasions to have influenced his friends, to the extent of throwing them into a hypnotic sleep, or impelling them to come into the room where he was seated, by the mere exercise of his silent will.[2] Dr. Ashburner,[3] Dr. Haddock,[4] and other contemporary writers record instances of the kind. In many of these cases it seems probable that the subject may have become aware of the operator's intention. In very few instances does it appear that the conditions of the experiment were so contrived as to exclude this possibility. The following case, however, quoted from Townshend's *Facts in Mesmerism*,[5] seems worth consideration. Townshend was one of the most careful experimenters of the time. Two previous trials of the same kind with the same patient had been completely successful. It will be observed that both the beginning and the end of the sleep are alleged to have coincided with Townshend's effort of will.

"The third trial that I made to mesmerise this patient from a distance was still more remarkable and decisive.

---

[1] *Mesmerism in India*, p. 92.
[2] See his articles in the *Zoist*, vols. iii. p. 319, v. p. 253, and elsewhere.
[3] *Zoist*, vol. v. p. 260.
[4] *Somnolism and Psycheism*, p. 92.
[5] P. 314.

"One evening, when sitting with my family, the idea occurred to me, 'Could I mesmerise Anna M—— there as I then was, while she was in her own house?' to which I knew she was just then confined by slight indisposition. Acting on this thought, I begged all the party present to note the hour (it was exactly nine o'clock), and to bear me witness that then and there I attempted a mesmeric experiment.

"This time I attempted to bring before my imagination very vividly the person of my sleepwaker, and even aided the concentration of my thoughts by the usual mesmeric gestures ; I also at the end of an hour said, 'I will now awake Anna,' and used appropriate gestures. We now awaited with more curiosity than confidence the result of this process.

"The following morning Anna made her appearance, just as we were at breakfast, exclaiming, 'Oh, sir! did you magnetise me last night ? About nine o'clock I fell asleep, and mother and sisters say they could not wake me with all their shaking of me, and they were quite frightened ; but after an hour I woke of myself ; and I think from all this that my sleep must have been magnetic. It also did me a great deal of good, for I felt quite recovered from my cold after it. After a natural sleep I never feel so much refreshed. When I sleep for an hour in magnetism, it is as if I had rested a whole night.' These were the words of Anna M——, noted down at the time as accurately as possible."

But Townshend was a better observer and recorder than most of his contemporaries ; and, taken as a whole, the numerous reports of similar cases scattered through the mesmeric literature of this date would scarcely call for consideration on their merits. They seem to have more significance, however, in the light of the experiments in the production of sleep conducted by several French men of science in recent times. Of these recent experiments the most striking are those made at Havre in 1885 and 1886 by Professor Janet and Dr. Gibert, with Madame B. (Léonie) as the subject. The distance between agent and subject in these experiments varied from a quarter-mile to one mile. The sensitive, Madame B., was staying in the Pavilion at Havre, a house occupied by Dr. Gibert's sister, who, herself ignorant of the hour fixed for the experiment, was able to report the results. The operator was sometimes Dr. Gibert, sometimes Professor Janet. The hour of the experiments was sometimes chosen by lot, or suggested by a third person ;

they ranged from 11 a.m. to 11.35 p.m.; precautions were taken to prevent Madame B. from having any suspicion of the time selected. The result willed by the experimenter was usually the induction of hypnotic sleep; but on three occasions he willed that Madame B. should leave the house and come to him. Out of twenty-five trials eighteen were completely successful, and there were four partial or doubtful successes.

It should be added that during the period of the experiments Madame B. only twice fell spontaneously into the hypnotic sleep—once on looking at a picture of Dr. Gibert; and that she never left the house in the evenings except on the three occasions on which she did so in apparent response to the operator's will. There seems little ground, therefore, for attributing the results to chance.[1]

[1] See Janet's article in *Revue Philosophique*, February, 1886. *Proceedings S.P.R.*, vol. iv. pp. 128, *seqq.* Some further experiments with the same subject are reported by Professor Richet, *Revue de l'Hypnotisme*, February, 1888.

CHAPTER IX

CLAIRVOYANCE

Community of sensation and clairvoyance partly explicable by
thought-transference—Clairvoyance at close quarters largely fraudulent
—But probably in some cases due to hyperæsthesia of vision—The case
of Alexis Didier—His card-playing and reading in closed books—
Houdin's testimony—Alexis probably an automatist—His description of
sealed packets and of distant scenes possibly indicative of supernormal
power—Other examples of probably telepathic clairvoyance given by
Lee, Haddock, Gregory—Many Mesmerists see in these demonstrations
proof of the action of the soul apart from the body.

IN the last chapter we have briefly referred to the survival
in byways of contemporary thought of the belief in the
manifestation of magnetic, odylic, or other imponder-
able effluences which formed the foundation of the Mesmerists'
creed in 1840–1850. It has been suggested that the extraordinary persistence of the belief, in face of repeated
demonstrations that the sensations on which it is based are
imaginary, may be due to some communication taking place
between the nervous system of the experimenter and the
percipient. This hypothesis is strengthened by the consideration of the numerous experiments in the induction of sleep at
a distance, especially those conducted twenty years ago by
Janet and Gibert. For nearly thirty years past the investigators of the Society for Psychical Research have worked at
the subject and have brought forward a body of evidence,
based partly on experiment, partly on observation, sufficient
at any rate to establish thought-transference or telepathy
as a working hypothesis. In the present chapter we shall

endeavour to show that this hypothesis will go far to explain many other marvels which must otherwise be rejected as altogether incredible, or accepted—as was actually the case with most of the Mesmerists of the period under review—as the basis of theories far more dubious.

These so-called "higher phenomena" may be roughly classed under the categories of community of sensation; clairvoyance at close quarters, or seeing without eyes; and clairvoyance at a distance. It is obvious that the hypothesis of an indifferent physical agency was inadequate to explain such manifestations. Some, indeed, of the earlier Magnetists, as already stated, did attempt to explain vision through opaque bodies as due to the all-penetrating action of the hypothetical fluid and "transference of sensation" as due to concentration of nerve-force. But the explanation is purely a juggle with words. It is clear that they had not attempted to conceive the *modus operandi*; and in the case of clairvoyance at a distance the attempt at a physical explanation was for the most part abandoned. The more sober-minded investigators at this period, amongst whom we must reckon Elliotson, and generally those who had not witnessed in their own persons any conclusive illustration of the supposed faculty, were content to keep an open mind upon the subject. Others—and they were the majority — looked upon the manifestations as a certain proof of the action of the soul apart from the body—a belief which is crystallised in the name "travelling clairvoyance."

The problems dealt with in the last chapter are of a comparatively simple kind. There can be no reasonable doubt that the odylic flames, the magnetic thrills, and all the protean manifestations of the mysterious fluid were elaborated by the imagination of the percipient. The demonstration, to those who have eyes to see and ears to hear, is so far complete. But some of the problems presented by these higher phenomena still await solution, and the investigation is unusually complicated and difficult. No good ground has been shown for imputing to the numerous company of Reichenbach's sensitives deliberate

deception. There was little fame and no money
to be gained by seeing flames from a magnet. But,
unfortunately, there is and always has been money in
clairvoyance; and — what is to many minds an even
stronger motive than money—there is the pleasure of
exciting wonder and admiration. In studying the records
of clairvoyance it is hardly too much to say that fraud is
the first explanation to be considered. But it need not
necessarily be the last.

The so-called community of sensation between mesmerist
and subject first came into prominence at this period. It
had, indeed, been observed, in the special form of communication of the symptoms of disease from patient to
clairvoyant, as early as 1784. As shown in Chapter V.,
Bertrand believed the occurrence of the faculty in the
somnambulic state to be well established, giving from his
own observations several instances of its exercise. But with
the English Mesmerists the faculty took a new direction.
It was no longer confined to morbid sensations; and the
sympathy was no longer exercised, as before, exclusively
between patient and clairvoyant. The sympathies of the
entranced somnambule were now turned to the mesmerist: she would feel what he felt, taste what he tasted, see
what he saw. Innumerable illustrations of this power, real
or imaginary, are to be found in the literature of the period.
But it is not necessary to dwell on these earlier results, since
they add but slight corroboration to the more striking and
more rigorous experiments in the same field made by Mrs. H.
Sidgwick and other recent investigators.

The demonstrations of clairvoyance at close quarters stand
upon a very different footing. The experience of the Burdin
Commission, described in Chapter VI., would seem conclusive,
so far as negative evidence can be conclusive, as to the
non-reality of the alleged faculty. Nevertheless, the marvel
obtained an extraordinary vogue in England at this time,
not only amongst the uninstructed crowd who thronged
the performances of itinerant lecturers, but with medical
men and sober-minded investigators like Townshend. It

obtains a certain amount of credence even at the present day.[1]

Devices more or less ingenious, but all relying for success mainly upon their audacity and the simplicity of the victims, were used by some of the clairvoyants of this period. George Goble, whose case is related by Sir John Forbes,[2] opened sealed boxes under the shelter of a friendly pillow. Major Buckley found forty-four sensitives, most of them young ladies of good social position, who could read the mottoes enclosed in nuts—hazel-nuts or walnuts filled with sweets—before they were opened. The trick in this case was, no doubt, performed by substituting, for the nuts just bought from the confectioner's, other nuts which had been already opened, so that the mottoes might be learnt by heart.[3]

Most, however, of the mesmeric clairvoyants of this type had their eyes bandaged, as was the case with the French subjects described in Chapter VI. It is not clear that these cases were necessarily fraudulent. The trance may have been genuine—there are indications in some cases that it was so—and the subject may in some cases have been ignorant of the means by which he obtained the information displayed. In some experiments made to test the existence of Reichenbach's magnetic effluence Messrs. Jastrow and Nuttall found that the subject may derive knowledge from sensations too faint to rise to the level of consciousness.[4] Again, in the course of some experiments in reading cards by the touch alone, Mrs. Verrall found that a picture of the card would appear before her mental vision, and that, after a certain

---

[1] See, for instance, Myers' *Human Personality*, vol. i. p. 556, where the testimony of Major Buckley is cited, and Dr. Alfred Russel Wallace's remarks on Alexis Didier, *Proc. S.P.R.*, vol. xiv.

[2] *Illustrations of Modern Mesmerism*, 1845.

[3] The proof of the statement in the text, since Major Buckley's young ladies were never, as far as I am aware, caught *flagrante delicto*, is purely circumstantial. But for those who read the records with care it is, I think, sufficient. For accounts of these experiments see *Zoist*, vol. vi. pp. 96 and 380, vol. viii. p. 265 ; Gregory's *Letters on Animal Magnetism*, p. 362 ; Ashburner, *On the Philosophy of Animal Magnetism*, p. 301.

[4] *Proceedings American S.P.R.* (1885), p. 116.

degree of proficiency had been attained in interpreting her tactile sensations, she ceased to be conscious of the process by which she learnt what the cards were.[1]

Further, there are a few experiments which would appear to indicate abnormal powers of vision on the part of some of the sensitives. Townshend's subject, a French youth of fifteen, was able to distinguish cards in a cupboard which to ordinary senses was perfectly dark.[2] Ellen Dawson, in a dark room, is said to have accurately described the coloured plates in Cuvier's *Animal Kingdom*.[3]

The best illustrations, not only of the so-called clairvoyance at close quarters, but of the more problematic clairvoyance at a distance, were given by a young Frenchman, Alexis Didier. Alexis was about nineteen when he first came to England in 1844, and we have reports of his performances extending over seven or eight years. His mesmerist was one Marcillet, a man of good education and social address. Marcillet was accepted as a friend by Elliotson and the Mesmeric school of the period, and was implicitly trusted by them—a fact which should be borne in mind in considering the clairvoyant's performances. Alexis gave numerous receptions, under the guidance of Marcillet, in London in the summer of 1844, and again at Brighton and Hastings in January, 1849.[4] His fee is said[5] to have been five guineas a sitting, and he sometimes gave three or four sittings a day. The performances were generally given in private houses, but as from twenty to forty people appear as a rule to have attended, the conditions were not favourable for exact observation. Marcillet was invariably present; and the members of the company were not always known to each other. Forbes's[;] conjecture that confederates may have been present to assist the tricks was not therefore unreasonable. The performance always followed a regular order. It began with an exhibition of the

[1] *Proc. S.P.R.*, vol. xi. p. 176.
[2] Townshend, *Facts in Mesmerism*.
[3] *Zoist*, vol. iii. p. 229. The experimenter was W. Hands, a surgeon.
[4] An account of these later demonstrations is given by Edwin Lee, M.D. (*Animal Magnetism*, 1866).
[5] By Sir John Forbes, *Illustrations of Modern Mesmerism*.

phenomenon of cataleptic rigidity. Alexis would be seated in a chair, his legs extended horizontally in front of him, entirely unsupported, and a heavy man would stand upon his thighs. Then began the clairvoyant performance. (1) The subject's eyes would be bandaged, and he would play écarté. (2) He would remove the bandages, a book would be opened and, holding his finger on a given part of the page, he would read words in a corresponding part, ten, twenty, or forty pages further on. (3) He would describe the contents of sealed packets presented to him. (4) He would give descriptions of absent persons, and diagnose their ailments; would describe the houses, furniture, and pictures of his questioners.

As regards the playing at écarté there is little to be said. Alexis was bandaged with cotton-wool, leather pads, and silk handkerchiefs. But, as shown, no bandaging of this kind can ever be satisfactory; and several witnesses testify that Alexis habitually interfered and fidgeted with his bandages. There need be no question that he could, and did, see through interstices in the bandaging, but it is astonishing how much he saw, and with what rapidity and accuracy. On two occasions the celebrated Robert Houdin had private sittings with Alexis. On each occasion he brought in his pocket an unopened pack of cards, broke the stamped covering at the table, and himself dealt the cards. After the very first deal, while the ten cards still lay face downwards on the table, untouched by Alexis, he correctly named every card. On the second occasion Houdin brought with him a trusted friend, to correct his own observations. Again and again Alexis, bandaged with all the conjuror's skill, showed complete knowledge, not simply of the cards in his own hand, but of those of his adversary, sometimes, again, of the cards still face downwards on the table.

Houdin was completely staggered, and professed himself unable to explain what he had seen by any means within the resources of his art.[1]

[1] Houdin's testimony is given in De Mirville's book, *Des Esprits et leurs Manifestations fluidiques* (Paris, 1854), vol. i. pp. 18–32 ; quoted in *Proc. S.P.R.*, vol. xiv. pp. 373–381.

Probably if Alexis had simply seen his own cards when held in his hand Houdin would have arrived at the true explanation. What staggered him, no doubt, was that Alexis should see so much more than this. I take it that the explanation probably lay in Alexis seeing the reflection of the cards as they fell on a polished surface. The reflecting surface may have been the table. In not one of the numerous accounts which I have read is the table described, except sometimes as a " card table." But highly glazed cards would no doubt serve the purpose. Houdin does not describe his own cards. But in the accounts of the English experiments of 1844 one writer mentions that the backs of the cards were glazed.[1] One would have expected an eminent conjuror to have been alive to this possibility. But Alexis's extraordinary, though not uniform, success in this particular performance indicates that he must have been possessed of an almost incredible acuteness of vision.[2]

A like extreme acuteness of vision was demonstrated in the next item of the programme. In Robert Houdin's second sitting this part of the performance is described as follows :—

"R. Houdin, after taking off the somnambulist's useless bandages, draws a book of his own from his pocket, and asks him to read eight pages further on, starting from a given place. Alexis pricks the page two-thirds of the way down with a pin and reads, ' Après cette triste cérémonie.'

"' Stop,' says R. Houdin ; ' that is enough, I will look.'

---

[1] *Zoist,* vol. ii. p. 496.

[2] Some years ago I paid several visits to an amateur clairvoyant who professed to be able to tell cards by looking at their backs. The clairvoyant's own cards were marked. When my pack was used the clairvoyance consisted in reading the reflection of the card, which was placed on a highly polished cloth-bound book. But the cards were taken up one by one, and the whole performance was very slow and hesitating. The performance in this case took place sometimes by daylight, sometimes by artificial light. I observed that the clairvoyant was very particular in the arrangement of the illumination. Alexis was, of course, always free to choose his position with reference to the source of light. Mrs. Verrall's experiments (*Proc. S.P.R.,* vol. xi. p. 174) indicate that with practice considerable facility can be attained in reading cards by reflection from polished surfaces.

"Nothing like it on the eighth page, but on the next page at the same height are the words, 'après cette triste cérémonie.'
" 'That's enough,' says Houdin ; 'what a marvel !' "

But the account was written by de Mirville. Houdin indeed attests that the incidents actually took place as described by de Mirville, but we cannot hold him as fully responsible for all the details as if he had himself written the account.

From the accounts given by Forbes and others it appears that what generally took place was as follows : A book would be presented to Alexis by one of those present. If not presented open he would open it himself, and instantly placing his hand or handkerchief over the open page, would offer to read from any part of the covered surface. This performance frequently took place with the eyes still bandaged. He would now remove the bandage, and, taking up the book, would hold it before his eyes whilst he rapidly separated a sheaf of some twenty to one hundred pages. He would then read correctly a few words, sometimes in a part of the page chosen by himself, sometimes in a part chosen by the audience. The words read would be found in a corresponding position several pages further on—sometimes five, sometimes one hundred—and Alexis would profess to indicate, and sometimes with approximate correctness, how far on they were.[1]

We must suppose that Alexis, in separating a portion of the book for the purpose of the experiment, was able to perceive words and sentences as he moved the pages rapidly

---

[1] See the account by Forbes (*op. cit.*) of these experiments. Forbes paid several visits to Alexis, accompanied by Carpenter (see *Mesmerism, Spiritualism*, &c., by Carpenter, 1877, p. 77). The Mesmerists give few details of the experiments, and rarely mention that Alexis handled the book at all. In some cases even it is expressly stated that he had no opportunity of turning over the leaves, or even of touching the book (see, *e.g.*, *Zoist*, ii. p. 500).

In such cases we are, no doubt, entitled to assume as probable an error of memory or observation on the part of the recorder. Reading the twelfth line from the bottom in a page of which top and side were uncut is perhaps within the bounds of possibility. (Lee, *op. cit.*, p. 278).

sideways before his eyes. But his movements were so rapid as to escape the suspicion of most observers; and the frequency of his success, even when he allowed the spectators to choose the part of the page, was very remarkable. There is one curious detail in this experiment the significance of which neither Sir John Forbes nor the Mesmerists appear to have appreciated. When challenged to read a sentence several pages deep Alexis, instead of saying the words aloud, generally took a pencil and wrote them down.[1] Why did he do this? If the thing was simply a clever conjuring trick, and Alexis was reproducing sentences which he had deliberately committed to memory, he would naturally prefer to speak them, first, because the act of speaking would involve less effort and, secondly, because, if the words were written, it would be impossible to explain away mistakes. The fact that he preferred to write them is an almost certain indication that the performance was not a trick, but an instance of automatic reaction, or, in Carpenter's phraseology, unconscious cerebration. It is well known that latent memories and other subconscious impressions are frequently and easily reproduced in automatic writing. But automatic speech is a much rarer phenomenon, and indicates generally a more serious dissociation of consciousness.

Both the feat just described and the feat of reading the cards face downwards point to a rapidity and acuteness of vision beyond the normal, and taken in conjunction with the preference for writing rather than speech, seem to make it almost certain that Alexis was not in the strict sense a conjuror, but belonged rather to the class of persons whom the Spiritualists call mediums, and to whom we may apply

[1] Roughly, this was the case in two experiments out of three, so far as Dr. Lee's account shows. The wording of the reports of 1844 is as a rule ambiguous; but even from these it appears that Alexis sometimes wrote instead of speaking the words, and he may have done so generally. In his experiments with Houdin he not only appears to have *read* the words, but he further pricked the part of the page where they would be found. This action, though it is occasionally recorded, is unusual, and taken in conjunction with the reading aloud, probably indicates that Alexis's perception was clearer than usual.

the non-committal term of Automatists. Further, it is not improbable that he was himself unaware of the channel through which his information reached him.

The feats so far described do not, however, point to any new faculty. The annals of Hypnotism contain many instances, as yet indeed very imperfectly investigated, of extraordinary acuteness of the special senses, and we need not go beyond this explanation. But automatic perception, even supplemented by hyperæsthesia, seems hardly an adequate explanation for the next item in Alexis's programme. No doubt some of the circumstances are very suggestive of fraud. Alexis would not accept a packet at the hands of any one who was antipathetic to him. If he were pressed to try such a packet, it must be opened and its contents shown—no doubt within the possible range of prying eyes—to some sympathetic spectator.[1] When Alexis took the packet his conduct was again suspicious. He would twist and turn it over in his hand, apply it successively to his forehead, the back of his head, the stomach, or even the toes. He would on occasion attempt, if not prevented, to break the seal. By these means, no doubt, he was enabled to feel the shape and frequently to make a shrewd guess at the contents. If he had to deal with a word in one or two folds of paper or a single sealed envelope, it is probable that in the course of his manipulations he was generally able to read it either by means of a gap, or through a single fold of paper. That he did, in fact, sometimes decipher the words by ordinary vision is proved by his occasionally, as a further test, driving pins through the envelope and transfixing particular letters.[2] But though Alexis, no doubt, used his eyes and his fingers when he could, and though he probably gained some information by " fishing " questions and by thinking aloud, it seems certain that in many cases the solution must be sought in some other direction. The records of 1844 are very fragmentary and the

---

[1] Sir John Forbes was one of those whom Alexis found antipathetic ; so was the Rev. F. Robertson, of Brighton (Lee, *op. cit.*, p. 258).

[2] See, *e.g., Zoist,* vol. ii. pp. 294 and 510–524, and Forbes's and Carpenter's books already cited.

N

marvels are mostly described at secondhand. The following incident, however, is well attested. The meeting was held at the house of Mr. Dupuis, in Welbeck Street, on July 2, 1844, and the account was drawn up by Lord Adare.

"Colonel Llewellyn, who was, I believe, rather sceptical, produced a morocco case, something like a surgical instrument case. Alexis took it, placed it to his stomach, and said, 'The object is a hard substance, not white, enclosed in something more white than itself; it is a bone taken from a greater body; a human bone—yours. It has been separated, and cut so as to leave a flat side.' Alexis opened the case, took out a piece of bone wrapped in silver paper, and said, 'The ball struck here; it was an extraordinary ball in effect; you received three separate injuries at the same moment; the bone was broken in three pieces; you were wounded early in the day whilst engaged in charging the enemy.' He also described the dress of the soldiers, and was right in all these particulars. This excited the astonishment of all the bystanders, especially the gallant colonel. This account is drawn up, not only from my own notes, but from Colonel Llewellyn's statement made after the *séance*, and from a written account given me by a lady who was sitting close by." [1]

A corresponding but rather fuller account of the incident was sent to the *Medical Times* by the Rev. G. Sandby (" Clericus "). It seems clear from the concurrent testimony of the two witnesses that Alexis did not open the packet until he had fully described the contents, and that he did not gain his information from hints inadvertently let drop by the bystanders. There remains the possibility that Alexis had somehow learnt particulars of the proposed test beforehand. Colonel Llewellyn may have unsuspectingly taken the respectable M. Marcillet into his confidence; or Alexis and his manager may have bribed servants or employed private inquiry agents. There is no doubt that information could be gained by such means; and as Alexis was more or less free to exercise his choice amongst the numerous articles presented to him at any sitting, the chances of success are, of course, much increased. But the systematic record by Dr. Lee of thirteen *séances* held at Brighton and Hastings in January, 1849, seems to put this last explanation practically

[1] *Zoist*, vol. ii. p. 510.

out of court. Dr. Lee is, no doubt, a convinced and, it must be admitted, credulous Mesmerist, and his reports are very condensed.[1] But he expressly says that he had recorded all the failures, total or partial.[2] In the thirteen *séances*, sixty-seven closed envelopes or packets are recorded to have been offered to Alexis for trial. In twenty-two cases he failed to decipher the contents ; in forty-five cases he succeeded.[3]

[1] It need hardly be pointed out that condensation can only be achieved by omission of detail. Dr. Lee was, no doubt, honest, and intended to omit only details which were irrelevant. But, in dealing with matters of this kind, only the expert can say what is really relevant. It is possible that some of the details omitted would have given us important clues. Unluckily, we can only now and then check Lee's statements. But two or three significant omissions may be pointed out. On p. 258 he describes a case of successful reading twenty pages in advance in a book presented by the Rev. F. Robertson. Two pages later, at the end of the account, he mentions incidentally that the first trial of reading, also proposed by Mr. Robertson, had been a failure.

In two instances we have records from other hands of the *séances* described by Lee, and we are thus enabled to discover other omissions. Thus (p. 258) Lee writes : " Sir R—— G—— then gave a morocco case, which Alexis said contained," &c. In an account of the same sitting by Mr. Parsons, of Brighton (*Zoist*, vol. vii. pp. 92–93), the incident is thus described : " Sir. R. Grant presented a packet containing a portrait, which had been before presented by a sceptic, and Alexis could then make nothing of it. Marcillet then proposed that the packet should be put into the hands of any other gentleman who was not a sceptic, and that the contents should be exhibited to that other person in another room. Sir. R. Grant volunteered, and this was done," &c. In another case (p. 269) Lee simply says that the right name—Blake—was " at length " written, but a journalist who reported the same *séance* states that Alexis wrote " one letter after another until he made out the word "—an important detail (p. 271).

[2] *Op. cit.*, p. 278, *note.*

[3] In the forty-five successful cases are included a few cases of partial but decisive success—*e.g.*, in one such case Alexis wrote " Mort," but was unable to continue ; the word was " Mortemar." The twenty-two " failures " are made up as follows: In one case Alexis refused to accept the packet because it was presented by a sceptic (the Rev. F. Robertson, possibly the celebrated divine of that name). In eight cases he failed to give any indication at all of the nature of the contents ; in three cases he gave descriptions which were incorrect. In seven cases the description was partly correct, but not sufficiently

It is possible, of course, that the failures may have been more numerous than are set down, because Lee is more likely to have forgotten a failure than a success. The successes must also be to some extent discounted, because though Lee claims to have recorded all the "total or partial failures," he states that he did not record "the erroneous impressions, which, owing to the variety of tests proposed, often pass through the mind of a somnambulist, to which he may give utterance before definitely deciding upon the test before him."[1] It is much to be regretted that we have not a full record of all the remarks made, both by Alexis and his interlocutors. A complete record would have great value. But in view of the nature of some of the tests proposed, and the nature of the replies given, the record, even as it stands, seems to point to the exercise of some supernormal faculty. Alexis, as said, attached considerable importance to the packet being presented by a "sympathetic" person ; the questioner was generally asked to give his hand to Alexis, or even to sit by him hand in hand for a time. As in the case of the sentences read in the book, Alexis seems to have preferred to write or draw his answer. Among the words correctly written were *Paris, pensée, Alexis, incredule, amie, Montespan, Verona, Edward Street.*

so to justify the attempt being counted as successful. In three cases sufficient details are not given to enable us to determine the exact nature of the failure. Amongst the "failures" were two packets containing bank-notes. In one case Alexis gave wrong indications ; in the other the propounder of the test refused to say whether the word written by Alexis was right or wrong.

[1] *Op. cit.*, p. 278, *note.* Of course, these erroneous impressions, when uttered aloud, may have served to elicit important information from the bystanders, if they were not on their guard. Forbes and Carpenter both point out the possibility, and are inclined thus to explain the partial successes witnessed by them. But Lee elsewhere (p. 267) expressly says that the parties only replied " No " if Alexis was wrong, and gave him no other assistance. It is not clear, however, that this statement is intended to apply to the whole series of *séances* recorded by him. But I cannot myself understand how any amount of " fishing " or "muscle-reading " could account for some of the results recorded.

On January 23rd a man handed Alexis an envelope containing the word " clairvoyance," which was correctly read. On reflection, it occurred to him that Alexis might have read the word through the envelope, and on the following day he presented a second packet, consisting of several envelopes one inside the other, to preclude all possibility of the words being read by ordinary vision. Alexis wrote " Louis Napoleon," which was correct.

Sometimes the word was written slowly, with hesitation, or letter by letter, but in two cases Lee mentions that the words were written spasmodically, or as if by a sudden inspiration.

As a variant of the experiments with sealed packets Alexis was frequently given a letter, or a lock of hair, or a trinket, and asked to describe the person to whom it belonged. The descriptions were acknowledged to be wonderfully accurate, even to such personal peculiarities as the loss of an eye or a limb. In these experiments also, when asked for a proper name or a date, Alexis generally took a pencil in his hand and wrote. One trial of this kind, as described by Houdin, may be given. Houdin handed Alexis a letter, which the latter placed successively on his stomach and the top of his head. He then gave a fairly accurate description of the writer and his surroundings. Houdin then asked—

" Where does the letter come from ? "

Alexis : " From ——."

" Ah ! " says R. Houdin ; "and the postmark. I never thought of that. But since you see the house, can you tell me in what street it stands ? "

Alexis : " Wait. Give me a pencil." After five minutes' reflection he wrote rapidly, " Rue d'A——, Number ——."

" This is too much," says R. Houdin. " It is beyond me. I don't want any more."

It is not stated whether the address was contained in the letter itself. But it can hardly be supposed that Alexis could, in Houdin's presence, have opened the letter and read the address undetected.

Generally, towards the end of the sitting, Alexis would be asked by one of those present to describe his house. Thus, to quote one such case, Mr. W. asked for the description of a house. Alexis said—

" ' It was sixty leagues to the right of London, about a league from a railroad ; the sea on one side, and sands along the shore ; the house very old ; of stone ; an inscription engraved on it in stone, in Latin ; five words ; five letters in the second word.' At length, after some effort, Alexis, having been correct in the former particulars, wrote the words ' Non nobis, Domine,' in characters similar to the inscription. He tried hard at the other words, but seemed confused, which was accounted for on the words being stated. The two first were repeated thus : ' Non nobis, Domine, non nobis.' He further said that ' the house was two storeys high ; that one portion was much newer than the other ; that there was a servant living in the stables, about forty years old, not good-looking ' (he is much marked with the small-pox) ; ' a large dining-room in the house, with three windows, they look out on trees on either side; there are two wells in the grounds ; the oldest well contains good water ; the newer one is dry, or has at times brackish or rain-water. In the park, near the entrance, a pillar or column, with something on the top ; a transverse cross-bar,' of which he drew a representation. (The object was, as I understood, a high post with a frame to hold a slate for marking the points at archery shooting.) ' There was no game in the park.' All correct."[1]

This is only one of many similar cases in Dr. Lee's book. Other records of the same kind at first hand are contributed to the pages of the *Medical Times*, the *Zoist*, and other periodicals. Thus Dr. Costello was told that he had on the previous day operated for the stone, and a description of the room, &c., was given.[2] Lord FitzClarence was given a description of an excursion taken two days previously ; the account was correct in the minutest details, down even to the nature of his lunch at a *pâtisserie*.[3] The Rev. C. H. Townshend and a brother clergyman, the Rev. H. B. Sims, received full descriptions of their houses, including the subjects of the pictures on their walls. In Townshend's case the detail was added that one picture, the subject of which was

[1] Lee, *op. cit.*, pp. 268–269.
[2] *Medical Times*, vol. x. p. 356 (July, 1844).
[3] *Zoist*, vol. vi. p. 418.

fully described, was painted on stone, and that the stone was bulged (*bombé*) at the back.[1]

I have chosen the case reported by Dr. Lee even though it lacks Mr. W.'s corroboration, because of the significant detail of the writing and drawing.

In a few cases Alexis is reported to have given information about scenes and events at a distance unknown to his interlocutor. De Mirville records an instance of this at Houdin's interview. Townshend relates a case of the kind in his own experience—the clairvoyant, however, being Adolphe Didier, brother of Alexis.[2] Several other cases are given, but not at first hand, in the *Zoist*. Dr. Lee gives one illustration which is worth quoting. In November, 1848, some atrocious murders had been committed in Norfolk by a man called Rush. The investigation was still proceeding in January, 1849, and somebody suggested to the coroner that he should consult Alexis. Without much expectation of any result, he wrote to Dr. Lee, proposing as a preliminary test that Alexis should be asked to state the contents of a tin box in the coroner's office. The letter was handed by Dr. Lee—himself, of course, entirely ignorant of the object to be described—to Alexis, who gave, to quote Lee's report, "a description of the coroner, his residence and the office in his house, the tin box which had been proposed as a test, which he said he saw confusedly—but there was in it some blue cloth or stuff and flannel." In his answer, which Lee unfortunately does not give in full, the coroner stated that "in some particulars, both as regarded himself and his office, the description was accurate," and also that the box contained a hat "lined with purple or bluish cloth and south-wester lined with flannel."[3]

---

[1] Townshend's case is given in the *Zoist*, vol. ix. p. 403, Sims's in vol. ii. p. 517. The latter case is in one respect the more striking of the two. Townshend was well known as a writer on Mesmerism, and the facts in his case may conceivably have been got up beforehand. But Sims tells us that he had no interest in the subject until the day before the meeting, which took place in Paris, the house described being in England.

[2] *Zoist*, vol. xi. p. 75.   [3] *Animal Magnetism*, p. 257.

The literature of the time teems with instances of similar clairvoyance. Of course in most cases fraud is the first explanation to be considered, and exaggeration on the part of the recorder the second. That fraud was frequently practised we know on the testimony of Elliotson himself. In his valedictory address in the last number of the *Zoist*[1] he writes: "Examples of clairvoyance abound, . . . but though the phenomenon appears unquestionable we well know that gross imposition is hourly practised in regard to it both by professional clairvoyants and private individuals influenced by vanity or wickedness. . . . The assertions of a clairvoyant should be believed . . . (only when) they are free from the possibility of lucky guesses or trickery, and are verified by ascertainment of the facts."

A case recorded by Miss Martineau furnishes an instructive illustration of spurious clairvoyance. In her *Letters on Mesmerism* she relates that a vague report had come on Sunday, October 13, 1844, to the house at Tynemouth, where she was then lodging, that the boat in which a cousin of her clairvoyant subject, Jane, was sailing had been wrecked. On the Tuesday evening no authentic news as to the fate of the sailors had, according to Miss Martineau, reached the house up till 8 p.m. At that hour a *séance* was held, and the entranced Jane gave the joyful news that all on board were saved, except one boy, and that the boat which rescued them was a foreign one. At the very hour, Miss Martineau adds, when this intelligence was being delivered in her sitting-room, the sailor's mother, who had come in after the commencement of the *séance*, and without the knowledge of Miss Martineau and her circle, was telling the same story in the kitchen, two floors below. Forbes shows, on the evidence of a local doctor and of one of the witnesses at the *séance*, that the good news was actually known in the house three hours before the sitting, and that the lady mesmerist had apparently conspired with the clairvoyant Jane to deceive her hostess.

[1] Vol. xiii. p. 443.

Miss Martineau's deafness no doubt facilitated the deception.[1]

In the case of the descriptions of houses of well-known persons it is of course in many cases conceivable that the facts given could have been acquired beforehand by gossip from servants and so on. But this explanation is much less probable in the case of the chief private clairvoyants of the period, patients of respectable physicians, than in the case of a professional like Alexis, for the two reasons already indicated, that Alexis had money to spend on inquiries, and that he was free within certain limits to choose the persons to whom he should give information. In many cases, moreover, the nature of the facts attested seems to preclude fraud, though the reports are still too often open to the suspicion of exaggeration or misdescription.

Sometimes, in order to convince sceptical inquirers, the faculty was tested by direct experiment. Thus Gregory was present when a small boy of nine was thrown into a trance in the house of his master, Dr. Schmitz, Rector of the High School in Edinburgh. At Gregory's suggestion the Rector and his son retired to another room and there moved about, gesticulated with their arms and performed grotesque antics, all of which were faithfully described by the sleeping boy.[2] W. Topham, a barrister, the mesmerist who had induced anæsthesia in Wombell's case (see Chapter VII.), relates that he requested a friend, De Gex, to go upstairs to the room above and hold up the window curtain in order to test his subject's clairvoyance. The clairvoyant described De Gex as entering the room and taking hold of Topham's

[1] *Illustrations of Modern Mesmerism* (1845), pp. 99–101. In her *Autobiography* (edition of 1877, vol. ii. p. 198) Miss Martineau, referring to Forbes's action in the matter, states that she holds a legal declaration which " establishes the main fact on which the somnambule's story of shipwreck was attempted to be overthrown." But she gives no particulars, nor attempts to refute Dr. Forbes's exposure in detail.

[2] *Letters on Animal Magnetism*, by William Gregory, M.D., F.R.S.E., Professor of Chemistry at the University of Edinburgh, 1851, p. 424.

father by the shoulder—which, in fact, was what De Gex had done, instead of carrying out the action originally suggested.[1] Another well-known mesmerist of the period, T. B. Brindley, carried out several experiments of this kind. In concert with a sceptical friend he rearranged the furniture of his sitting-room and tied the cat on a chair. Then, locking the door, he went off straightway to the clairvoyant's house, who as soon as she was entranced reproached him for his treatment of the cat.[2] Lord Ducie, at the opening of the Bristol Mesmeric Institute, described how a clairvoyant had given him a circumstantial inventory of his country house and an adjacent farm.[3] Professor de Morgan, immediately after his return home, received from a little girl, a patient of Mrs. de Morgan's, a precise description of the manner in which he had spent his evening at a friend's house.[4] The Hon. Caroline Boyle, visiting a London surgeon, W. Hands, received from his somnambulic patient, Ellen Dawson, a description accurate to the minutest detail of her house and surroundings in Somersetshire, also of a church in Rouen which she had visited the previous year and of the robes and sacred vessels in the sacristy to which she had been admitted by the priest.[5]

But it would be tedious to continue the enumeration of the many striking illustrations of this faculty given in the pages of the *Zoist* and by Gregory, Haddock,[6] and other writers of the period. It is true that the evidence is not set forth with the particularity which we are entitled to demand of those who recount facts so new and strange. Contemporary notes, if made, are rarely cited, and the recorder seldom thinks it necessary to confirm his own version by adducing the testimony of other witnesses. But even if we felt ourselves justified in rejecting the testimony of so many trustworthy witnesses standing alone, the more recent observations made

[1] *Zoist*, vol. v. p. 128.
[2] *Ibid.*, ii. p. 139. See also p. 138 and vol. i. p. 467.
[3] *Ibid.*, vol. vii. pp. 154, 155.
[4] *Memoirs of Augustus de Morgan*, 1882, pp. 206–208.
  Zoist, vol. iii. p. 236.
  Somnolism and Psycheism, by J. W. Haddock, M.D. (2nd ed., 1851).

by the Society for Psychical Research add powerful confirmation to these earlier records.

The excuse for the somewhat slovenly fashion in which many of the records are presented is, no doubt, that to the observer of fifty years ago the possession by many somnambules of a faculty which enabled them to read the thoughts of those present seemed too well established to need further proof. When the facts seemed to point to a faculty of a more transcendent kind—the actual seeing of events at a distance—the evidence is in most cases more complete. Haddock sets forth in detail, with corroborative evidence, three cases in which a somnambulic patient of his, Emma, was instrumental in recovering lost property. The cashier of a business firm in Bolton had to pay into the local bank a sum of £650. Some weeks later, on making up the accounts it was found that the bank had no entry of the payment. Fruitless search was made at the bank, and finally as a last resource the cashier came with his principal to consult the clairvoyant, who, after correctly describing the missing papers —two bank-notes and a bill—claimed to see them in an envelope with a number of other papers in a private room at the bank. Renewed search was made, and the missing notes and bill were actually discovered, having been inadvertently set on one side amongst a mass of unimportant papers.[1] In the two other cases the money had been stolen ; Emma correctly indicated the thief, and the money was restored.[2] A valuable brooch was recovered through the agency of another clairvoyant, Ellen Dawson. In this case also the thief confessed, and it was proved that the clairvoyant had been correct in her statement of some circumstances attending the theft.[3] It is, of course, possible in each of these

[1] *Bolton Chronicle,* September 8, 1849.
[2] *Somnolism and Psycheism,* pp. 112–128. In one case the person indicated confessed ; in the other case he denied the crime ; but the stolen money was thrown into the house next day by an unseen hand. See *Zoist,* vii. p. 323, for corroborative evidence in one case.
[3] *Zoist,* vii. pp. 95–101. See also the *Belle Assemblée,* vol. xxii., No. 2, pp. 108, 109.

cases that the clairvoyant in indicating the thief was guided by latent suspicions on the part of those who consulted her. But in two of the cases details are given, afterwards verified by the confession of the culprit, which could not have been known beforehand. If the clairvoyant's vision was inspired by thought-transference, it would seem that we must then apparently trace the originating impulse to the mind of the thief. In another case the clairvoyant indicated, after a fruitless search had been made for nearly three weeks, where the body of a drowned girl would be found.[1] And there are a few other cases reported at this time resembling some of the incidents recorded in connection with the modern clairvoyant, Mrs. Piper, which compel us at least to enlarge the meaning of thought-transference. Thus, G. Toulmin, the conductor of the *Bolton Chronicle*, consulted Haddock's clairvoyant, Emma, as to a friend, named Willey, who had gone to California. Full notes of the sittings were taken and printed immediately. Emma gave a description of the doings and sufferings not only of Willey, but of his companion Morgan. Amongst other details which could not have been derived from the minds of those present, and which were verified by subsequent correspondence, she saw Willey constantly rubbing his arms (for rheumatism), and she expressed considerable alarm at seeing him climb the rigging—he had, in fact, done so on one occasion to help in furling the sails; she saw that Morgan had fallen overboard into the water and had had a fever, and in course of the fever had a vision of his wife. The whole record, which is too long to be reproduced here, is worth studying as a very curious illustration of the workings of a clairvoyant's mind.[2]

In the following case, again, the record of which, it will be

---

[1] *Huddersfield and Holmfirth Examiner*, January 13, 1855, and *Zoist*, vol. xiii. p. 54.

[2] The contemporary notes are reprinted by Haddock in his *Somnolism and Psycheism*, pp. 132–139. Willey himself on his return to England at a personal interview assured Haddock of the accuracy of the facts; unfortunately, Haddock did not think it necessary to procure a written attestation, but contented himself with recording the fact.

seen, is based on letters written immediately after the event, the facts related could clearly not have been derived from the minds of those present :—

Professor Gregory describes a visit paid by him to a friend in a town about thirty miles from Edinburgh six or seven months previously. He there met a lady who had been twice mesmerised by his friend and who exhibited considerable clairvoyant powers. At Gregory's request, this lady—who was personally unknown to him—began by giving him a minute description of his own house in Edinburgh, and then of his brother's house, near the same city, and his brother's occupation at the moment. The details given proved on inquiry to be correct. Gregory then continues :—

"I now asked her to go to Greenock, forty or fifty miles from where we were (Edinburgh was nearly thirty miles distant), and to visit my son, who resides there with a friend. She soon found him, and described him accurately, being much interested in the boy, whom she had never seen nor heard of. She saw him, she said, playing in a field outside of a small garden in which stood the cottage, at some distance from the town, on a rising ground. He was playing with a dog. I knew there was a dog, but had no idea of what kind, so I asked her. She said it was a large but young Newfoundland, black, with one or two white spots. It was very fond of the boy and played with him, 'Oh,' she cried suddenly, 'it has jumped up and knocked off his cap.' She saw in the garden a gentleman reading a book and looking on. He was not old, but had white hair, while his eyebrows and whiskers were black. She took him for a clergyman, but said he was not of the Established Church, nor Episcopalian, but a Presbyterian Dissenter. (He is, in fact, a clergyman of the highly respectable Cameronian body, who, as is well known, are Presbyterians, and adhere to the Covenant.) Being asked to enter the cottage, she did so, and described the sitting-room. In the kitchen she saw a young maidservant preparing dinner, for which meal a leg of mutton was roasting at the fire, yet not quite ready. She also saw another elderly female. On looking again for the boy, she saw him playing with the dog in front of the door, while the gentleman stood in the porch and looked on. Then she saw the boy run upstairs to the kitchen, which she observed with surprise was on the upper floor of the cottage (which it is), and receive something to eat from the servant, she thought a potato.

"I immediately wrote all these details down and sent them to the gentleman, whose answer assured me that all, down to the minutest, were exact, save that the boy did not get a potato but a small biscuit from the cook. The dog was what she described ; it did knock off the boy's cap at the time and in the place mentioned ; he himself was in the garden with a book looking on ; there was a leg of mutton roasting and not quite ready; there was an elderly female in the kitchen at that time, although not of the household. Every one of which facts was entirely unknown to me, and could not, therefore, have been perceived by thought-reading, although, had they been so, as I have already stated, this would not have been a less wonderful, but only a different phenomenon.

"The above case I regard as a very satisfactory one, inasmuch as I did not know beforehand that I was to try any experiments at all, and had never seen the lady before.

"WILLIAM GREGORY.[1]

"Dec., 1851."

The coincidences here are too exact to be due to chance ; if the record is accurate, we must look for the explanation in some action of distant minds on the sensitive clairvoyant— whether directly or mediately through Professor Gregory. In the records of Mrs. Piper's trance utterances there are many cases which compel us to look for a similar explanation.

To sum up, the so-called clairvoyance at close quarters, when not due to fraud, would seem to indicate extreme acuteness of vision, the result sometimes of training, sometimes apparently of hyperæsthesia in the trance. But the manifestations of community of sensation and of clairvoyance at a distance, so far as they appear to be genuine, furnish some support to the hypothesis of thought-transference.

But to Gregory and some of his contemporaries, as to some students in recent times, such incidents seemed to point to faculties transcending the ordinary course of nature and not susceptible of explanation in physical terms. Many of the writers on Mesmerism at this period are emphatic in their declaration that the facts of clairvoyance prove that the soul can act apart from and independently of the bodily organism.

Townshend, in particular, one of the most critical writers on the subject, employs the argument afterwards developed with such force by Myers in his *Human Personality.*

"Would wings," he asks, "be folded in the worm if they were not one day to enable it to fly ? We cannot think so poorly of creative

---

[1] *Zoist*, vol. ix. pp. 423, 424.

wisdom or of thrifty Nature. Throughout her realms there is no mockery of unmeaning displays of power; and, if so, then is Mesmerism a pledge irrefragable of a future state of existence, calculated from the exhibition of those energies which are but a promise here." [1]

More definite proof of a future life was found in the trance revelations of certain clairvoyants. Cahagnet's book had been well received by some of the English Mesmerists. In the course of the same year, 1848, in which the first volume of the *Arcanes* appeared, Haddock's clairvoyant, Emma, passed into trances of a nature very similar to those described by Cahagnet, and gave similar descriptions of angels, of glorified men and women, and of celestial scenery.[2] Both Gregory [3] and Haddock, if unprepared to accept these revelations as unquestionably authentic, are still less disposed to dismiss them as mere random productions of the ecstatics' imagination. In subsequent chapters we shall see how these marvels of clairvoyance and these trance revelations prepared the way for the reception of the gospel of modern Spiritualism.

[1] *Facts in Mesmerism*, p. 366.

[2] The first of these ecstasies took place in July, 1848. It does not appear whether Haddock at that date was acquainted with Cahagnet's book, which had been published in Paris the preceding January. But at any rate Emma was not, for she was quite uneducated and could not, of course, read French; and it is not probable that Haddock, a judicious observer, would have gone out of his way to talk to his subject about the book. Probably Emma's ecstasies originated independently.

[3] *Letters on Animal Magnetism* (1851), pp. 224–227.

CHAPTER X

SPIRITUALISM IN FRANCE

The physical theories of Animal Magnetism gradually found to be inadequate : clairvoyance, prevision, and other faculties interpreted as pointing to a world transcending sense—Views of Tardy, Puységur, Deleuze—The Exegetical Society of Stockholm in 1788 held converse with spirits through the mouths of entranced mediums—Their views adopted by some French Magnetists—Alphonse Cahagnet (1847) and his somnambules : their celestial visions : their interviews with deceased persons : the effect on Modern Spiritualism.

FOR more than two generations, as we have seen, save for the suggestive theories of Faria and Bertrand, the explanations advanced by the French Magnetists were based upon the assumption of a fluid amenable to physical laws. But the hypothesis of an indifferent universal fluid was framed under a very imperfect apprehension of the facts. It seems probable that it was partly shaped under the influence of a reaction from the purely Spiritualist view of Gassner, the great healer who had immediately preceded Mesmer, and that in the famous Propositions the physical aspect was expressly emphasised in order to conciliate the rationalist temper of the time. It would appear at any rate from Puységur's statement that Mesmer's exposition of his own theory was designedly incomplete, inasmuch as it omitted the essential human contribution. However that may be, the Propositions were published before the discovery of the somnambulic state, and after that discovery the theory proved clearly inadequate to explain the multifarious phenomena which engaged the attention of Mesmer's followers. Even Tardy de Montravel, writing in 1785, the year after

Puységur's discovery, claims that Somnambulism has revealed the existence in man of a sixth sense, more sure in its operation and of wider scope than the familiar five senses. And though he essays to explain clairvoyance and prevision of comparatively remote pathological events on a physical basis, as due to this sixth sense interpreting the indications afforded by the magnetic fluid, he is constrained to admit that the facts are scarcely reconcilable with a materialistic explanation. "If the spirituality of the soul needs a fresh proof, magnetic somnambulism furnishes one such as even the most obstinate materialist can scarcely refuse to recognise." [1]

We have seen already how Puységur was led by his personal experiences to modify the conception of an all-potent fluid which he had inherited from Mesmer, until he came to believe in the soul as the motive power, and was content to pass over, as of minor importance, the question whether the soul acted through a fluid or by some other means. Again, writing in 1818, Deleuze is forced to recognise that Mesmer's system has fallen into ruins. Yet Deleuze, like Tardy, essays a naturalistic explanation of the phenomena of somnambulism. Up to a certain point, indeed, the fluid theory—if we are content to postulate the existence of an agent which responds to no objective test—can be stretched to explain the phenomena. If the subject essayed to describe his own disease, it was, the Fluidist would say, because, owing to the concentration of magnetic fluid in the brain, he became sensitive to special bodily sensations which passed unheeded in the normal state. If the description given was preposterous, as when the somnambule talked of worms biting the heart, or abscesses discharging by impossible routes, there was no need to impute bad faith. The sensation was really felt; it was only the interpretation which was at fault; and which of us would not be at fault in like case? The explanation of thought-transference, again, presents no difficulties.

" Dans l'action magnétique ma pensée modifie l'organe intérieur, lequel imprime un mouvement au principe que nous designons sous le

---

[1] *Essai sur la Théorie du Somnambulisme Magnétique*, p. 38.

nom de fluide magnétique ; et ce fluide traversant tous les corps, parvient directement à l'organe intérieur de celui qui est au rapport avec moi. Il y produit immédiatement toutes les modifications qui ne l'auraient été que par un intermédiaire." [1]

If we substitute the hypothetical ether for the hypothetical magnetic fluid, we might accept this statement at the present time as indicating the general lines on which a physical explanation must probably be sought. The phenomenon, or rather pseudo-phenomenon, of seeing without eyes presented, however, greater difficulties. In Petetin's experiments the card or other object appears to have been placed in almost immediate contact with the patient's body ; and it was possible therefore to explain the "vision" as due to the transfer of sensation to the nerves of the epigastrium or other part concerned. But the explanation is clearly inapplicable to later experiments, in which the object was frequently placed at some distance from the part of the body assumed to exercise the faculty of vision. In most of Petetin's trials a sensitive surface was all that was required. But if the later results are to be explained in terms of ordinary physiology, where are we to find the machinery for focussing the divergent rays proceeding from the object? The term "transference of sensation" becomes clearly inapplicable here ; and it is noticeable that after Petetin's time the phrase " vision without the aid of the eyes" seems to have been preferred. It was manifestations of this class which apparently led Georget to renounce his materialism and to proclaim his belief in the immortality of the soul.

Prevision, so far as it related only to events within the seer's organism, could, as already shown, be explained as an instinct, or *pressensation*, on the assumption that the perceptions of organic processes and the power of drawing correct inference are alike heightened in the magnetic trance. It is so that Tardy, Puységur, and Deleuze explain the phenomena. It was so, as we have seen in a previous chapter, that Bertrand also essayed to explain them until he hit upon the true interpretation of the facts. But the power

[1] Deleuze in *Bibliothèque du Magnétisme animal*, vol. v. p. 36.

of prevision was alleged occasionally to be concerned with events outside the subject's organism ; and of such predictions the most elastic fluid could scarcely render an adequate explanation. Clairvoyance at a distance, a phenomenon which, whatever its explanation, cannot, as we have endeavoured to show, be summarily dismissed as the product of fraud or iilusion, seems hardly to have been recognised in France during the early years of Magnetism. One or two instances are, however, recorded by the Strasbourg Society. M. Mouilleseaux, a member of that Society, relates that in October, 1785, a patient of his in the trance at Strasbourg professed to see M——, then in Paris. She saw him lying in bed with a headache, and a handkerchief bound round his forehead. At a later *séance* the somnambule explained that she had seen a stream of magnetic fluid which, on following it to its source, she found to proceed from M——, who was earnestly desiring to get into *rapport* with the magnetiser.[1] Another typical case of the same date is recorded by Puységur. The chronicler is a M. Segrettier, a *proprietaire* at Nantes, who does not, however, apparently write as an eyewitness of what he describes. The Baron de B——, according to M. Segrettier, had magnetised his niece, and becoming alarmed at her state, from which he was unable to rouse her, left the château and went to Nantes to consult a physician. During the whole of the outward journey the niece followed his movements and described them to those around her. The Baron stayed in Nantes overnight and returned with the physician the following day. His niece again followed his movements step by step. She saw his companion, described his dress and conversation ; gave a detailed account of all the incidents of the journey, dwelling especially on a dispute, which nearly came to blows, between her uncle and a tall man dressed in grey. Finally, she announced that they had dismounted some distance from the château—that they were in the courtyard—on the staircase, and when the doctor entered the room alone she insisted that her uncle was in the next room, as proved to be the case.[2]

---

[1] *Annals du Magnétisme* (1816), vol. iv. p. 164.
[2] Puységur, *Du Magnétisme animal*, p 225.

It need scarcely be said that in a case of this kind, reported at second or third hand, we should not be justified in assuming that the facts are accurately stated, or that any supernormal knowledge was actually displayed by the somnambule. The narrative is cited here as testifying to the belief, amongst some of the early Magnetists, in a faculty which later attracted considerable interest, especially in Germany and England, and of which examples not infrequently occur at the present time. When not due solely to the imagination of the seer, the facts may possibly be attributed, as suggested in the preceding chapter, to thought-transference from the person whose actions and surroundings are described.

Puységur realised the difficulty which the interpretation of such facts presented on the fluidic hypothesis, and in the same volume in which M. Segrettier's letter appears he explains that he had withheld from publication for the present a journal containing many instances of lucidity for fear of affording to ignorance and superstition " le droit de les interpréter d'après les erreurs de leurs systèmes ou l'exagération de leurs idées." [1] Thirty years later, however, the manifestation had become fairly common. Puységur himself records a case in Paris in 1818,[2] and the periodicals of that date contain several typical cases, mostly, however, quoted from German and other foreign sources.[3] Deleuze accepts the facts of clairvoyance at a distance, comparing it to the Scotch " Second Sight," and explains it on the assumption that our soul is in relation with the whole material world, through the medium of a universal fluid infinitely more subtle than light.[4]

It is not surprising that, confronted by this bewildering mass of phenomena, the true significance of which the science

---

[1] *Op. cit.*, p. 332.

[2] *Bibliothèque du Magnétisme animal*, vol. vii. p. 246.

[3] See, *e.g.*, the long account of Anna Nillson, a patient of the Swedish Doctor Ekman, who made journeys to a distance to the school where her master's son was employed and described his dress and occupations, and so forth (*Bibliothèque du Magnétisme animal*, vol. viii. p. 190, &c.).

[4] *Bibliothèque*, &c., vol. v. p. 31.

of that date was scarcely competent to disentangle, even those Magnetists who still professed scientific orthodoxy should feel that the purely physical conception was too narrow. Deleuze, even while attempting to explain clairvoyance at a distance by the intermediation of the all-powerful fluid, thinks that the phenomena of somnambulism prove clearly the spiritual nature of the soul, the division between the soul and the body, between Man as seen from within and Man as seen from without. He thinks they prove also that the soul,

" though it generally makes use of the sense organs, can in certain states receive ideas and sensations without the mediation of those organs. . . . This principle once recognised, the strongest argument, nay, the only argument, against the immortality of the soul is destroyed. I do not assert that this alone is sufficient to demonstrate the immortality of the soul, but it materially strengthens other proofs, by removing all difficulties. In short, it is much to have incontrovertibly established that the soul can feel, think, know, and reason without the aid of the bodily organs ; and that those organs, which in its ordinary state it uses as its instruments, often prove obstacles to the knowledge which it can acquire by immediate apprehension unstained by transmission through the organs of sense." [1]

If a man gifted with such sobriety of judgment as Deleuze could write in that strain, it is not to be wondered at that less cautious students should see in the magnetic trance an open door into the spiritual world. Swedenborg had taught his disciples that in his spontaneous trances he had intercourse with angels and spirits, and some fellow-countrymen of the Swedish seer looked for and—since in this region all who seek shall find—soon discovered in the somnambulic trance manifest proof of like communication. In 1788 the Société Exégétique et Philanthropique of Stockholm had some correspondence with the Society at Strasbourg founded by Puységur for the study of Magnetism ; and in a letter dated March 25th [2] they explained that they had for some time been receiving through the mouths of their somnambules

[1] *Loc. cit.*, p. 14.
[2] Afterwards published in the *Annales du Magnétisme animal*, No. xxv., 1816.

news of the spirit world and of their friends and acquaintances recently deceased. For the assurance of the friends
at Strasbourg they sent extracts from their Journals recording the conversations held. In the presence of the Prince
Royal, several members of the nobility, and other distinguished
persons, questions were put to two or three somnambules.
The intelligence answering through the mouth of the entranced
woman professed in each case to be the spirit of a deceased
person—in one case the infant daughter of the somnambule,
in another case the child of a neighbour. The spirits affirmed
generally the truth of the doctrines taught by Swedenborg.
In particular they explained that the spirits who spoke
through the lips of entranced persons were not devils, but
either good spirits or spirits of mixed character—*i.e.*, recently
deceased persons still in the *chemin de milieu*, or intermediate
state, from which they would ultimately be drafted, according
to the development of their characters, to the Swedenborgian
heaven or hell. The spirits undertook in several cases to
prescribe for the diseases, even of persons not actually present
in the room. Some of the spectators took occasion to ask
after the welfare of their deceased friends. In reply the com-
municating spirit stated that the late King was in a state of
happiness. The late Captain Sparfvenfeldt was, however,
described as "still floating." Concerning the condition of
the late Queen and the late Count de Stenbock no information could be furnished.

There is no ground for attributing these so-called spirit
communications to any other cause than the imagination of
the somnambules. That they were not so regarded by the
spectators is due to several causes. In the first place, there
is a natural inclination to give credit to the speaker, especially
when he deals with matters held sacred both by himself and
his hearers. Moreover, it was a very general view amongst
the early students that a person in the state of somnambulism
could not but speak the truth. And there is indeed no
reason to question the good faith of these early spirit mediums.
Further, all the concomitant circumstances must have seemed
to the inquirers of a hundred years ago to endorse the claim

made. The entranced person was in a state obviously differing very widely from either normal sleep or normal wakefulness; in the waking state she herself retained no recollection of what happened in the trance; in the trance she habitually spoke of her waking self in the third person, as of some one else; the intelligence which manifested in the trance possessed powers of expression and intellectual resources in some directions far greater than any displayed by the waking subject. Add to this that the trance intelligence habitually reflected the religious orthodoxy of its interlocutors; that on occasion it showed knowledge of their thoughts and intentions which could not apparently have been acquired by normal means; that it was, in particular, extraordinarily skilful in diagnosing, prescribing for, and occasionally foretelling the course of diseases in its own body and others—the proof must have seemed to the bystanders complete.

But, all these considerations notwithstanding, the Spiritualist interpretation found few articulate champions in France, as compared with its prevalence in Germany and Scandinavia. We find only scattered hints here and there of the existence of the Spiritualist Magnetiser. Tardy de Montravel in 1787 published a series of letters controverting the view that in the trance the soul was freed from its earthly bonds, and able to soar into the spiritual world. In 1793 Keleph Ben Nathan published his *Philosophie divine*, written from the Christian standpoint, in which, recognising the reality of somnambulism, he condemned the practice of Magnetism as being in reality trafficking with evil spirits—a view, it may be said, held by Roman Catholic divines at the present time. We learn from the writings of Deleuze that in the second decade of the nineteenth century there were several societies of Illuminati or Theosophists in France, who professed to heal by Divine power, and to hold intercourse in some fashion with the world of spirits by means of the trance. Again, there were professional clairvoyants in Paris, as in the present day, who were willing for a suitable fee to reveal the secrets of the other world to their clients. One speaker at the meeting of the Royal Academy of Medicine in February, 1826, mentioned that he had recently visited in Paris a child who in the trance was sent by the magnetiser into Paradise, and there saw two great prophets, whose names were—Rousseau and Voltaire![1]

Ten years later M. de Petriconi, a magistrate at Calvi, wrote to the Burdin Commission giving some account of his clairvoyant experiences. Three of his subjects, one of them at least a man of good social position, and under circumstances which made deception improbable, professed in the trance to have voyaged to the moon. They gave descriptions, more or less concordant, of what they saw there—rivers, lakes, beautiful forests, with the trees larger and the fruits finer than any on earth; men about three feet high, very ugly, with faces shaped like snouts, ill-clothed, dwelling in huts, and living without agriculture on the spontaneous fruits of the earth. Petriconi records these and many other details in pure simplicity, and asks the Burdin Commission to move Government to take up the wonderful discovery.[2] Deleuze himself, as already shown, accepted in 1818 many of the Spiritualists' premises, though unable to agree with their conclusion. In his later years he appears to have been almost converted to the Spiritualist interpretation by the experiences of one Dr. Billot.[3]

The most remarkable case of "spirit communications" in France occurred, however, some years later, on the eve of the outbreak in America of the movement of Modern Spiritualism. Alphonse Cahagnet was a cabinetmaker and restorer of old furniture living in the Rue St. Denis. He practised Mesmerism in the first instance for curative purposes. But one of his early somnambules, Bruno, soon fell into deep trances or ecstasies in which he professed to see the spirits of his deceased friends, and on occasion to be admitted into heaven. Cahagnet appears to have had some acquaintance with the works of Swedenborg, and no doubt with the revelations of the German Spiritualists of whom some account

[1] Foissac, *op. cit.*, p. 58.

[2] *Hist. acad.*, pp. 568–571.

[3] *Recherches psychologiques . . . ou correspondance sur le magnétisme vital entre un Solitaire et M. Deleuze* (Paris, 1839).

is given in the next chapter. It seems probable, therefore, that the medium's visions were inspired partly by hints from Cahagnet himself, partly by memories of lessons learnt in childhood, and of pictures and images in Catholic churches.

Here, for instance, is an account of a vision of heaven vouchsafed to Bruno :—

"I was in a place without any horizon, illuminated by a superb light. Before me was a being who, I believe, was God, seated on a throne ; his head was covered with a shining turban, his beard was grey. *I think* his arm was resting on the arm of his chair. He was robed in crimson velvet studded with golden fleurs-de-lis. His mien was majestic ; he was speaking to his ministers, six or seven in number. I did not count them. They were all seated on the steps of the throne, and were clothed in robes of the same material and the same colour as the robe of God ; but I do not think there was any gold embroidery on them. All round them and in the distance walked a multitude of beings. Oh ! how ugly are the men of the earth in comparison with those beautiful faces, those fair skins ! A gauze-like scarf covered one shoulder, and, besides that, they had a little skirt of such transparent gauze that every limb was easily distinguishable. Their feet were shod with sandals, fastened with broad laces (*cothurnes*) ; but, oh, God ! how beautiful it was ! I was lifted up into the air, I beheld the earth under my feet, and all these little men, so proud, so vainglorious, how ill-favoured and poor they seemed to me by the side of those divine beings around me ! " [1]

At a later sitting Bruno was given to understand that the figure seated on the throne was the Angel Gabriel.

Bruno's revelations never went beyond this stage, and the experiments with him soon ceased. Cahagnet, however, found other subjects, all of whom experienced similar ecstatic visions, and gave like descriptions of celestial scenery. The most remarkable was a young woman named Adèle Maginot, who had been a natural somnambulist from her childhood. She came to Cahagnet in the first instance in order that he might cure her of the liability to these spontaneous attacks, which were impairing her health. Cahagnet soon found that she had remarkable gifts for diagnosing and prescribing for disease in others, and he

[1] *Arcanes*, vol. i. pp. 18, 19.

employed her for a time in that capacity. He notes that, though, like himself, a humble member of the working classes, she gave her services freely and took nothing in return. Her ecstatic visions took in the first instance the same direction as those of Cahagnet's other somnambules. She began by seeing and conversing with deceased relatives, and describing the scenery of heaven.

Cahagnet seems to have prized these curious visions as authentic revelations of the spirit world. But for modern students, and for the more discerning of his contemporaries, the really valuable part of his work will be found in the later experiments with Adèle Maginot. It soon appeared that Adèle could see not only her own deceased relatives, but the friends and relations of other persons who came to consult her. Naturally these other persons demanded some proof that the invisible figure with whom Adèle pretended to hold converse was not simply the creature of her own imagination. To convince them Adèle would give a description of the dress of the deceased and of the manner of his death. Cahagnet kept careful notes of what was said, and afterwards drew up an account of the interview, which he submitted to the inquirer for his attestation. These accounts do not profess to be verbatim ; they are obviously much condensed ; and it is probable that in many cases the information given by the somnambule might have been elicited by leading questions, or that the gestures and manner of the questioner may have given a clue to the answer expected. Nevertheless, the descriptions were in some cases so detailed and so exact, and the proportion of successful *séances* seems to have been so high, that it is difficult to suppose their correspondence with the facts can entirely be accounted for by such means. The inquirers were in many cases persons of good education and of a critical temper. They came by no means disposed to accord unquestioning belief to the somnambulic revelations, and occasionally, as will be seen, they armed themselves beforehand with test questions. Cahagnet's good faith was unquestionable. The medium had at any rate no pecuniary motive for fraud. But, in fact, it is difficult to see how the most ingenious fraud could explain the results. The following is a typical case :—

"No. 129.[1] M. Petiet asks for M. Jérôme Petiet. Adèle sees a young man, about twenty-four or twenty-six years of age (he was thirty) ; not so tall as his brother now present ; auburn hair, rather long, open forehead ; arched and very pronounced eyebrows ; brown and rather sunken eyes ; nose rather long, pretty well formed ; complexion fresh ; skin very white and delicate ; medium-sized, round, and dimpled chin. 'He was weak in the chest ; he would have been very strong but for this. He wears a rough grey vest, buttons with a shank and eye, such as are no longer worn. I do not think they are made of brass, nor of the same stuff as the vest, they don't look to me very bright. His pantaloons are of a dark colour, and he wears low-quartered shoes without any instep.

"'This man was of a stubborn disposition, selfish, without any fine feelings ; had a sinister look, was not very communicative, devoid of candour, and had but little affection for any one. He had suffered with his heart. His death was natural, but sudden, he died of suffocation.' Adèle chokes as the man choked, and coughs as he did. She says that 'he must have had moxas or a plaster applied to his back, and this accounts for the sore I see there. He had no disease, however, in that part, the spine was sound. Those who applied this remedy did not know the seat of the disease. He holds himself badly. His back is round without being humped.'

"M. Petiet finds nothing to alter in these details, which are very exact, and confirm him in his belief that the application of the plaster, advised by a man who was not a doctor, brought on his brother's death, which was almost sudden.

"'Signed the present report as very exact.

"'PETIET,

"'19, Rue Neuve Coquenard.'

"NOTE.—The buttons that Adèle was unable to describe were of metal, a dirty white ground, and surrounded by a blue circle. In the apparition there is a remarkable fact to be noted—viz., that Adèle experienced the same kind of illness as this man. I was obliged to release her by passes. She suffered terribly."

As the description given by Adèle faithfully represented the image of the dead man present in the mind of his brother it might conceivably—if we exclude the possibility

[1] *Arcanes de la vie future dévoilés*, vol. ii. p. 170.

204 MESMERISM AND CHRISTIAN SCIENCE

of fraud—be attributed to thought-transference. But some of the more intelligent witnesses devised special tests to exclude thought-transference. Thus:—

"No. 122.[1] Pastor Rostan, who is referred to in the preceding *séance* in connection with the conversion of M. l'Abbé A——, desired in his turn to obtain an apparition. . . . He asked his maid-servant to give him the name of one of her acquaintances who had been dead some time; he came armed with this name, and asked for Jeannette Jex. Adèle replied, 'I see a woman who is not tall. She may be between thirty and forty years of age; if she is not hump-backed she must be crook-backed, for she carries herself very badly. I cannot make her turn round. Her hair is auburn, approaching to red; she has small grey eyes, a thick nose. She is not good-looking. She has a prominent chin, a receding mouth, thin lips; her dress is countrified. I see that she has a cap with two flat bands, rounded over the ears. She must have suffered from a flow of blood to the head; she has had indigestion. I see she has a swelling in the abdomen on one side, and in the glands of one breast. She has been ill a long time.'

"M. Rostan handed the report to his servant, and gave it back to me after adding his signature and the following remark:—

"'This is correct as regards stature, age, dress, carriage, the disease and deformed figure.

"'(Signed) J. J. ROSTAN.'"

M. Rostan appears to have been satisfied with the result of the test; but some of his friends were still disposed to attribute the results to thought-transference. Apart from these test cases, which are too few to allow us to base any conclusion on them, there seems no reason to go beyond thought-transference to explain Adèle's revelations. That was not the view, however, taken by less critical readers, either in France or elsewhere. The somnambulist's out-pourings were widely accepted as authentic revelations from the world of spirits, and Cahagnet's book had a powerful influence in shaping the destinies of Modern Spiritualism.

[1] *Arcanes*, vol. ii. pp. 142–144. See also the case of Abbé A—— vol. ii. pp. 98, 99.

CHAPTER XI

SPIRITUALISM IN GERMANY

Animal Magnetism more widely practised by medical men in Germany than in France or England—Prevalence, at first, of physical theories, gradually yielding to Spiritualist views—Wesermann's experiments in transference of thought : many cases of clairvoyance—The case of Julie recorded by Strombeck : her visits to heaven : her predictions of her illness : the method of treatment prescribed in the trance : her dictatorial attitude—Other somnambules described by Römer, Werner, and others—The Seeress of Prevorst : her supernormal powers : her conversations with spirits : her revelations on spiritual matters—The Spiritualist view widely accepted in Germany by writers of some standing

SINCE 1784, when the practice of Animal Magnetism had been so severely condemned by the official medical corporation, few medical men in France of any standing ventured even to let their interest in the subject be known. But in Germany, as we have already learnt from the discussion at the Academy of Medicine at Paris in 1826, matters stood on a different footing. There was no strong central body, as in France, to impose its restrictions on the physicians throughout the scattered empire. On such matters every principality was, no doubt, a law to itself. As a matter of fact we find that from 1810 onwards Animal Magnetism was increasingly employed throughout Germany in private practice ; whilst Court physicians and professors of medicine and surgery at many universities published treatises on the subject. The periodical, *Archiv für den thierischen Magnetismus*, which commenced in 1816, was edited jointly by Eschenmayer, Kieser, and Nasse, professors at Tübingen,

Jena, and Halle respectively. Amongst others who had written on the subject, or who openly included it in their medical practice in the second decade of the nineteenth century, were Wolfart and Kluge, professors at the University of Berlin ; Ennemoser, Professor at Bonn ; Hufeland, chief physician to the King of Prussia, who had established a hospital for pursuing the treatment ; Stieglitz, physician to our own George III. at Hanover ; Reil, professor at Halle ; W. Arndt, secretary to the Oberland gericht of Prussia ; J. U. Bährens, Hofrath of Baden, and doctor of medicine and philosophy. By most of these men, as by the older writers on the subject, such as Gmelin and Wienholt, Magnetism was regarded principally as an adjunct to the art of healing, and in their physical conception of the subject they followed closely on the lines of the French Magnetisers. Experiments and observations such as we have already become familiar with in reading the works of Tardy de Montravel, Petetin, and Deleuze, were repeated again and again by the German investigators. The magnetic fluid could be seen radiating as a stream of light from the eyes and the fingers of the operator and the poles of a magnet, from the heart of a living frog or the spinal marrow of a newly killed ox. Metals exercised severally characteristic effects on somnambules at a distance of ten or fifteen paces ; the poles of a magnet could be distinguished by the different sensations to which they gave rise. To the clairvoyant somnambule her whole body, irradiated by the magnetic fluid, seemed transparent. She could see her heart beating, could trace the course of the nerves and the blood flowing through the arteries. The thaumaturgic fluid was invoked to explain wonders greater than these, for its action, if perhaps diminished in efficacy, was at all events not annulled by distance. One of the most thoroughgoing advocates of the physical transmission theory was Herr Wesermann, Government Inspector and Chief Assessor of Roads at Düsseldorf. In 1822 he published a small book, *Der Magnetismus und die allgemeine Weltsprache*, in which he records some experiments of his own in action at a distance. Even the fluid emanating from the mineral

magnet will, he points out, pass through solid opaque substances without losing its virtue ; the fluid which streams
from our own bodies has no less penetrating power. Moreover, this animal fluid can act at a much greater distance.
Agrippa, four hundred years ago, had taught that from every
body there proceed images of an indestructible nature which
extend themselves endlessly through space, and by this means
bodies can act upon each other, though very far off, so that a
man can share his thoughts with a friend one hundred miles
away.[1] And Mesmer, as Wesermann reminds us, was of
opinion that a man through his inner sense could learn what
was happening to a friend at a distance, if, as is the case
under magnetic influence, the more insistent appeals of the
external sensory world could be stilled.

Moved by these considerations, Wesermann set himself to
influence some of his acquaintances by means of his thoughts.
He made five successful experiments, the distance varying
from a furlong to nine miles. In the first four experiments
the percipient was asleep, and his dream reproduced the
image willed by Wesermann.

In the fifth experiment the apparition of a human figure
was seen by the percipient, who happened to be awake.

Marvellous though the incident may seem, there are several
close parallels amongst the more recent cases investigated
by the Society for Psychical Research. And Wesermann's
explanation of these occurrences has anticipated with curious
exactness that offered by later inquirers. The figure seen,
though with the eyes open, is not a ghost but a dream ; the
dream was produced by the thought of the distant experimenter. We have only to substitute for Wesermann's
hypothetical stream of magnetic fluid the more modern conception of ethereal undulations originating in the molecular
changes of the agent's brain accompanying the act of
thought.[2]

---

[1] Quoted by Wesermann, *op. cit.*, p. 33.

[2] It is to be regretted that Wesermann has not given us fuller
information about his experiments ; from a subsequent letter, published
in Nasse's *Zeitschrift für psychische Ärzte*, vol. iii. p. 758, it is to be

Clairvoyance at a distance was apparently much commoner in Germany and Northern Europe generally at this time than in France. The cases quoted are rarely, however, recorded with sufficient detail to serve any purpose other than that of attesting the prevalence of the belief, and some of the instances are strongly suggestive of collusion.

The special contribution of the German nation, however, to the early history of Animal Magnetism consists of the revelations concerning the spiritual world dictated by several somnambules in the state of ecstasy. One of the earliest somnambules to receive the honour of a verbatim report was Fräulein Julie, an account of whose case was published by Baron von Strombeck in 1813.[1] No "magnetic" procedure was indeed employed in this case to induce the trance. Fräulein Julie afforded one of those curious exhibitions of spontaneous dissociation of personality with which the investigations of French, German, and American physicians in recent times have made us comparatively familiar. But in correlating the manifestations with those of the induced trance the observers of 1813 showed a sound judgment, though instead of referring the spontaneous psychological phenomena to Magnetism we should now class the manifestations of the so-called magnetic trance under the heading of psycho-physiology.

Fräulein Julie was a young woman of seventeen who came in 1810 to act as governess and companion in the household of Baron von Strombeck, president of a judicial tribunal in Zell, Prussia. From the summer of 1812 onwards Baron von Strombeck himself took careful—in the latter part of the period almost verbatim—notes of the proceedings. There were present as witnesses on most

inferred that he had made other experiments, of which some at least, as was to be anticipated, had failed ; and that apparitions such as that above described could seldom be produced. Two of his friends, however, he tells us, succeeded in like manner in influencing persons at a distance. See the note on Wesermann's experiments in the *Journal S.P.R.* for March, 1890.

[1] I have followed the French translation, *Histoire de la Guérison d'une ieune personne* (Paris, 1814).

occasions of importance several other persons of standing, including three physicians, Marcard, Köler, and Schmidt, all of whom furnished independent accounts of what they witnessed. When Julie came to Strombeck's house in 1810 she soon gained the affections of the family by her charming character; she was a bright talker, an admirable reciter and actress; she on one occasion took the leading part in a little musical play written in iambic verse by Strombeck, and her singing and acting won universal applause. At her first coming she seemed in perfect health. But in the summer of 1811 she had several attacks of convulsions. Dr. Köler, the family physician, was called in, but found her a very intractable patient. She laced very tight, and absolutely refused to give up the practice, which the physician pointed out to her must seriously aggravate her ailment. It was with the utmost difficulty that he could induce her to take any medicine at all. Her sense of smell was very highly developed; she disliked the odour of most of the drugs proposed and would have nothing to do with them. She refused to be bled or to submit to other methods of treatment proposed, and was very unwilling to give the doctor any details of her personal or family history. Ultimately, in the summer of 1812, she consented to be bled and to undergo a course of treatment, baths, &c., and thereafter remained almost perfectly well for six months. In January, 1813, however, her attacks were renewed. She then in the trance undertook her own treatment, laid down a very exact dietary for herself, and was finally cured in about a fortnight.

During her earlier attacks in 1811 she commonly passed, after the convulsions, into a state of trance, in which she would believe herself to be voyaging in air over the surface of the globe, watching the rising of the sun or admiring the beauty of the moon on the ocean. Sometimes she believed herself to be in heaven, holding converse with angels and the souls of the just; or she would offer prayer and praise in the most exquisite language. During these celestial visions her utterances were habitually cast in the form of iambic verse,

P

apparently suggested by the play referred to ; and Strombeck testifies that her rhythm was practically faultless—he only once detected a halting line. Occasionally she carried her visionary interpretation into the real world around her, mistook Strombeck and his family for discarnated spirits, and was astonished to find them already dead. Strombeck was profoundly moved by these scenes, and could almost believe himself already in the society of the blessed. But Julie warned him that he might find it dull in heaven in the absence of his regular occupation in the law-courts.

During this period Strombeck distinguished four different stages in her condition in the trance, in one only of which the patient kept her eyes closed. In the other three she appears to have had her eyes open [1] and to have taken part in the ordinary affairs of life. Her bearing and conduct were marked by certain differences, and each state was characterised by an exclusive memory. The memory of the normal life was, however, common to all four states. From the midsummer of 1812 until the end of the year, as already said, these attacks almost entirely ceased. But in the evening of January 4, 1813, something happened to put her out. Dr. Köler had already noted that her equilibrium was easily upset if anything occurred to cross her. On this occasion she suddenly fell at the supper-table into the second state, a kind of delirium. She was undressed and put to bed, and then passed into a profound sleep, from which she did not wake until midday on the 5th. A large part of the next two or three days was passed in alternations of fainting-fits and delirium with heavy slumber. Dr. Köler was called in, but could do nothing ; and Strombeck himself recognised that it was in the patient's own power at least partially to control her attacks, if she chose to do so.[2]

On the evening of the 7th she fell again into the trance, and in that state announced that she would be completely restored to health in a few days. To secure this happy ending, however, it was absolutely necessary to follow implicitly

[1] This is not expressly stated of the fourth state, *op. cit.*, p. 30.
[2] *Op. cit.*, p. 34.

the directions which she would herself issue for her treatment. In effect during the following days the entranced Julie dictated to the obedient watchers at her bedside predictions as to the course of her malady and minute directions as to the treatment to be followed. At such an hour or minute she would wake; at such another hour she would fall into strong convulsions or into delirium ; the attack would last so many hours; and so on. As the clock struck 8.30 she was to have a cup of strong coffee with precisely four teaspoonfuls of milk ; at such another time three cups of camomile tea, or half a glass of wine, with sugar; sago soup, or a glass of iced water from the spring. She must take certain baths, must be placed in a certain bed; on such and such an evening her attendants must find her some distraction—a concert would do, but something more exciting would be better. At another time they must bathe the patient's forehead with eau-de-Cologne, and give her half a glass of Malaga to drink. But for Heaven's sake they must not on any account let iron touch her, or attempt to bleed her, or in the minutest detail fall short of or exceed their instructions, for in that event madness or death might follow.

Poor Strombeck and his wife yielded unquestioning obedience to these instructions. So anxious were they not to overlook any detail that Strombeck would read his notes aloud over and over again that the somnambule might correct them, and on an important occasion he made two copies of the inspired instructions, one for his own use and one for that of his wife. For the next ten days they were kept fully occupied, for the treatment would occasionally be modified at short notice, and any act of omission might entail terrible consequences. On one occasion, owing to some uncertainty as to the precise instructions, the invalid did not drink the glass of wine which she had previously prescribed for herself, and at intervals during the next few days she bitterly reproached Strombeck for the omission, and called him to witness the increased suffering brought on her by his negligence. Equally serious consequences ensued when Strombeck, at the instance of one of his friends, ventured so far as to address a question to the entranced patient without having received instructions to do so.

The last command was that Strombeck should have a heavy gold ring made for the patient; it had to be made at forty-eight hours' notice after a prescribed pattern, and must on no account be made at Zell. The infatuated Strombeck sent his servant on horseback to Hanover, some thirty miles distant, to execute the commission, and found too late that he had forgotten to give him the pattern. He dispatched a friend's servant after him to remedy the omission, and then passed two days of acute anxiety, because the second messenger failed to overtake the first. But the somnambule in the sequel was graciously pleased to overlook this omission.

At precisely 10.30 on the morning of Sunday, January 17, 1813, Strombeck placed the ring on the prescribed finger of the patient. Julie promptly yawned, awoke from her trance, and was cured from that hour. She professed to have no recollection of anything which had taken place since the evening of Monday, January 4th.

In view of what we have since learnt of these unstable hysterical personalities we can recognise that the facts above described do not necessarily imply deliberate fraud on the part of the patient. But of course in any case of this kind it is practically impossible to draw a clear line between not quite unconscious self-suggestion and the not quite conscious playing of a part, and it would not be surprising if Strombeck's contemporaries generally wrote him down as the victim of a designing minx. But apart from the strong affection which Strombeck and his wife obviously felt for the patient, they had, as they held, other grounds for giving her implicit trust, in the tokens of supernormal intelligence apparently displayed. So far as her own power of self-healing and the prediction of the phases of her own illness were concerned, enough has already been said in previous chapters. They were, of course, simply results of self-suggestion.[1] But to the spectators of 1813 they carried con-

---

[1] Bertrand cites Strombeck's case as a typical illustration of self-suggested crises simulating prediction.

viction of faculties transcending those of ordinary humanity, a conviction which was strengthened by the apparent display of clairvoyant powers in the course of the illness.

It was not until Julie descended to practical affairs, and gave directions for her own curative treatment, that Strombeck, as will be seen, thought her sayings worth recording verbatim. If he had regarded her ecstatic visions of heaven as equally worthy of attention, we should, no doubt, have had as full revelations from her as from other somnambules of this period whose utterances were reverently taken down by their obedient magnetisers. Auguste Müller, a patient of Dr. Meier, not only gave many illustrations of clairvoyance at a distance, but conversed on occasion with the spirit of her dead mother.[1] Another somnambule, Fräulein Römer, daughter of Dr. C. Römer, who records the case, advanced a little further into the realms of the unknown.[2] Under the guidance now of some dead relative, now of the spirit of a still living companion, the young lady repeatedly voyaged to the moon, and there met her deceased grandparents, and learnt that her younger sisters had already gone on to Juno. Miss Römer's description of lunar scenery and of the astronomical phenomena attendant on her voyage are not such as to inspire us with confidence in her revelations, though her father records them in all seriousness as deeming them, if not authentic, at least worthy of consideration. He mentions, indeed, that the descriptions of other worlds given by his daughter accord with those given by other clairvoyants.

Heinrich Werner's somnambule, R. D., had terrible interviews with a wicked monk, and a Jesuit to boot, who by his own confession had murdered his five children and buried them one by one in a cloister. From the too near approach of this fearsome being R. D. was shielded by her guardian spirit, the angel-pure Albert, who gave Werner several remarkable proofs of his existence. On one occasion the

---

[1] *Höchst merkwürdige Geschichte der magnetisch hellsehenden Auguste Müller* (Stuttgart, 1818).

[2] *Ausfuhrliche historische Darstellung einer höchst merkwürdigen Somnambule*, &c., &c., von C. Römer, Ph.D., &c. (Stuttgart, 1821).

wicked monk overthrew two flower-pots in an empty room at Werner's lodgings, and would have done more damage but for the restraining hand of Albert.[1]

But the best-known somnambule of the period, in whom all these marvels culminated, was Frederica Hauffe, the Seeress of Prevorst, whose sayings and doings have been fully chronicled by Kerner.

Justinus Kerner, a well-known poet of that generation and a physician of some distinction, had his attention early called to the trance and its value in therapeutics. Towards the end of 1826 there came to him at Weinsberg, to be treated by him, one Frau Frederica Hauffe. A full history of her remarkable trances was published by Kerner in 1829, shortly after the death of the Seeress.[2]

From her childhood she had been delicate, had suffered from convulsive attacks, had fallen into spontaneous trance, and seen visions. She had already been magnetised, with more or less success, by different persons. After her arrival at Weinsberg she spent the greater part of her existence in somnambulism—the trance, or secondary condition, lasting on one occasion for about a year. Kerner records several instances of clairvoyant and prophetic dreams and visions; but the evidence is in all cases inconclusive, and sometimes indicative of collusion with members of the Seeress's family.

But the Seeress's supernormal faculties found their most characteristic field of activity in seeing and holding conversations with phantasmal figures, the spirits of deceased men and women, who came to her mostly for help, guidance, and prayer. In this manner she made the spiritual acquaintance of a former burgomaster, who had died in the middle of the preceding century, also of a recently deceased solicitor, of ill repute, and of other deceased citizens of Weinsberg, and

---

[1] *Die Schutzgeister,* by Heinrich Werner (Stuttgart and Tübingen, 1839).

[2] *Die Seherin von Prevorst: Eroffnungen über das innere Leben des Menschen un über das Hereinragen einer Geisterwelt in die Unsere* (Stuttgart and Tübingen). A second edition, to which reference is made in this account, was published in 1832, and two others in 1838 and 1846 respectively. An English translation, greatly abridged, by Mrs. Crowe, was published in London in 1845.

received from them much information on their affairs and family history.

These ghostly figures, which purported constantly to appear to the Seeress herself, both by night and by day, were occasionally visible to Kerner and other inmates of the house. Further, the household was constantly disturbed by raps, knockings on the walls, and other noises; also stones were thrown about, a lamp shade, a knitting needle, a stool; the Seeress's boots and other objects flew through the air, just as in a modern Poltergeist entertainment. It must seem to many difficult of comprehension that a man of education and intelligence should have seen in puerile performances of this kind signs of the intervention of a spiritual world, or should have taken the rhapsodical utterances of hysteria and diseased egotism as the foundation of a new mystical philosophy. Yet such in fact was the case. Kerner regards himself as highly privileged in being chosen to witness these marvels and to record the wisdom which fell from the lips of the Seeress. He chronicles for us all that she told of sun-circles and life-circles and the mystic relation of numbers. He reproduces for us portentous designs of interlacing circles

> " With centric and eccentric scribbled o'er,
> Cycle and epicycle, orb in orb,"

with the Seeress's interpretations thereof, partly in cypher, partly in the primitive universal language written in the primitive ideographs.

In the early part of the century Jung-Stilling, in his *Theorie der Geister-Kunde*, had discerned in the phenomena of the trance new proofs of the immortality of the soul. According to him Animal Magnetism proves incontrovertibly that man consists of an innermost essence or soul, which is a spark of the divine fire, an immortal spirit possessing reason and will, and of a luminous body (*Lichtshülle*) which is inseparable from it. These two are temporarily comprised in a body of flesh, and in ordinary waking life their powers are cribbed and confined by that conjunction. But in profound sleep, trance, or ecstasy the inner spirit may loosen its hold upon the body; the vital functions will go on of themselves, and the emancipated soul may rise to the world of real existence, and so gain new powers of comprehension and hold converse with its fellows. Even amongst the more sober-minded investigators of Animal Magnetism, who rejected the crudely Spiritualistic view, there were many, such as Wienholt, Kieser, and Kluge—to mention no others —who held that in the higher stages of the trance the soul approaches the threshold of the universal life, and seems partly to free itself from the shackles of space and time;[1] whilst Nasse goes further, and frankly claims that in somnambulism we have to deal with a fact of the spiritual order, and that any attempt to correlate its laws with those of the physical universe must end in failure.[2] It is clear, indeed, that men who believed in the reality of clairvoyance at a distance (as distinguished from reading the thoughts of those present) must have been hard put to it to find an explanation in physical terms.

But Jung Stilling's views were further defined and materialised by the Seeress of Prevorst and the other somnambules of the period. The psychic body, or *Nervengeist*, was clearly more of the nature of body than of spirit, since not only could it be seen by the eyes of the clairvoyant, but in the case of specially gross or earth-bound spirits it could even be discerned by ordinary eyes as the spectre in a haunted house or hovering as a faint cloud round a newly made grave. Even the spirit of man—the innermost vital spark—was not wholly immaterial. That is reserved for Deity alone.

The influence of the Seeress of Provorst did not cease with her death. In a series of volumes entitled *Leaves from Prevorst* a little circle of mystics, of whom Kerner himself, Görres, and Eschenmayer were the chief, continued for some

---

[1] Wienholt, *Lectures on Somnambulism* (translated). Kieser, *System des Tellurismus oder thierischen Magnetismus*. Kluge, *Versuch einer Darstellung des an. Mag.*, pp. 259–306.

[2] *Archiv für den th. Mag.*, vol. i. part iii. pp. 3–22.

years to expound and illustrate her teachings. They were interpreted and confirmed, now by the philosophical writings of Plato and Pythagoras, or the works of more recent mystics, now by fresh revelations from other contemporary seeresses. The conception of the spiritual world and its relation with our own, thus familiarised by the writings of Kerner and his contemporaries, unquestionably did much to prepare the way for the advent within less than a generation of the gospel of Modern Spiritualism.

CHAPTER XII

THE COMING OF THE PROPHETS

By the middle of the nineteenth century the trance is widely recognised as opening a door to the spiritual world—Characteristics of the movement in America—Andrew Jackson Davis: his childhood and youth—He dictates *Nature's Divine Revelations*—The doctrines taught in the book—They accurately reflect ideas on scientific, social, and religious subjects which were "in the air."—His view of disease as a discord, a thing having no existence in itself—His views on marriage.

THE final stage in the history of the science founded by Mesmer has now been reached. From this time onwards Animal Magnetism gradually disappears from view. The fluidic theory, as we have seen, has been breaking down. Since 1784 the attention of Animal Magnetists has year after year been turned more towards the trance, and the phenomena associated with the trance have of late come to seem irreconcilable with any theory of a physical effluence. The trance itself, originally regarded primarily as a valuable aid towards the recovery of the patient, and secondarily as a means of diagnosing and prescribing for the ailments of others, has in the course of these two generations assumed a new significance. At the date at which we are now arrived, the fifth decade of the nineteenth century, its chief interest for many practitioners lies no longer in its therapeutic possibilities, but in the promise which it holds forth of spiritual revelations. From this time onwards the entranced clairvoyant will be consulted less and less frequently as a physician and more and more as a seer of things hidden from the vulgar gaze.

Again, the political convulsions which marked the fateful years 1847 and 1848 throughout the civilised world appear to have awakened echoes in the world of thought which affected most powerfully the little band of dreamers and enthusiasts whose doings we have been considering. Both in Europe and America we seem to be aware of an almost conscious expectation of some new outpouring of spiritual forces. The *Divine Revelations* of Andrew Jackson Davis were published in the summer of 1847. In the following year appeared the first volume of Cahagnet's *Arcanes*, and the same year saw the outbreak at Hydesville of those mysterious knockings which formed the beginning of the singular epidemic of Modern Spiritualism. It would be foreign to the purpose of this book to trace the later sensational developments of that movement. But in its early stages it is intimately connected with our subject-matter—being, in fact, a direct outgrowth from the mesmeric propaganda of the previous decade.

The history of Mesmerism or Animal Magnetism in America ran on parallel lines with its course in this country. As was the case in England, its first effectual introduction to the United States dates from the visit of a French Magnetist, Charles Poyen, who lectured in various New England towns in 1838. His platform demonstrations set an example which was widely followed, and the next decade saw the growth of a movement similar in most respects to that whose course we have traced in a previous chapter in this country. The leading practitioners in America, however—Grimes, Sunderland, Collyer, Dods, Buchanan—were men for the most part of less general culture and possessing inferior qualifications for scientific investigation, so that the movement was marked by greater extravagance, and seems to have obtained even less scientific recognition in America than in Europe.

After the outbreak of the Hydesville or Rochester rappings in 1848 most of the Mesmerists were absorbed in the larger movement. But the belief in a fluid, which had been supported in the previous decade by experiments outshining in grotesqueness any of those reported by Elliotson or Reichenbach, still persisted ; and for the first few years the question of Fluids *versus* Spirits as an explanation of the marvellous doings at dark *séances* was hotly debated in the American Spiritualist journals. Gradually, however, the Spiritualist view prevailed, the theory of a magnetic fluid suffered euthanasia, and the clairvoyants were left in possession of the field.

After 1848 the movement in America presents one remarkable feature in which it differs from the European. The entranced subjects of Haddock or Cahagnet laid claim in their waking hours to no special sanctity, they arrogated to themselves no spiritual authority ; they were looked upon simply as channels for the conveyance of information. And when, a few years later, magnetic clairvoyants were transformed into spirit mediums this characteristic was preserved. The medium was regarded, and was content to be regarded, simply as the mouthpiece of higher intelligences. Even in Germany, notwithstanding the almost incredible arrogance displayed by the magnetic subjects of Strombeck and Kerner, these hysterical young women never ceased to be to some extent subject to their magnetisers. They remained primarily " seers," and their seeing was intermittent and dependent as a rule, on another's will. But in the land of democracy we are confronted with a singular development unknown to the older monarchies. The transatlantic seers constantly tend to be independent ; they assume the authority of the prophet ; they grasp at a spiritual autocracy—an autocracy by no means confined to the spiritual concerns of those subject to it. The supreme example of this spiritual autocracy will, of course, be found in the person of Mrs. Eddy, the founder of " Christian Science." But its practical significance can best be understood if we follow its origin and development in the course of two earlier ecstatics, each of whom, though born some years after Mrs. Eddy, reached the culmination of his career as a prophet before her reign had well begun.

Andrew Jackson Davis was born in Blooming Grove,

Orange Co., New York, on August 11, 1826. His father, by turns weaver and shoemaker, eked out his insufficient earnings from those trades by odd jobs at harvesting; a shiftless, unstable man, much given to drink, according to his son's account, at one period of his married life. For the first few years of the prophet's existence the family lived somewhere near the margin of subsistence, and the young Andrew Jackson could rarely have tasted plenty. His mother was a gentle, loving woman of strongly religious temperament—a believer, withal, in omens and spiritual monitions. Young Jackson was a delicate, dreamy, indolent child; he had little regular schooling—for the family were constantly moving their home from one nascent township to another—was extremely backward in his studies, and generally stupid and unhandy. With a body no doubt permanently undernourished, he grew up an anæmic, spiritless lad, always ready to turn the other cheek to the smiter, and comically frightened when, in his seventeenth year, a forward maiden proposed to walk out with him.

It was, indeed, according to his own account, an entirely unromantic childhood; his early years came too near the hard facts of life to admit any perception of their beauty or spiritual significance. In one of the passages of real human interest which occasionally break through the studied pose of the prophet's autobiography he tells us that as a child he valued animals, trees and fruit, sunshine and shade, rain and snow, and even human affection, only in so far as they ministered to sensual needs. His mind was eminently matter-of-fact, and as a child he seems to have been little under the influence of religious hopes, or even fears. Nevertheless, when at the age of twelve he attended a Sunday-school class in connection with the Reformed Dutch Church, he claims to have argued against the doctrines of predestination and eternal damnation, and to have confounded his venerable teacher.[1]

Shortly after this date his own spiritual experiences began.

[1] *The Magic Staff: an Autobiography*, by Andrew Jackson Davis, p. 161, thirteenth edition (New York, 1876).

In 1839, when the boy was thirteen years old, the family removed to Poughkeepsie, and there remained four years. Jackson received a few months' further teaching in the Lancasterian School, being himself appointed monitor over the A B C Class. At some periods of his early childhood he was much given to sleep-walking, and occasionally heard mysterious voices of warning or encouragement. One incident of the kind occurred when he was about seven or eight years old. Conceiving himself ill-used, he had run out of the cottage one evening and vented his anger in a loud oath, containing all the bad words he knew. Presently he heard a voice cry reproachfully, "Why, Jackson!" The child naturally thought it was his mother's voice, but going indoors, he found that his mother had not called him, and knew nothing of what had passed. At Poughkeepsie the counsels of the inner voice assumed a more definite shape. One day, being out of work, he had been round begging unsuccessfully for food, when he heard the voice say, "A little leaven leaveneth the whole lump." The boy's matter-of-fact mind interpreted this as a command to peddle yeast, and brought thereby some profit to the family purse. A few months later the solemn accents were heard again, "Eat plenty of bread and molasses"; and again the future prophet obeyed. To such lofty ends are the appetites of youthful prophets guided. Two or three years later, moved apparently by the sentiment that religious faith would be a desirable possession, young Davis attended a series of revival meetings in a Methodist Church, but failed to realise salvation. His nature, in effect, if we may trust his own account of the matter, was in boyhood, as certainly in maturer years, curiously insensible to the religious appeal. At no time of his life does he seem to have been conscious of any inward deficiency, or to have felt any urgent craving for guidance and help. His attitude to the spiritual world finds its counterpart in the complacent parochialism of Mr. Lafayette Kettle surveying the visible universe from the lofty standpoint of an American citizen.

But a crisis in the boy's life was at hand. In 1843, when he was seventeen years old, Professor Grimes, a well-known lecturer on Mesmerism, gave a performance at Poughkeepsie. After his departure, a tailor, William Levingston, operated on young Davis and sent him into the trance. It soon appeared that the youth possessed clairvoyant powers; he read a newspaper placed to his forehead, told the time on the watches of those present, and diagnosed diseases.

For about eighteen months Davis remained with Levingston, prescribing for all who came to consult him. In the clairvoyant state Davis claimed that not only the human body but the whole of nature became transparent to his spiritual vision. He could see the blood and the nerve currents coursing through the body in their several channels; he could trace every fibre in leaf and tree; he could see veins of metal as rivers of fire running under the earth; his eyes could roam over the whole surface of the globe, and track the tiger hunting his prey in Indian forests.

Amongst the substances which the spiritual eye, thus roaming over boundless nature, selected for the cure of diseases were rats' and frogs' skins, and the fat of thirty-two weasels. But he did not at this period of his career eschew the use of drugs, and the knowledge which the unlettered youth displayed of medical practice and terminology amazed his clients. His own explanation of the matter is as follows:—

" By looking through space (*i.e.*, in the trance) directly into Nature's laboratory, or else into medical establishments, I easily acquired the common (and even the Greek and Latin) names of various medicines, and also of many parts of the human structure, its anatomy, its physiology, its neurology." [1]

At some time during this period he fell into a prolonged trance, in the course of which he was conveyed—whether in the body or in the spirit is not quite clear—to a cemetery where two reverend figures, whom he afterwards recognised as Galen and Swedenborg, came to him and offered their help and counsel. Later Galen appeared again and promised a *Magic Staff*. The promise was fulfilled by the display,

[1] *The Magic Staff*, p. 253.

in radiant letters, before the seer's inner vision of the legend :—

BEHOLD
HERE IS THY MAGIC STAFF.
UNDER ALL CIRCUMSTANCES KEEP AN EVEN MIND.

The revelation reveals, if nothing else, the temperament of the prophet and the limitations of his spiritual outlook.

During his stay with Levingston Davis dictated in the trance a series of lectures, which were published under the title *Clairmativeness.* The matter dictated was taken down from the seer's lips by a Universalist minister, the Rev. Gibson Smith, who corrected the grammar and edited the book for publication.

In the summer of 1845 Davis, in obedience to an inward monition, forsook Levingston and chose as his mesmeriser, or operator, one Dr. Lyon, a physician whose acquaintance he had already made in the course of his travels for healing purposes. To him the youthful prophet announced the coming of a fresh revelation. Another scribe, the Rev. W. Fishbough, was found. The three took lodgings in New York, supporting themselves on Davis's earnings as a medical clairvoyant. On November 28, 1845, Davis entered for the first time the "superior condition"—a self-induced trance—in which from that date onwards all his works were produced.[1] He prefaced the dictation of his first chapter with the following announcement: "To the great centre of intelligence, to the positive sphere of thought, to that Force which treasures up all the knowledge of human worlds, to the Spiritual Sun of the spiritual sphere, I go to receive my information." The dictation was spread over about fifteen months, and the results were published in the summer of 1847 in a portly volume entitled *The Principles of Nature, Her Divine Revelations, and a Voice to Mankind.*

---

[1] In later years the dissociation of consciousness seems to have become less complete ; the "superior condition" was apparently one of reverie rather than of trance.

The *Divine Revelations*, the most important section of the book, opens as follows :—

" In the beginning the Univercœlum was one boundless, undefinable, and unimaginable ocean of Liquid Fire ! The most vigorous and ambitious imagination is not capable of forming an adequate conception of the height and depth and length and breadth thereof. There was one vast expanse of liquid substance. It was without bounds—inconceivable—and with qualities and essences incomprehensible. This was the original condition of Matter. It was without forms, for it was but *one* Form. It had not motions, but it was an eternity of Motion. It was without parts, for it was a Whole. Particles did not exist, but the Whole was as *one* Particle. There were not suns, but it was one Eternal Sun. It had no beginning, and it was without end. It had not length, for it was a Vortex of one Eternity. It had not circles, for it was one Infinite Circle. It had not disconnected power, but it was the very essence of all Power. Its inconceivable magnitude and constitution were such as not to develop forces, but Omnipotent Power.

"Matter and Power were existing as a whole, inseparable. The *Matter* contained the substance to produce all suns, all worlds, and systems of worlds, throughout the immensity of Space. It contained the qualities to produce all things that are existing upon each of those worlds. The *Power* contained Wisdom and Goodness, Justice, Mercy, and Truth. It contained the original and essential Principle that is displayed throughout the immensity of Space, controlling worlds and systems of worlds, and producing Motion, Life, Sensation, and Intelligence, to be impartially disseminated upon their surfaces as Ultimates." [1]

From these opening sentences the entranced clairvoyant proceeded on successive evenings to trace the gradual evolution of the ordered universe by the condensation of the primæval nebula into systems of suns and planets, passing on to a sketch of the geological progression upon the earth, and of the early history of the human race, as recorded for us in the " Primitive History," the term invariably used for the Old Testament. The terminus of the great cosmic process, it was explained, is the individualisation of Spirit, the production of Man, the Ultimate, to the end that communion and sympathy may be established between the Creator and the created.

[1] *Op. cit.* (thirty-fourth American edition, Boston, 1876), pp. 121, 122.

Q

" Man, the final cause of Nature, is in himself a microcosm ; he is composed of particles and essences of all things else existing—all below Man must of necessity enter into the composition of his being." In other passages man's place in the scheme of things is more precisely defined. " The Universe must be united by a Living Spirit, to form, as a whole, ONE GRAND MAN. That spirit is the cause of its present form, and is the Disseminator of motion, life, sensation, and intelligence throughout all the ramifications of the One Grand Man." To this universal spirit the whole visible frame of things serves as a Body ; " Man is a part of the great Body of the Divine Mind. He is a gland or minute organ which performs specific functions, and receives life and animation from the interior moving Divine Principle." As such he can have no free will, for if independent action were possible to him " the Universe would be no longer an organised system of beauty and grandeur, but an incomprehensible ocean of chaos and confusion."

Of Christ the book teaches that He was " a noble and unparalleled moral Reformer," but in no special sense divine. Naturally Davis rejects popular theology. Its four pillars, as he describes them, are the doctrines of Original Sin, the Atonement, Faith, and Regeneration. The first he calls a " repulsive blasphemy," the second " an unrighteous and immoral " doctrine ; faith is devoid of merit ; and regeneration is scientifically untrue.

The Bible he interprets as giving in symbolism an account of the early history of mankind. Adam and Eve stand for the primitive human race. Originally men conversed freely without speech ; but when they had eaten of the tree of knowledge they learnt how to conceal their thoughts by " arbitrary vocal sounds," thus wrapping them " in deceptive aprons of obscurity." " The animal of the saurian species (*i.e.*, the Serpent) . . . corresponds to the secret imperceptible progress of an unfavourable and unhappy mental development." [1] The story of the Flood " is an entire spiritual

---

[1] Mrs. Eddy finds that the Serpent means *Malicious Animal Magnetism.*

correspondence." As there is no free will there can be no sin ; the race, Davis says, " was merely misdirected in youth . . . I discover that all moral disorder results from the misdirection of Love and Will." Disease, again, is as unreal as sin. But if sin and disease are illusions, matter is only a symbol.

" It is highly necessary that the human mind should comprehend the great truth that nothing exists in the outer world except as it is produced and developed by an interior essence, and that of this essence the *exterior* is the perfect representation. . . . Forms do not exist with the mechanic or with the artist merely as productions of the outer combination of Matter ; but every form invented by Man is a precise representation of the interior thought which is the *cause* of its creation."

The third and final section of Davis's inspired book, entitled a *Voice to Mankind*, is occupied with the existing state of the body politic and with forecasts of a more equitable scheme on Socialist lines. The very heavens, he claims, are witnesses on the side of the coming revolution in the affairs of man :—

"The beauty and harmony displayed in the motions (of the celestial spheres) with respect to each other and around their respective centres, the perfect precision manifested in every line and path in which they travel, the constant reciprocal and universal sympathy which they display, manifest in their general indications the divine attributes of Meekness, Compassion, and Mercy. Each motion, action, and force observed in the planetary system is a true and correct signal of distributive Justice and infinite Mercy."

Besides Lyon and Fishbough, three other witnesses—the Rev. J. N. Parker, Theron R. Lapham, and Dr. T. Lea Smith —were appointed to be present at each dictation, and sign the report. Other witnesses were occasionally admitted, of whom the most notable were Thomas Lake Harris, Albert Brisbane the Socialist, and the Rev. George Bush, Professor of Hebrew in the University of New York, and a well-known Swedenborgian. Bush vouches in the most emphatic terms for the good faith of the author and his circle. On more than one occasion he had put impromptu questions to the clair-voyant which were answered correctly. Bush was profoundly impressed with the book.

"For grandeur of conception," he writes, "soundness of principle, clearness of illustration, order of arrangement, and encyclopædic range of subjects, I know of no work of any single mind that will bear away the palm. . . . In every [theme] the speaker appears to be equally at home, and utters himself with the easy confidence of one who has made each subject the exclusive study of a whole life."

John Chapman, the well-known editor of the *Westminster Review*, who was the English publisher, gives testimony hardly less striking. "The aim of the work," he writes, "is so exalted, the style and thought are so impressive and digni-fied," that he finds it impossible to doubt the genuineness of the author. He goes on to point out that the philosophy of the *Revelations* was akin to that of Kant, Fichte, Schelling, and Hegel; while the scientific conceptions advocated were confirmed by the views enunciated by Goethe, Oken, and the Evolutionists generally, as well as by recent discoveries in astronomy.[1]

Whatever view we may take of its origin, the book is, no doubt, an extraordinary production for a youth under twenty years of age. That minor defects of grammar and con-struction were corrected by the scribe is admitted. Indeed, two or three years later Davis confessed himself still un-willing to trust his own unaided grammar and orthography (*Magic Staff*, p. 428). But the testimony of the witnesses makes it clear that, apart from such corrections, the printed work accurately represents the utterances of the clairvoyant. Nothing, indeed, in the ideas presented is strictly original. The *Voice to Mankind* reflects with more or less exactness the exotic Socialism which had taken root in American soil a few, years previously. The rest of the book embodies philosophical and theological views which were in the air. The doctrine of the Grand Man, the science of Correspon-

[1] *Brief Outlines and Review of " The Principles of Nature,"* &c. (London, John Chapman, 1847

dences, the relations between the world of Spirit and the world of Matter—in a word, the greater part of the theological scheme—are derived from Swedenborg. The striking picture of the evolution of the Cosmos, which had so impressed the English publisher, contained in itself nothing novel, except mistakes in scientific terminology. The *Vestiges of Creation*, which had given in popular language an account of the nebular hypothesis and of the main features of the geological progression, had been published in 1844. It is not possible to prove that Davis had read the book, and he himself expressly denies having done so. But the ideas contained in it were, at any rate, public property. Given a memory of extraordinary retentiveness for words and phrases, and the capacity to understand and reproduce current social, scientific, and philosophic conceptions, and it is at least possible to understand how Davis's *Revelations* came into existence. All the materials were at hand.

But Davis claimed to have derived the matter of his revelations from direct intuition, and asserts that up to the time of their publication he had read no book except a trivial novel, *The Three Spaniards*. In his *Autobiography* he dwells frequently on the meagreness of his schooling, a few months at most, which sufficed for even less than the beggarly elements, and makes several ingenious attempts to explain away the evidence of book learning. Apart, however, from the enormous improbability involved in the claim, we have direct proof that the clairvoyant's statements are not accurate. An early friend, the Rev. A. Bartlett, who had known the boy intimately from 1842 to 1845, says that he

"possessed an inquiring mind, loved books, especially controversial religious works, which he always preferred when he could borrow them, and obtain leisure for their perusal. Hence he was indebted to his individual exertions for some creditable advances which he made in knowledge."[1]

---

[1] *Nature's Divine Revelations* (Introduction), p. x. Davis in his *Autobiography* (pp. 199, 200), referring to this passage, says that he borrowed the books to lend them to his friends, but had neither time nor inclination to read them himself.

Further, Bush states that in a letter written to him from Poughkeepsie before the publication of the *Revelations* Davis quoted a passage from Swedenborg's *Arcana Cœlestia*, giving the exact reference. Again, the coincidence in the language between the *Revelations* and Swedenborg's writings in certain passages is, according to Bush, "all but absolutely verbal."[1] In some of Davis's later works, written in what is claimed to have been the "superior condition" under spiritual impression, two or three cases of wholesale plagiarism have been detected.[2] It may be taken, then, that the book is the result of the reading and pondering of an imperfectly trained mind, equipped with a memory of extraordinary retentiveness, and liable to be rapt into a condition of spontaneous ecstasy, in which the intellectual powers reached a high degree of exaltation. The larger outlines have been seized and reproduced with something more than mechanical accuracy ; the student has made them his own and enlarged their

---

[1] Letters to the *New York Tribune*, November 15, 1846, and August 1, 1847.

[2] The most striking case of the kind is the parallelism of certain passages in the *Great Harmonia* (vol. iii., published in 1852) and in Sunderland's *Pathetism* (1847). That Davis should have deliberately copied those passages, half a page at a time, and that he should have chosen for the purpose a book written by a fellow-believer, which contained, moreover, a criticism on his own writings, and would certainly be familiar to many of those who read his own book, argues a want of foresight which is scarcely credible. See Sunderland, *The Trance*, p. 104 ; and compare *The Great Harmonia*, vol. iii. pp. 92, 93, 96, 101, 102, 136, with *Pathetism*, pp. 74, 75, 105, 101, 102, 111. See also, for other cases, Mattison, *Spirit Rappings*, &c., pp. 121, 122, 126 ; Asa Mahan, *Modern Mysteries*, &c., p. 30. In *Human Nature* (London, 1868), vol. ii. p. 321, the authoress of *Primœval Man*, an "inspirational" work published in 1864, shows that Davis, in his *Arabula* (1867), had quoted several paragraphs from the earlier book with a few verbal alterations. Davis, writing to *Human Nature* later in the same year (p. 407), explains that he got perplexed in the proof-reading by various quotation marks which had been misplaced, and that he imagined himself in this passage to have summarised the views of the authoress, not to have made a direct quotation. He further excuses his mistake by pointing out that if he cannot claim the credit of the passage referred to, neither can his victim, since her book was admittedly "inspirational." Davis, in his *Autobiography* (p. 451), deals with Mahan's charge of plagiarism.

interpretation. But details have been imperfectly mastered, and the scientific vocabulary is hopelessly at fault.[1]

Davis cannot, of course, be wholly acquitted of disingenuousness in the matter. But his preposterous claim that the book was evolved wholly out of his inner consciousness, though it no doubt originated in the inordinate vanity characteristic of prophets, does not perhaps imply so deliberate a falsehood as would be implied in the case of a normally constituted mind. It is not possible to judge such a case by ordinary rules. The state of trance in which he dictated the *Revelations* was essentially an abnormal one, and it seems not unlikely that there may have been some dissociation of consciousness even in his ordinary life. His memory of the mere mechanical act of reading may have been half obliterated by spontaneous ecstasies, such as he describes more than once in his *Autobiography*, in which all that he had learnt, from whatever source, was fused together and transformed into a kind of apocalyptic vision. At any rate, it seems clear that in composing and dictating the *Revelations* he wielded intellectual powers of far wider range than those which sufficed for his daily needs—he was, to that extent, inspired in his work.

Originally, like other prophets, he claimed infallibility for his utterances in the superior condition. But his critics were quick to point out that he had claimed a like infallibility for his earlier work, on *Clairmativeness*, and that the views of the two books on the subject of Christianity were irreconcilable. Later, Davis modified his claim to infallibility, and prefaced his utterances in the superior state with " I am impressed."

In *Nature's Divine Revelations* Davis makes merely a passing reference to the phenomenon of disease. But he had begun his public career as a clairvoyant healer, and he continued for many years to practise healing. When, after the publication of his great work, his friends established a paper

---

[1] The section of the book which describes the geological progression contains a wild hotch-potch of technical terms, names of species, and statements of fact or theory, imperfectly understood, and still more imperfectly remembered. Some quotations are given in the author's *Modern Spiritualism*, vol. i. pp. 161, 162.

—the *Univercœlum*—to form the mouthpiece of the new philosophy, the prophet's first contribution consisted of a series of
papers on specific diseases and their treatment, afterwards
republished as vol. i. of the *Great Harmonia*, under the
title, *The Physician*. In this work he expounds his philosophy of the subject.

" Disease," he tells us, "is a want of equilibrium in the circulation of
the spiritual principle through the physical organisation. In plainer
language, disease is a discord, and the discord must exist *primarily*
in the spiritual forces by which the organism is actuated and governed."

In order to heal this disease the original spiritual harmony
must be restored. Cathartics, injections, leeches, blisters,
the lancet, and all the rest of the physician's armoury are
" unqualifiedly erroneous " ; doctors distinguish hundreds of
diseases, but all are variations of one, and that one " is not
an entity, not a something to fight down with medicinal
weapons," but a discord.

Like all prophets of the period, Davis had a message to
deliver on the relations between the sexes. His enemies
accused him of free-love. His own statement of his views
is that for each man or woman there is waiting the pre-
destined partner, the perfect complement of his nature.
When the two come together their union is indissoluble.
Until, however, that spiritual affinity is discovered, he would
permit a certain freedom of divorce. Davis himself was
twice married. His first wife, a lady some years older
than himself, who had assisted to finance his early publications, died a few years after marriage. The prophet then
discovered his spiritual affinity in a lady who, unfortunately,
had a husband living. But Davis had the courage of his
convictions, and as both parties were quite willing to
recognise the prophet's prior claim, an Indiana divorce
was arranged. The affair, however, caused some scandal,
and, no doubt, alienated from Davis many of his followers.
A certain scandal in connection with his first marriage had
formed the beginning of the rupture with the poet Thomas
Lake Harris, who had at the outset yielded implicit allegiance

to the youthful seer's inspiration.   The rupture in that case
was, however, sooner or later inevitable.   For to Harris, no
doubt, had already come dim forewarnings of a long career
as a prophet on his own account.

Davis in any case was the least of all the prophets, and his
inspiration, such as it was, soon deserted him—

> " He sang himself hoarse to the stars very early,
>   And cracked a weak voice with too lofty a tune."

His followers were never numerous, nor, except at the outset,
enthusiastic.   His theological scheme, as will have been seen,
is derived from Swedenborg, and in temperament he strongly
resembled the Swedish seer.   But not even Swedenborg's
religion was so matter-of-fact ; and his horizons, of course,
were far wider.   The poverty of blood which marked poor
Andrew Jackson's childhood was reflected in his spiritual life.
Surely to few other seers has been granted so limited and so
purblind a vision of things celestial.   He was almost wholly
lacking in passion, human or Divine.   His ideal of conduct
was an emasculated stoicism, his highest virtue a milk-and-
watery benevolence, his God a progressive nebula.

CHAPTER XIII

THOMAS LAKE HARRIS

His character and early years—His inspired preaching—In 1867 he founds the Community of Brocton—Career of his chief disciple, Laurence Oliphant—Breach between Harris and Oliphant—Harris's doctrines : the Inner Breathing, Regeneration, the Celestial Marriage, Immortality, a social and religious Millennium—His "inspired" poems.

THE prophet whose career we have next to consider, Thomas Lake Harris, the companion and disciple for a time of the youthful Andrew Jackson Davis, belonged to a different type. He was a man not merely of intellectual distinction, but of marked spiritual force. His "inspired" lyrics, whatever their deficiencies, are characterised generally by an exquisite verbal melody. His mystical prose writings, notwithstanding frequent incoherences and extravagances, have the note of literature, and rise frequently, when informed by pity or indignation, to passages of real beauty. This, in fact, is the feature which distinguishes Harris from the other "inspired" writers of the last two generations. He was a man at his best of generous human instincts and full of a passionate idealism. In a more fortunate age he might have led a Crusade, have lashed himself into a saint, or won a martyr's death. His ambiguous career, the gradual degeneration and hardening of his character, represent a reaction, perhaps inevitable, from a more complex social environment. He came too late into too old a world.

Thomas Lake Harris was born at Fenny Stratford, Bucks, in 1823. Thence four years later he went with his parents to

America, where the rest of his life was spent. His childhood was comforted by visions. When about eighteen years of age the image of his dead mother appeared to him in a trance, and impressed upon his mind, as he tells us, the central truth, that God is our Father and all men our brothers. In 1844 he became a preacher in the Universalist denomination. His attitude to the revelations of Andrew Jackson Davis has already been recorded. In 1848, after the break with the Poughkeepsie seer, he became the minister of an Independent Church. To the same year belongs his first automatic or "inspirational" production, a sermon on the text "Suffer little children to come unto Me," which produced a profound impression, and indirectly led to the founding of the New York Juvenile Asylum.[1] Harris never made a profession of healing, but both at this date and later he occasionally exercised the gift of curing ailments by laying on of hands and prayer. It is, of course, generally characteristic of the prophets of this period that they were healers as well as teachers. In Harris's case the connection was more intimate; for, as will be shown later, in his philosophy the regeneration of the spirit involved the rejuvenescence of the body. For some time during the years 1850–1853 Harris was associated with one James Scott, a minister of the sect of Seventh Day Baptists. Scott, under professedly Divine inspiration, founded in 1851 a Socialist Community at Mountain Cove, Virginia, and Harris for a time joined him there, and was named in Scott's inspirational utterances as joint leader. The word of the Lord through the mouth of Scott had, however, prior apparently to Harris's appearance on the scene, required the disciples to divest themselves of all their worldly goods, and hand them over to the head of the Community. The natural man rebelled against the enforcement of the inspired decree, and the Community finally broke up in 1853. The history of the Community is so fragmentary and obscure that it is impossible to

---

[1] These and other details of Harris's early life are taken from *The Brotherhood of the New Life and Thomas Lake Harris*, by R. McCully (Glasgow, 1893).

discover how far Harris was directly implicated in Scott's proceedings.[1]

In 1858 appeared the first of Harris's "inspirational" poems, *A Lyric of the Morning Land,* followed a year or two later by the *Lyric of the Golden Age.* In 1857 was published the first of his prose writings, *The Arcana of Christianity,* in which he definitely broke away from the orthodox Sweden-borgianism which he appears to have professed for some years previously. His claim in effect was that to him had been revealed the "celestial" sense of the Bible, whereas Swedenborg had been permitted to know only the inferior spiritual interpretation. The book purported to be the product of direct inspiration from "the Lord." In 1859 Harris came to England and there delivered a course of sermons on the new doctrine. Of these sermons a witness who will scarcely be accused of a favourable bias writes that they are

"of a very remarkable character—full of lofty enthusiasm ; . . . not even the most careless could be unimpressed by the fervent and living nobility of faith, the high spiritual indignation against wrong-doing . . . with which the dingy pages, badly printed upon bad paper, and in the meanest form, still burn and glow."[2]

On his return to America a year or two later we find the prophet in a new capacity as a practical farmer, and President of the first National Bank of Amenia, Dutchess Co., New York. The impulse for Community building was, however, strong within him, and in 1867 he and his disciples —for he had for some years past been forming round him the Brotherhood of the New Life—purchased a tract of 1,600 acres at Brocton, Chautauqua Co., on the south shores of the Lake Erie. Harris, it is said, laid down half the

---

[1] The whole episode is passed over by McCully. For some account of the Mountain Cove Community see Noyes, *History of American Socialisms,* pp. 568–574, Capron, *Modern Spiritualism* (1855), chap. vi., and other Spiritualist sources.

[2] *Life of Laurence Oliphant,* vol. ii. p. 4, by Margaret O. W. Oliphant. The well-known novelist, who wrote the Life, was only a distant cousin of Laurence Oliphant, and did not share his peculiar views.

purchase money, his associates finding the rest. From this date until his death, which took place at Santa Rosa in 1906, he lived entirely within the walls of the Community, directing its affairs with a strong hand, and busied meanwhile in the constant inditing of inspired books.

The Community of Brocton, when visited in 1869 by a reporter of the *New York Sun*,[1] consisted of some sixty adult members, besides a number of children. Amongst the adults were five clergymen, some American ladies of good social position, and some Japanese.[2] But the most interesting members of the young Community were Lady Oliphant, the widow of an ex-Chief Justice of Ceylon, and her only son. Laurence Oliphant, who was at this date just forty years of age, had had an interesting and varied career. He had travelled much in little known parts of the world, and the books in which he described what he had seen had earned for him a considerable reputation. He had held various diplomatic appointments; he had been private secretary to Lord Elgin during his viceroyalty of Canada; he had accompanied his chief on special missions to Washington and Tokio, and had later been first Secretary of Legation in Japan. Wherever there had been war or political disturbances—the Crimea, Poland, Italy—Oliphant had rushed to the spot to see the fun, sometimes to take part in it, but always to observe and record it. He had been special correspondent for the *Times* in the Crimea and elsewhere. He knew everybody from royalty downwards who, in the current phrase, was worth knowing, and would seem to have done almost everything that was worth doing.

In 1865 Oliphant was elected M.P. for the Stirling Burghs, and his friends expected that a man of such brilliant parts, a ready and practised speaker, with exceptional first-hand knowledge of foreign affairs, would have a distinguished

---

[1] The report is quoted in Noyes's *History of American Socialisms*, pp. 578–586.

[2] It is stated that Harris had been a member of the American Legation in Japan in 1861; see Mrs. Oliphant's *Life of Laurence Oliphant*, vol. ii. p. 1, *note*.

career before him. He falsified all expectations by maintaining during the two years of his parliamentary life an unbroken silence. He had already met his Master, and this silence had been imposed upon him as the first pledge of implicit obedience. In the autumn of 1867 the time had come, in the opinion of the autocrat, for a more severe probation. Oliphant suddenly disappeared from the political and social world, not returning to London until some three years later, in 1870. He had been summoned by Thomas Lake Harris to Brocton. On his arrival there he was set forthwith to clean out a stable. The task must have been of Augean dimensions, for we are told that it occupied many days of absolute loneliness. He slept in a loft, furnished only with a mattress and some empty orange-boxes. During all those weary days he spoke to no one ; his very meals were brought to him in the midst of his repulsive surroundings by a silent messenger. Mother and son were devoted to each other, and had passed all their lives in the most intimate communion. But in the eyes of the prophet the bonds of natural affection constituted the strongest obstacle to spiritual growth, and Lady Oliphant and her son were allowed to meet but rarely, and then only as mere acquaintances.

Oliphant acted as war correspondent for the *Times* during the Franco-German War, but always holding himself in readiness to return to Brocton on a summons from Harris. In 1872 he met his future wife. The affair was immediately laid before the Master, who for long withheld his consent to marriage. But the lady made her complete submission to the prophet and placed all her property unreservedly in his hands, to dispose of as he thought fit. The marriage was then permitted to take place. Shortly after Lady Oliphant and the young couple were summoned to Brocton ; the two ladies were set to do housework, and Oliphant was despatched to New York to labour for the Community as director of a Cable Company. For years the prophet contrived to keep husband and wife apart, each willingly acquiescing in the burden laid upon them. For a space of three years Oliphant was not permitted to see his wife at all ; she during that time had been sent out of the Community penniless and alone to earn her living—and had gone gladly. In 1880 they were permitted to rejoin each other in Europe. Meanwhile Harris had bought fresh territory and had migrated with part of the Community to Santa Rosa, California. There some scandal arose because of his relations with a lady whom he afterwards married. Oliphant went over in 1881 to find his mother dying. Her death, the rumours against the prophet's fair fame, and other causes at length broke the spell, and Oliphant threw off the allegiance which had bound him for more than sixteen years. His friends with difficulty recovered the property which he had invested in the Community.

It is by the mere accident of his social position and his literary connections that we have so full a record of the enslavement of Oliphant and two members of his family. From the vague rumours which have reached the outer world there is no reason to think that the sway exercised by Harris over the rest of the Community was less autocratic. But the very circumstances which gave him such absolute dominion over the few who were fit to become disciples necessarily prevented any wide diffusion of that dominion. In fact, Harris's gospel admitted of no compromise. Those who listened to the message were bidden to come out from the world, to give up all worldly possessions, to break all human ties, and to undergo a long and severe probation, to fit them for the higher Use. But his influence was by no means confined within the narrow radius of the Brocton Community. His writings, indeed, never attained a wide circulation ; they were not distributed through the ordinary channels. They were not, in fact, sold at all. To any inquirer, however, who was adjudged fitted for its reception the printed word of the new revelation was given freely, under certain restrictions as to secrecy. In this way Harris obtained some following in this country. His disciples throughout the world are said to have numbered thousands.

Harris's teaching occupies a position in some respects intermediate between that of Davis and the later gospel of

Christian Science. Like the *Divine Revelations*, Harris's theology was essentially a development from Swedenborgianism. But he accepted the inspiration of the Bible and the Divinity of Christ, whilst claiming for himself, as already stated, a higher place amongst the prophets than Swedenborg.

Harris's prose writings consist mainly of the interpretation, in accordance with the revelation specially accorded to him, of the Bible, especially of the Apocalypse. His characteristic tenet is the doctrine of the Fall and the nature of the subsequent Regeneration. " God manifested in the Flesh is not Male merely nor Female merely, but the Two in One . . . in whose spiritual and physical likeness we seek to be reborn." [1] Elsewhere he speaks of our Father and our Mother God.[2] Before the Fall, Man and Woman were conjoined in the likeness of God. At the Fall this bi-sexual unity was divided. The idea is, of course, a modern re-statement of an old Platonic myth. Again, as a sequel to the Fall, mankind lost the faculty of internal respiration. Originally, they had been connected with the Divine Nature by a kind of respiratory umbilical cord, through which the whole spiritual nature was nourished and strengthened. The first and essential step towards Regeneration is the recovery of this dormant faculty of Inner Breathing. It is a fact that Harris, Laurence Oliphant, and other members of the Society claimed to exercise, not continuously but fitfully, this faculty of Inner Breathing. I have myself talked with persons in this country who claimed it. It is probable that the claim was based on actual physical sensations—the Inner Breathing possibly consisted in a more extensive use of the diaphragm and the respiratory apparatus generally. Dr. Garth Wilkinson testifies that Harris's chest was peculiarly formed. On first examination, it appeared weak and contracted—the sternum depressed, the lower ribs folded in

---

[1] Letter from Harris to W. A. Hinds, in 1877, quoted by McCully (*Brotherhood of the New Life*, p. 132).

[2] And again, " God the Wife is the Mother of us all " (*The Lord, the Two in One*, p. 92).

under each other. But it was capable of enormous expansion. " I never saw such capacity of respiration in any other person." [1]

When the continual influx of spiritual power had been re-established by the full development of the Inner Breathing the Regeneration would be complete; the true union of the sexes would be restored, and death would be overcome. In the letter already quoted Harris explains to a sympathetic inquirer that "among my people, as they enter into the peculiar physical evolution that constitutes the new life, two things decrease—the propagation of the species and physical death." He proceeds to quote statistics in support of these assertions. Some years later, in June, 1891, Harris claims to have realised the spiritual and physical regeneration in his own person; the Inner Breathing, he writes, is now completely established; his own body has regained the outward semblance and internal vigour of youth. "He is re-incorporated into the potency and promise of psychophysical immortality. He is in the youth and spring and morning of the new existence."

During these latter years, he explains, he had been engaged in studying the problem " By what process shall man overcome the universal racial tendency towards physical deterioration and decease ? . . . how, in a word, without passing through physical decease shall man practically embody and realise the resurrection ? " [2] It was the shock to Oliphant's faith caused by the discovery that the prophet could not avert death from one of his most faithful disciples that is said to have been partly responsible for the breach between the two men.

Harris had already, some years previously, claimed to have

---

[1] Quoted by McCully, *op. cit.*, p. 67. The doctrine of Internal Breathing is derived from Swedenborg.

[2] *Brotherhood of the New Life*, a pamphlet by Harris. As regards the claim to physical rejuvenation, see the description given by Laurence Oliphant in his *Masollam* of the hero's extraordinary power of passing at will from the apparent feebleness of age to the full vigour of manhood. "Masollam" is understood to be a portrait of T. L. Harris.

been united in a true mystical marriage with his celestial counterpart, the Lily Queen.[1] But the ordinary union of the sexes he regarded as a hindrance to spiritual regeneration. It was not absolutely forbidden to the neophyte, but it was discouraged, and the prophet, as we have seen, consistently set himself to keep married persons apart, and to prevent the natural fruit of the union. For marriage on the natural plane, the normal human union of the sexes, was a direct consequence of the Fall—a " terrible " thing, as it is called in a letter written under Harris's direction to Lady Oliphant ;[2] " so long as men are unregenerated there is no absolute purity in any sex relation." [3]

"We think," he writes elsewhere, "that generation must cease until the sons and daughters of God are prepared for the higher generation by revolution into structural bi-sexual completeness, above the plane of sin, of disease, and of natural mortality." [4]

As already said, Harris's writings strike a note which is almost wholly wanting in the utterances of the other "prophets" of his generation. We find him in a passionate indignation against wrong-doing ; a passionate realisation of the ineffectual struggles and sufferings of mankind ; an altogether human sense of tragedy and pity, and of human fellowship.

"One almost sees," he writes, "the Lord uplifted in spirit upon that great industrial cross, whereon His faith was to be crucified through nineteen centuries of inversion in the broken hearts and bleeding bodies of the innumerable toilers of the globe." [5]

Here, again, is a passage from *The Lord the Two in One* :—

---

[1] See *The Lord the Two in One*, published in 1876.
[2] *Life of Oliphant*, vol. ii. p. 93.
[3] *Arcana of Christianity : the Apocalypse*, vol. i. p. 156.
[4] Letter to Hinds, McCully, *op. cit.*, p. 131. It is interesting to note that Oliphant himself in his later mystical writings—*Sympneumata* and *Scientific Religion*—preached a somewhat similar view of marriage.
[5] *Arcana of Christianity : the Apocalypse* (1867), vol. i. p. 199.

"Aspiration when it falls into the power of circumstance is an angel broken upon the wheel. We are slaves of the events. The years make wholesale slaughter among the sons of God. Paradise is always suspended in the atmosphere. There are two Kingdoms of God : one within, waiting to come forth ; one above, waiting to come down. When the Divine Humanity meets Divine Society, that which is within shall have come forth, and that which is above shall have descended. This shall be the end of every captivity, the Marriage of the Earth and skies.

"Our hopes by their vastness put to scorn the littleness of our performance. What is Hamlet, what the sad and splendid procession of the Shakespearean drama, when measured by the great and awful tragedy of humanity ? We travel over the deserts of the world's broken hopes. What valour and vigour of virtue, what wealth of learning, what holiness of philanthropy poured themselves through the French Revolution ! What angels descended into the bottomless pit of dead corrupted monarchy ! Earth's holiest word, Fraternity, the word that makes Heaven vibrate responsive with each kindred Heaven, the word Fraternity, which contains in itself the essence of all Gospels, and the fulfilment of all Revelation, was preached to the spirits in prison, and Hades seemed for a moment to open its bosom to the advent of immortal life. Yet the end came : the Angel descended to the grave of buried Abel, to call him from the ground ; but Cain rose instead of Abel."[1]

Here, again, is a description of mankind put into the mouth of Christ :—

"When men see lambs upon the hillside perishing with cold, they see the Nations of the world as I behold them. When men see fishes of the sea torn with hooks, caught in nets and impaled upon spears, they see the people of the nations as I behold them. When men see idiots gibbering in the market-place, clothed in fantastic particoloured rags of finery, they see the priesthoods of the world as I behold them. When men see butchers smeared with the blood of the shambles, and dogs trained to tear the passer-by, they see the military chieftains of the world as I behold them."[2]

Of the regeneration of the individual we have already spoken. But Harris did not summon his followers to the practice of a barren holiness. For Christ's Gospel, he tells us, was originally "a great Health Service," with Sermons

---

[1] Pp. 133–135. Slightly abridged.   [2] *Id.*, p. 90.

on the Mount and the like for accompaniment. "The Kingdom of God," he continues, "as it now unfolds in our midst is the same Use . . . based on production, organising production, truly a sheep-feeding institution."

The spiritual regeneration, in short, is to be accompanied by a material reorganisation, a kind of glorified but rather vaguely indicated Socialism. The new Gospel

"proposes to serve men by organising them into the hierarchy of industries ; . . . it is the gospel of cotton and of cotton mills ; of sheep and wool and woollen factories ; the gospel of farmhouses and farm-fields, of the vineyard and the garden. It is the gospel of building and of all carpentry ; the gospel of the home and all domestic eco-nomies. It is thrift and care, it creates and saves. . . . It is so full of God that its words overflow with joy and hope into splendour and happiness ; so full of strength, that it rejoices setting forth to the world's deliverance, as the bridegroom to his nuptials, or the strong man to run his race."

Such in brief outline was the message with which Harris was charged. A few words remain to be said on the nature of the inspiration which he claimed. The genesis of his first considerable work, *A Lyric of the Morning Land*, a poem of some five thousand lines, is thus described :—

"On the 1st Jan., 1854, at the hour of noon, the archetypal ideas were internally inwrought by spiritual agency into the innermost mind of the Medium, he at that time having passed into a spiritual or interior condition. From that time till the fourth of August, fed by continual influxes of celestial life, these archetypal ideas internally unfolded within his interior or spiritual self ; until at length, having attained to their maturity, they descended into the externals of the mind, uttered themselves in speech, and were transcribed as spoken by the Medium, he, by spiritual agencies, being temporarily elevated to the spiritual degree of the mind for that purpose, and the external form being rendered quiet by a process which is analogous to physical death.

" The Poem was dictated at intervals during parts of about fourteen days, the actual time occupied by its delivery being about thirty hours."

Harris claims that he himself had " no knowledge or con-ception of any part of the poem " until it was actually spoken by his lips.

The poem itself is characterised by a grandiloquence, a
kind of intoxication of verbosity, common to most "inspirational" writings. But the rhythm is nearly always well
maintained, and there are many lyric passages of considerable beauty. It is, however, full of echoes from earlier
writers, as is apt to be the case with young poets, "inspirational" or not. The following extracts will give some idea
of the poem.

Here is the opening stanza from the *Hymn of Life's Completeness* :—

> "Golden Age of Harmony,
>   Thou shalt from the Heaven descend,
>   Earth shall rise and welcome thee,
>   Man to man be Angel-friend ;
> And the trumpets that blow when the Battle's red star
> 'Whelms the world with its blood, as it bursts from afar;
>   And the bugles that peal
>   To the crossing of steel,
> When the Demon of Wrath drives his scythe-armed car,
>   And the war-drums that roll
>   In the shock of the battle,
>   And the death-bells that toll
>   O'er men slaughtered like cattle ;
> And the death-smitten eyes that look up at the sun,
> And see only the cannon-smoke darkling and dun ;
> And the lips that in dying hurl curses at those
> Whom the Father made brethren, but evil made foes ;
> The death-shot that scatters the ranks of the flying ;
> The wild, fierce hurrah, when the Fratricide host
> Have driven their brethren to Hades' red coast—
>   They shall cease, they shall cease,
>   For the Angel of Peace
> Shall whiten the Earth, not with bones of the slain,
> But with flowers for the garland and sheaves for the wain."

Here are two stanzas from *The Song of Saturn* :—

> "I am the Patriarch Star ; I stand
>   And view, entranced, that Wondrous Land,·
>   That worlds ascend to when they rise
>   From outward space to inward skies.
>   I am the eldest child of Space,
>   And gaze into the Sun's bright face,
>   And in the Sun, prophetic, see
>   My own approaching destiny.

I am the Prophet Orb; I gaze
Through the far Future's unknown ways;
Mysterious wisdom thrills me deep ;
Not always shall Destruction keep
A lingering foothold, and with curse
And wailing jar the Universe ;
I see the end of Death and Sin ;
I see the golden years begin
For happy Earth, our sister sphere ;
Rejoice, O Heavens! her Spring is near."

And here, in a less heroic vein, are some verses from the
Marriage of Apollo :—

" Echo, Echo, thou dost hide
    In the mountain coverts dim,
Where the spotted fauns abide,
    And the wood-birds chant their hymn,
Thou a sylvan sprite shouldst be,
Dwelling with thy sisters three—
Mild and melancholy Night,
Glad and sparkling Morning Light,
Evening Lustre calmly bright.
Echo, Echo, thou dost dwell
In some shady woodbine dell,
Where the strawberry, luscious-sweet,
Tinges red thy whitest feet,
And the tendrils of the vine
Round thy temples twine and twine.

Echo, Echo, wake, I pray,
Wave the drowsy sleep away ;
I would chant a mellow strain
For thy lips to breathe again,
Where the wood-birds brood and haunt,
Where the young fauns throb and pant,
Where the cowslips feed the bees,
Where the leafy forest seas
Wave and ripple in the sun,
Reaching t'wards the horizon.

Wake, sweet wood-nymphs, Light and Shade—
One a dusky Indian Maid,
One a white-browed Sylph, with eyes
Clear as May-dew, when it lies
Sparkling in the violet's ear,
Fairy diamond in its sphere.

Ye who run your cheerful race
With the Seasons, as they pace,
And the golden-footed Days,
O'er the grand Titanian ways—
Light and Shadow, twins divine,
Nursed at either breast of Time :
Light that hides with laughing lips
In the glowing Sun's eclipse ;
Shade that wings herself away
In the yellow blooms of day :
Come, sweet Spirits, ye shall be
Crowned with roses preciously."

Of the exact nature of the inspirational process in his later prose works I am not aware that he gives any account. But it seems probable that the process, as it became more and more familiar, became also more fully conscious, as was the case with A. J. Davis. It will be remembered that Harris's "inspiration," unlike that of his predecessors, owed nothing to Mesmerism ; it does not appear that his trances or ecstasies were at any time of his life other than spontaneous.

Of the numerous other inspired writers and prophets of the period two call for a passing mention. Charles Linton, a young blacksmith, a man of good intelligence but very limited education, after acting for some time as a medium for the spirits of Daniel Webster, William Shakespeare, and others, was called to a loftier theme. In the course of four months in 1853 he wrote under "inspiration"—that is, automatically, and without consciousness on his part of the meaning of what he was writing—a manuscript containing considerably over 100,000 words, afterwards published under the title *The Healing of the Nations.* The book is a kind of religious rhapsody, an ecstatic outpouring, without definite plan or logical sequence, of ideas and imagery drawn from the Bible and various religious works. The work is not without literary merit of a kind. The choice of language is mainly biblical, and the writing maintains a certain dignity and sonorous rhythm. But it is wholly without originality ; it is a mere echo. Such as it is, however, it is the best of the minor inspired gospels of the time.[1]

[1] For some account of these curious productions see the author's *Modern Spiritualism* (1902), vol. i. pp. 263–282.

A prophet of a somewhat different type was J. T. Mahan, of Cincinnati, a Magnetic clairvoyant, who "brought forth a system of physical and intellectual science" rivalling the *Revelations* of Andrew Jackson Davis. Mahan's message was, however, of a more practical kind. Under his inspired leadership some wealthy citizens of Cincinnati formed a Co-operative Agricultural Community, and purchased in 1846 a large property on the Ohio river. Mahan's personal character, however, appears to have degenerated, and the Community had but a brief and disastrous existence.[1]

Enough has been said to show that there were many at this period who in all honesty claimed inspiration from superhuman intelligences, and found no lack of followers to approve their claim, with credit and with cash.

[1] See my *Modern Spiritualism*, i. p. 175, and Noyes, *History of American Socialisms*, p. 374.

CHAPTER XIV

THE RISE OF MENTAL-HEALING

Common origin of Hypnotism and the Mind-cure—Phineas Parkhurst
Quimby : his career : his practice in healing : testimonials from patients,
including Mrs. Eddy : his philosophy—Disease an ancient delusion—
Quimby's disciples: the Rev. W. F. Evans, H. W. Dresser, and the
leaders of the New Thought Movement—The doctrines of the New
Thought : mental invasion or obsession.

AS already stated, a large number of those who had
hitherto practised Animal Magnetism or Mesmerism, whether in America or Europe, were sooner
or later absorbed in the ranks of the Spiritualists. But there
remained some whose interest in healing was greater than
their love of the marvellous. From 1860 onwards the healers
again began to be divided into two camps. In both alike
the fluidic theory, if not altogether rejected, has at least been
allowed to sink into the background, and attention is being
more and more concentrated on the psychical side of the
question.

On the one hand, originating with Braid and Liébeault,
we have the respectable science and the respectable practitioners of Hypnotism. Hypnotism, no doubt, implies a
particular physiological condition. But the older physical
explanations are already discarded. Nobody now believes
that the hypnotic state is due to prolonged monotonous
stimulation of certain sensory nerves inducing inhibition of the
higher cerebral centres. The three classic stages of the Grand
Hysteria find few supporters at the present day. Whatever
the physiological explanation of the phenomena may be, it

has now come to be recognised that the clue to the process must be sought first in the region of psychology. The leading Continental school has, indeed, rejected the term " Hypnotism " altogether, substituting for it " Suggestion." In fact, it is admitted on all hands that the phenomena of Hypnotism are due primarily to Suggestion. Now " Suggestion is only another name for the power of ideas, so far as they prove efficacious over belief and conduct."[1] When, therefore, we speak of healing by Hypnotism or Suggestion, we mean, in fact, healing by imagination, or healing by faith.

In the other camp we have the innumerable sects of Mental-healers, Mind-curers, Christian Scientists, or by whatever other name they may be called. All these have from the first fastened their attention on the internal or psychical side of the matter. They have all along recognised that the healing process was essentially an act of the patient's will, imagination, or faith. Science and Superstition can now almost shake hands, so narrow is the ditch that divides the two camps.

The earliest Mental-healer of this period of whom we have authentic record is Phineas Parkhurst Quimby.[2] Born at Lebanon, New Hampshire, on February 16, 1802, he removed with his parents as a young child to Belfast, Maine, where the greater part of his life was spent. Quimby's father was a poor blacksmith, and the boy himself had but little schooling. In his youth he was apprenticed to a clockmaker, and proved himself a successful and ingenious craftsman. He appears to have been a thoughtful and observant man; an inventor, moreover, and always open to new knowledge. In 1838 he was present at a lecture on Mesmerism by Charles Poyen. He was much struck by what he saw and heard,

---

[1] William James, *Varieties of Religious Experience*, p. 112.

[2] The account of Quimby's life and doctrine given in the text is derived mainly from *The Philosophy of P. P. Quimby*, by Annetta Gertrude Dresser (Mrs. Julius Dresser), 1895. I have made use also of the later material included in the articles on Christian Science published in *McLure's Magazine* in 1907 and 1908, and in Lyman Powell's useful book, *Christian Science, the Faith and its Founder* (1907).

made the acquaintance of the lecturer, and finally began to experiment in the new science on his own account. He was fortunate enough to find an admirable subject, one Lucius Burkmar, a youth of seventeen, and soon threw up his trade and became a professional Mesmerist, giving popular demonstrations and treating disease by clairvoyance. ·

After three or four years, however, Quimby became convinced that his clairvoyant's diagnoses were due to thought-reading—that, in fact, he simply reproduced the opinion which the patient or Quimby himself had formed of the disease, and that his prescriptions could be traced to the same source. Carrying out this line of thought, he convinced himself that the efficacy of the treatment prescribed by Burkmar was due entirely to the expectation of the patient, that any other person or thing which could inspire equal confidence in the patient would be equally efficacious—that, in short, the patients cured themselves. He dismissed Burkmar, discontinued the practice of Mesmerism, and, meditating upon his past experience, gradually evolved a new theory—that all disease was a delusion, an error of the mind. In 1859 he removed to Portland, Maine, where he opened an office, and was continually occupied until his death, in 1866, in the treatment of disease by the new method which he had elaborated in accordance with his theory. One of his early patients, Mrs. Julius Dresser, who came to him as a young girl after six years of hopeless illness, her case given up by all the doctors, thus describes his procedure:—

" He seemed to know that I had come to him feeling that he was a last resort and with little faith in him and his mode of treatment. But instead of telling me that I was not sick, he sat beside me and explained to me all my sickness was, how I got into the condition, and the way I could have been taken out of it through the right understanding. He seemed to see through the situation from the beginning and explained the cause and effect so clearly that I could see a little of what he meant. . . . He continued to explain the case from day to day. . . . I felt the spirit and life that came with his words, and I found myself gaining steadily."

The local papers of these years contain frequent references

to Quimby's theories.[1] Thus the *Bangor* (Maine) *Jeffersonian* writes in 1857: "He says the mind is what it thinks it is, and that if it contends against the thought of disease and creates for itself an ideal form of health, that form impresses itself upon the animal spirit and through that upon the body."

Again, in the *Lebanon Free Press* of December 3, 1860, we read: "The foundation of his theory is that disease is not self-existent nor created by God, but is purely an invention of man."

In the *Portland Advertiser* of February 13, 1862, there is a letter from Quimby himself. After explaining that he is not a Spiritualist or a Mesmeriser he goes on: "I deny disease as a truth, but admit it as a deception . . . handed down from generation to generation until the people believe in it." The patient's trouble, he adds, arises from "the poison of the doctor's opinion in admitting a disease."

One of his patients, Miss E. G. Ware, in a letter published in the same paper of March 22, 1862, amplifies this creed:—

"Instead of treating the body as an intelligent organisation with independent life, he [Quimby] finds the life and intelligence in the man who occupies it." Often, she adds, he tells the patient that "he has no real disease. . . . He refers (disease) directly to man himself under the dominion of errors invented by man. . . . To cure disease . . . is to destroy the error on which it is based."

But in view of later developments the most valuable, if not perhaps the most lucid, of the contemporary expositions of Quimby's theory is to be found in a letter from another grateful patient, Mrs. Mary M. Patterson, afterwards to be known throughout two hemispheres as the Rev. Mary Baker G. Eddy, the founder of Christian Science. The letter was published in the *Portland* (Maine) *Courier* of November 7,

---

[1] These extracts from the provincial papers quoted in the text are derived from Mrs. Dresser's book already referred to. It is hardly necessary to emphasise the importance of this disinterested contemporary testimony in view of the fierce controversy which has in recent years sprung up round Quimby's name.

1862.[1] Mrs. Patterson began by explaining that Quimby healed neither by Spiritualism nor by Animal Magnetism, and that the magnetiser who had previously treated her failed to effect a cure because "he believed in disease, independent of the mind, hence I could not be wiser than my Master." She then continues :—

"But now I can see, dimly at first and only as trees walking, the great principle which underlies Dr. Quimby's faith and works ; and just in proportion to my right perception of truth is my recovery. This truth which he opposes to the error of giving intelligence to matter and placing pain where it never placed itself, if received understandingly, changes the currents of the system to their normal action, and the mechanism of the body goes on undisturbed. That this is a science capable of demonstration becomes clear to the mind of those patients who reason upon the process of their cure. The truth which he establishes in the patient cures him (although he may be wholly unconscious thereof), and the body, which is full of light, is no longer in disease. At present I am too much in error to elucidate the truth, and can touch only the keynote for the Master hand to wake the harmony."

The exposition, as said, is not lucid. The writer sets out, as she tells us, to "analyse" the power by which she has been healed : she makes "great argument about it and about" without ever getting to the point. Imperfect as the testimony is, it is, however, sufficient.

From all the contemporary testimonies it is clear that so far back as the later fifties, at any rate, P. P. Quimby taught that disease was a non-entity, a delusion, an ancient error ; and that he carried out his teaching in practice by ministering, not to the body, but to the sick soul.

Quimby left behind him no systematic account of his doctrines. In any case he had no special power of expression, and his later years seem to have been occupied, to the extreme limits of his strength, in healing those who came to him for help. But he was in the habit of dictating to one or other of his disciples who acted as secretary or amanuensis, whenever he could find moments of leisure. These manuscripts, which fill several volumes, are still extant. From the

[1] Quoted in *McLure's Magazine* for February, 1907.

fragments which have been published by Mrs. Dresser and others it is clear that his philosophical ideas had never been worked out in a coherent system. The keynote of his thought, however, is a vivid realisation of the difference between what older philosophies have called Soul and Body, the Spiritual and the Natural Man. But Quimby conceived this opposition from a new point of view, and employed a novel terminology for the purpose of describing it. "Is a man spirit or matter?" he asks, and replies "Neither; he is Life." Though not an adherent of orthodox Christianity, he believed in Christ, and frequently describes his doctrine as the Science of Christ: he occasionally calls it "Christian Science." More generally, however, he refers to it as the "Science of Health" or the "Science of Health and Happiness." But both "Christ" and "Science" are used in a special sense. Thus he writes that Christ "separated Himself as Jesus the Man of opinion from Christ the scientific Man." Again, after explaining that the "senses are life—the senses are all that there is of a man," he proceeds: "Are the senses mind? I answer No. Mind and Senses are as distinct as light and darkness, and the same distinction holds good in wisdom and knowledge, Jesus and Christ. Christ, Wisdom, and Senses are synonyms. So likewise are Jesus, Knowledge, and Mind." Or again, "Mind is Matter—all knowledge that is of man is based on opinion. This I call the world of Matter."

Quimby's vocabulary, it will be seen, is somewhat confusing. The usage of centuries has accustomed us to conceive of "mind" and "matter" as complementary terms, as an alternative method of expressing the opposition between soul and body. But Quimby tells us that mind is matter. The statement, however, represents something more than the confusion of terminology natural in a self-educated man. In classing disease, mind, opinion, knowledge, Jesus, amongst the things that do not count, Quimby is really endeavouring to draw a new line between the things which are and the things which only seem to be. It is a line which everybody at some time of his life tries to draw in some fashion or another.   We must recognise here an heroic attempt to start from a new point, to draw the line higher up, to leave on the other side a good deal which most people have been content to include amongst the things that are. We are not here concerned with the success of the attempt. It is enough to bear in mind, in considering the development of later derivative philosophies, that Quimby is the first of whom it is recorded that he made such an attempt.

Quimby is one of those men, like Socrates or St. Simon, who live not in their books but in the lives of their disciples. He wrote his message not on the printed page, but on the minds and characters of living men and women.   One of his earliest pupils was the Rev. W. F. Evans, originally a Methodist minister, who for some years before as a patient he visited Quimby, in about 1863, had been studying the works of Swedenborg.   Evans quickly assimilated Quimby's theories, and between 1869 and 1886 published a number of books on Mental-healing.   It is not necessary to consider his teaching in detail.   His terminology and doctrine are strongly tinged with Swedenborgianism and differ considerably from Quimby's.   He can hardly, in fact, be said to be in the strict sense a disciple, though he acknowledges his personal debt to the Maine healer.   But he drew the line in a different place.   He does not identify mind with matter.   The following extract from his earliest book will, however, make it clear that in his view of the nature of disease he differs little from his teacher.   To cure disease, he says,

" all that is necessary is the power intuitively to detect the morbid state of the mind underlying the disease, and how to convert the patient to a more healthful inner life.   All disease is, in its cause, an insanity . . . its secret spring is some abnormality or unsoundness of the mind." [1]

Dr. Evans in his later life established a Mind-Cure Sanatorium in Salisbury, Mass.   He appears to have had a considerable following in his lifetime, and his influence still

[1] *The Mental Science Cure*, p. 80 (Glasgow, 1870).   The first American edition was published in 1869.

persists among the adherents of the "New Thought" Movement.[1]

Both Julius Dresser and his wife were patients of Quimby in about 1860, and their son, Horatio W. Dresser, is one of the ablest exponents of the unsectarian side of the Mind Cure or New Thought Movement at the present time ; another pupil of Dr. Quimby's, as said, is the founder and sole exponent of the philosophy of Christian Science.

Quimby is, then, in a sense, the founder of the whole modern movement of Mental-healing which in America has attained to such enormous proportions. But the Maine healer represents only one of the channels which connect the present with the past. The tide has been fed from many other sources. The Mind-curers, as already said, are the direct descendants of the Mesmerists, and in their speculative views we get in touch through the Animal Magnetists with the older mystics. Hindu philosophy has helped to swell the stream, and, as William James has pointed out, Berkeley and Emerson have contributed. The characteristic note of the movement is its deliberate optimism—an optimism of which we find other expressions in the gospel of Modern Spiritualism, in the writings of Walt Whitman, and generally in the popular interpretation of the scientific doctrine of Evolution—that all things work together for good. In the hackneyed phrase, the New Thought is a genuine offspring of the Zeitgeist.

To attempt an adequate description of the numerous phases of the movement would be tedious and unprofitable. It will suffice if we examine it as presented in the pages of H. W. Dresser, who is admittedly one of its ablest exponents, does not himself practise as a healer, and is therefore not liable to be biassed by commercial considerations in emphasising particular aspects of the doctrine, and, above all, is sufficiently broad-minded to quote with appreciation from the writings of others, such as Trine, Henry Wood, and Leander Whipple, who represent other phases of the movement.

Dresser, then, represents the New Thought in its sanest and

[1] See *McLure's Magazine* for February, 1908, p. 390.

most critical form. He has departed from the primitive simplicity of Quimby's theory. He believes in the reality of matter—that food can nourish, alcohol intoxicate, and drugs poison or heal the body. Naturally, therefore, he is sceptical of the omnipotence of the Mind-cure. " Some diseases, like typhoid," he writes, " apparently have to run their course, even under Mental treatment " ; and he is doubtful as to the power of the treatment to set broken bones.[1] In short, he recommends that, for the present at any rate, the Mental-healer should seek to co-operate with the regular physician rather than to replace him.

In another important point the modern Mind-healers tend to revert to the older Animal Magnetists. Quimby, as has been seen, appealed exclusively to the understanding of his patients. The modern hypnotist, according to the predominant scientific school, acts on the patient's imagination. A scarecrow to the eye of faith is as awe-inspiring as a ghost ; and a cunningly constructed automaton, which should flash an eye no less imperious and speak in accents as persuasive, ought to prove therapeutically as effective as a Nancy professor. But the Mind-curers generally believe in the specific action of the operator on the subject. A patient may be treated and healed without his consent and even without his knowledge. Dresser himself knows of persons who have under such conditions been cured of drunkenness.[2] "Absent " treatment is thus as efficacious as treatment when healer and patient sit and converse in the same room. In the tariff of a leading New York " Metaphysician " which lies before me " Present " and " Absent " attention are charged at the same rate—ten dollars an hour. Now, in a philosophy which allows a professional curer of diseases to call himself a Metaphysician, which opposes " mind and body " to " soul," which regards mind as only a finer form of matter, and speaks of it as "shading off gradually into brain and nerves "[3]—in such a philosophical scheme it is inevitable that the action between

[1] *Methods and Problems of Spiritual Healing* (1904), pp. 9, 35, &c.
[2] Dresser, *op. cit.*, p. 10.
[3] *Op. cit.*, p. 48.

S

healer and patient should be described in material terms and should, whether admittedly or not, be conceived of as itself of a material nature. Thus Dresser tells us that "the thought of the healer directs and focusses the [healing] power where it is most needed," and further explains that "in the healing process the communication . . . is of a vibratory character," analogous to the aerial waves by which sound is conveyed. The conception of an influence conveyed by undulations or vibrations is the last and most attenuated form of the doctrine of the Sympathetic system. And just as the Sympathetic system found its complement in the popular belief in witchcraft, so the modern Mind-curers have given life to a Frankenstein monster—the belief in injurious mental action at a distance. We find little trace of such a belief amongst the Animal Magnetists, no doubt because the fluid was generally supposed to be physical both in its origin and in its effects. But, so soon as the influence at a distance became conceived of as a process primarily affecting the mind of the patient, the fear of its abuse became inevitable. Of course, a power which could cure could also kill. But the ordinary citizen does not expect to come across a Catharine de Medicis or a Marquise de Brinvilliers. It is quite another thing to possess or to dread the possession by your neighbour of a power not merely to inflict discomfort and disease, but to influence will and affection for private ends. How powerfully the popular imagination has been impressed by this conception all alienists know. The conviction of persecution by distant enemies, operating by mesmerism or telepathy, is one of the commonest delusions of incipient insanity. But sane persons have not escaped the contagion of this panic fear. When Thomas Lake Harris fell out with Andrew Jackson Davis the poet commiserated the prophet as "the victim of a strange magnetism"; Mrs. Eddy is obsessed by the spectre of Malicious Mesmerism; and the Mental-healers are continually concerned about the danger of invasion or contamination by alien mental atmospheres. The contagion, Dresser explains, may be unconscious on each side, as when young people think themselves in love; or there may be a deliberate intention on the part of the invading or obsessing mind to secure domination over another personality. "Before one knows that there is a deep-laid scheme behind," the mischief is done, "and the mind is brought into subjection to the suggestion of another." "Vampires," he warns us, "are numerous, and one must take care of oneself." [1]

But bodily healing, though an essential part of the New Thought, is only one aspect of the gospel. Its message is one of good cheer for body and soul as well. Cast away all fear, direct your thoughts continually towards the good, strive continually to realise your identity with the Divine.

"The desideratum," says Dresser, "is to lift the entire process (of healing) to the spiritual plane, to live in thought with the ideal, to regard mind and body rather from the point of view of the soul, than to look upon the soul from the standpoint of the body. To live more with God, this it is spiritually to heal and to be healed. To aspire, to hope, to love, to co-operate with God. For healing is loving and renewing ; it is a part of the great creative work of the Universe." [2]

Says another exponent of the New Thought :—

" The great central fact in human life is the coming into a conscious vital realisation of our oneness with the Infinite Life, and the opening of ourselves fully to the Divine inflow. In just the degree that we come into a conscious realisation of our oneness with the Infinite Life, and open ourselves to the Divine Inflow, do we actualise in ourselves the qualities and powers of the Infinite Life, do we make ourselves channels through which the Infinite Intelligence and Power can work. In just the degree in which you realise your oneness with the Infinite Spirit, you will exchange dis-ease for ease, inharmony for harmony, suffering and pain for abounding health and strength. To recognise our own divinity and our intimate relation to the Universal, is to attach the belt of our machinery to the power-house of the Universe. One need remain in hell no longer than one chooses to ; we can rise to any heaven we ourselves choose ; and when we choose so to rise all the higher powers in the Universe combine to help us heavenwards." [3]

---

[1] *Op. cit.*, pp. 45, 51, &c.

[2] Dresser, *op. cit.*, p. 33.

[3] Ralph Waldo Trine, *In Tune with the Infinite*, quoted by W. James, *Varieties of Religious Experience*, p. 101. James's account of the

The New Thought, it will be seen, is something much more than a new hygiene. It is a rule for the guidance of life. It is, in short, a new religion. But it makes no claim to exclusive revelation. The divine illumination, the strength, and the healing are within the reach of all. But they are the reward of deliberate and constantly renewed effort. The whole energies of the mind must be concentrated on higher things; the outer world must be shut out; the seeker must enter into the silence, and keep his whole being open to the divine influx.

Probably the state thus indicated does not differ essentially from the "superior condition" of Andrew Jackson Davis, or the state of inspiration claimed by Harris and other prophets of the period.

But the question which will most interest the practical man is "Do the Mental-healers heal?" Unquestionably they do. There are, indeed, few statistics available. But the question has been carefully investigated by Dr. H. Goddard, of Clarke University,[1] who finds abundant evidence of cures, both by Faith-healers, commonly so called, such as Dowie and Schlatter, and by followers of the New Thought. He has satisfied himself that there are many cases where the cure is real. He quotes some statistics of a Mental Science Home, the records of which have been fairly and intelligently kept. Out of 71 cases, of which particulars are given, 24 were claimed as cured, 34 more or less improved, 13 not helped. Amongst the failures are cases of cancer, locomotor ataxy, Bright's disease, insanity, and melancholia.

Of course, such figures are of no value in indicating the proportion of cures, since several different processes of selection had, no doubt, been in operation before the patients were admitted to the Home. But they do prove that a favourable effect is produced in many cases. Dr. Goddard's general conclusion is that Faith-healing and Mental Science are effective in cases where Hypnotism would be effective, and

"Religion of Healthy Mindedness" should be studied by all who are interested in the New Thought Movement.

[1] *American Journal of Psychology*, vol. x. (1889), p. 431.

fail where Hypnotism also fails. In other words, in all alike the effect produced would appear to be due to Suggestion ; and it has not yet been proved that any one of the recognised modes of imparting the suggestion is conspicuously more effective than another.

CHAPTER XV

MARY BAKER EDDY

Birth and early years : marries (1843) G. W. Glover : marries (1853) Dr. Patterson—Visits Quimby and is cured : the fall on the ice—Begins to teach and practise healing—Richard Kennedy—Birth of Christian Science—Marries (1877) A. G. Eddy—In the law-courts : the new Witchcraft—The New Church : the Massachusetts Metaphysical College—*Science and Health*—The organisation of the Church, and Mrs. Eddy's part in it.

W E have now to trace the history of Quimby's most famous disciple, and of the school of Mental-healing which she has founded.[1] Mary A. Morse Baker, afterwards known successively as Mrs. Glover, Mrs. Patterson, and now as Mrs. Eddy, was born at Bow, New Hampshire, on July 16, 1821, her father being a farmer

---

[1] This account of Mrs. Eddy's life and the history of Christian Science is based partly on her own Autobiography, but mainly on the articles by Miss Georgine Milmine in *McLure's Magazine* for 1907 and 1908, already referred to. I do not propose, however, to follow the author of these extremely able articles in her account of Mrs. Eddy's early years. This part of her story is necessarily based either on tradition, or at best on the memories of the oldest inhabitants. An octogenarian's recollections of his own childhood and youth have an undoubted value, and may present us with an approximate picture of the reality. But the recollections of an octogenarian—perhaps even a nonagenarian—about some other person's childhood and youth ! That is quite another matter. Any reader who desires it may study the rather unpleasing picture of Mrs. Eddy's youth and early womanhood, as presented in the articles in question, and form his own conclusions.

It need hardly be said that these remarks do not apply to Miss Milmine's account of Mrs. Eddy's later career—an account which is

of the familiar New England type; a man of strong, if narrow, personality, much respected in the district. In her Autobiography [1] Mrs. Eddy tells us that her ancestors were connected with some distinguished Scotch families. But in one instance at least the claim has been denied by the British representative of the family in question.[2]

Mary Baker was the youngest of six; as a child she was gifted with great personal beauty, and appears to have been the pet of the family. Like the youthful Andrew Jackson Davis,[3] she tells us that at the age of eight she heard a voice repeatedly calling her name. She thought it was her mother's voice, but found that her mother had not called her. Again, Mrs. Eddy tells us that when, about the age of twelve, she was examined on the occasion of her formal reception into the Church, she refused to accept the doctrines of pre-destination and eternal damnation : "Even the oldest Church members wept at her eloquence . . . the good clergyman's heart also melted, and he received her into their communion." But Mary A. M. Baker, as appears from the official records of the Tilton Congregational Church, was received into the Church in 1838, when she was *seventeen* years old. It will be remembered that Andrew Jackson Davis relates a similar legend of himself at the same signifi-cant age of twelve. The prophetic imagination tends to conform to tradition.

not only judicial in tone, but supported at every step by contemporary letters, affidavits, official records, and other documentary evidence. A few further details of Mrs. Eddy's career will be found in a little book —*Christian Science : The Faith and its Founder*—published in 1907 by the Rev. Lyman P. Powell. Mr. Powell has made an independent study of the Quimby MSS. and other important documents in the case, and has personally interviewed many of the leading witnesses. There can be no reasonable doubt of the substantial accuracy of the account given by these two independent authorities of Mrs. Eddy's life-history.

[1] *Retrospection and Introspection* (thirtieth thousand, 1906).

[2] See *McLure's Magazine*, January, 1907, p. 237, *footnote*. Compare the claim of the celebrated Spirit Medium, D. D. Home, to be con-nected with the Earls of Home—again a Scotch family.

[3] This, it need scarcely be said, is not the parallel that loyal Christian Scientists have drawn.

One of the Baker brothers, Albert, was a man of considerable ability, who died at the age of thirty, at the opening of what promised to be a career of distinction. This brother, Mrs. Eddy tells us, taught her Greek, Latin, and Hebrew. The favourite studies of her childhood, she adds, were Natural Philosophy, Logic, and Moral Science. But all this worldly knowledge vanished like a dream when the revelation came. " Learning was so illumined that Grammar was eclipsed." So it was !

In December, 1843, at the age of twenty-two, Mary Baker married for the first time. Her husband, George Washington Glover, a bricklayer by trade, had left New England to settle in South Carolina, where wages were higher.[1] Six months after the marriage he died of yellow fever. A few months later a posthumous child was born. The boy was adopted by some neighbours, who in 1857 moved to Minnesota. Mrs. Glover, as we must now call her, did not see her son again until 1878, when he was thirty-four years old, and himself married, with two children.

From 1844 to 1853 Mrs. Glover lived either with her father or a married sister, Mrs. Tilton. In the latter year she married for the second time, her husband being Daniel Patterson, a travelling dentist. They lived together for some years in struggles and poverty, constantly moving from place to place. In 1862 Patterson, who had visited the battlefield merely as a spectator, was captured by the Confederate forces, and spent a year or two in a Southern prison. On his release he and his wife lived together again for a time, but finally separated in 1866. In 1873 Mrs. Glover-Patterson obtained a divorce on the ground of desertion.[2]

---

[1] *McLure's Magazine*, January, 1907, p. 239. Mrs. Eddy, in the Preface to her *Miscellaneous Writings*, p. viii, calls him " Colonel Glover, of Charleston, South Carolina."

[2] It should be stated that Mrs. Eddy's own account of her separation from Patterson, and of the subsequent divorce, differs from that given in the text. The same remark applies to other episodes related in Mrs. Eddy's *Retrospection and Introspection* and her other autobiographical writings. As the history of Mrs. Eddy given in *McLure's Magazine* is

But long before the separation the turning-point in Mrs. Patterson's life had come. For the greater part of her youth and womanhood she had been in delicate health, and during the later years was apparently a confirmed invalid. She left her sick-bed to marry Patterson, and for some years of her married life was practically bedridden. In October, 1861, Patterson wrote to Quimby, asking his help on behalf of his wife, whom he described as suffering for many years from a spinal disease. Mrs. Patterson could not at that time afford the expense of going to Portland, but in the following year, after Patterson's capture by the Southerners, she managed to journey thither by herself. She arrived in October, 1862. Mrs. Julius Dresser has left a record of her first appearance.[1] The invalid was so feeble that she had to be helped up the steps to Quimby's consulting-room. She was worn and emaciated, shabbily dressed and extremely poor. All her adult life, indeed, since her first few months of marriage in 1843, had been spent in poverty. She had for nearly twenty years been an invalid dependent on others. For forty years her life had been of the narrowest and barest kind; there had been no interests of wider scope than those of the home, and in these she seems to have found no outlet worthy of her restless energies. Of the nature of these energies no member of her circle, not even herself, could have been aware. From this date onwards all was changed. That Quimby restored her bodily health is much. But he did more. He gave her a purpose in life. He laid the world open to her. For some years Mrs. Patterson seems to have lost sight of her own personality in her enthusiasm for Quimby and his teaching. One of her early letters has been quoted in the previous chapter. In another letter, dated April, 1864, she tells Quimby that she is about to lecture in the Town Hall at Warren, on "P. P. Quimby's Spiritual Science Healing Disease, as opposed to Deism or Rochester Rapping

attested at nearly every point by sworn testimonies and citations of court records, &c., there is, of course, little ambiguity as to the real facts of the case.

[1] *The Philosophy of P. P. Quimby,* p. 50.

Spiritualism." On Quimby's death, in January, 1866, Mrs. Patterson published some memorial lines in a Lynn newspaper, which are remarkable for the extravagance of the personal devotion displayed. The first and last stanzas run as follows :—

> "Did sackcloth clothe the sun and day grow night,
>   All Matter mourn the hour with dewy eyes,
> When Truth, receding from our mortal sight,
>   Had paid to error her last sacrifice ?
>
> .   .   .   .
>
> Heaven but the happiness of that calm soul,
>   Growing in stature to the throne of God ;
> Rest should reward him who hath made us whole,
>   Seeking, though tremblers, where his footsteps trod."

A few days before these lines were written Mrs. Patterson, who was then residing with her husband in Lynn, Mass., slipped on the frosty pavement, and in her fall struck her back on the ice. She was taken up unconscious. Writing on February 1, 1866, two weeks after the accident, to her fellow-disciple, Julius Dresser, she says :—

"The physician attending said I had taken the last step I ever should, but in two days I got out of my bed *alone* and *will walk*, but yet I confess I was frightened, and out of that nervous heat my friends are forming, spite of me, the terrible spinal affection from which I have suffered so long and hopelessly . . . Now can't *you* help me ? I believe you can. I write this with this feeling. I believe that I could help another in my condition if they had not placed their intelligence in matter. This I have not done, and yet I am slowly failing. Won't you write me if you will undertake for me if I can get to you ?

"Respectfully,
"MARY M. PATTERSON."[1]

It is from this illness that Mrs. Eddy and her followers date the discovery of Christian Science. And, in fact, whatever share in the credit of the discovery we may assign to

---

[1] The text of this important letter is given in *McLure's Magazine* for February, 1907.

Mrs. Eddy, it seems probable that her mental independence originated in this incident. It is curious to reflect that if Quimby himself had lived a few months longer there might have been no Mother Church and no final revelation in 440 editions, Asa G. Eddy might have died a bachelor, and the Red Dragon [1] might still be sleeping in his cave. But when Mrs. Patterson fell upon the ice Quimby was dead or dying. And since Julius Dresser apparently could not come to Lynn there was none to help. Mrs. Eddy was forced to fight the illness and depression resulting from the accident with her own right hand, even if the weapon which brought victory had been forged by another. She speedily recovered her health; but in fact, as we learn from the affidavit of the doctor who attended her, the injury was not of a serious character.

Probably, as said, the beginnings of Mrs. Eddy's mental independence may be traced to this episode. It appears, nevertheless, from the testimony of many persons still living, that for the next four or five years she continued to regard herself as the pupil and disciple of Quimby, and to give him the credit of the new philosophy which she made it her business to preach to all who could be persuaded to listen. After her separation from Patterson she wandered about for four years living with different families, in Lynn, Amesbury, or some of the neighbouring towns. But she was never able to stay long in one family. She quarrelled successively with all her hostesses, and her departure from the house was heralded on two or three occasions by a violent scene. Her friends during these years were generally Spiritualists; she seems to have professed herself a Spiritualist, and to have taken part in *séances*. She was occasionally entranced, and had received "spirit communications" from her deceased brother Albert. Her first advertisement as a healer appeared in 1868, in the Spiritualist paper, *The Banner of Light*. During these years she carried about with her a copy of one of Quimby's manuscripts giving an abstract of his philo-

---

[1] One of Mrs. Eddy's names for Malicious Animal Magnetism. See *Revelation* xii. 3.

sophy. This manuscript she permitted some of her pupils to copy.

In 1870 Mrs. Patterson returned to Lynn, bringing with her the most promising of her pupils, one Richard Kennedy, a boy of twenty, whose acquaintance she had made two years previously. Kennedy and Mrs. Patterson took rooms together; Kennedy practising with much success as a healer, and Mrs. Patterson studying and conducting classes in the Science which she was now beginning to look upon as her own. The fee for the course of twelve lectures was originally fixed at one hundred dollars. Within a few weeks Mrs. Patterson was led, as she tells us under divine inspiration, to raise it to three hundred dollars, at which figure it seems to have remained.[1] Mrs. Patterson kept for herself the entire fees paid for her lectures. Of the fees paid to Richard Kennedy she took half of what remained after the expenses of the joint establishment had been paid. When the inevitable rupture came, early in 1872, Mrs. Patterson found herself for the first time in her life a comparatively rich woman, with about six thousand dollars in hand.

From 1870 until 1881 she remained in Lynn, preparing her book, *Science and Health*, the first edition of which appeared in 1875, teaching her pupils, and gradually collecting round her a small band of devoted followers. On January 1, 1877, she was married for the third time, to Asa Gilbert Eddy. Of the bridegroom it is enough to say that he did as he was told. Mrs. Eddy told him, the night before the marriage, that she intended to marry him the next day and he obeyed. He died five years later.

But if the annals of Mrs. Eddy's third marriage are vacant, the same cannot be said of her dealings with her disciples and her general activities during the decade 1870–1880. Favourite after favourite was installed in the place of honour, only to be cast out with contumely a year or two later. Lawsuit after lawsuit came into court, Mrs. Eddy figuring sometimes as plaintiff, sometimes as defendant—but always defeated.

[1] The number of lectures given in return for this fee was, however, in 1888 reduced from twelve to seven.

It will be remembered that Mesmer not only sold the secret of his healing at a high price, but conceived the idea of exacting from his pupils a proportion of the fees received by them in their practice. There is a curious similarity in Mrs. Eddy's early methods. When we remember, however, that many of her original students—who were asked to pay £60 for a course of twelve lectures—were simply shoe-hands employed in the neighbouring factories, and that few rose above the rank of artisan or small farmer, we can but wonder at Mesmer's moderation in exacting no more than one hundred louis from a marquis, a farmer-general, or an ambassador. Mrs. Eddy, again like her great predecessor, required her early students to enter into a bond not to reveal the secret; and some of them bound themselves to pay over to her 10 per cent. of the yearly income derived from their practice as healers.

Naturally, arrangements of this kind led to constant litigation. In 1872 a former pupil, Mrs. Vickery, brought an action against Mrs. Eddy to recover 150 dollars paid for tuition, which she alleged to be valueless; Mrs. Vickery won her case. In 1877 G. W. Barry, once a favoured disciple, brought an action for money due to him for copying and preparing MSS. for the press; he recovered 395 dollars. In 1878 Mrs. Eddy herself brought a suit against Kennedy to recover 750 dollars alleged to be due; she lost her case. She brought actions against three other pupils—Tuttle, Stanley, and Spofford—to recover unpaid tuition fees, and lost them all.

But not all Mrs. Eddy's appearances in court were of this squalid character. We have already traced the rise, amongst the Spiritualists and Mental-healers, of the strange doctrine of injurious mental influence. Malicious Animal Magnetism became from this date onwards the nightmare of Mrs. Eddy's existence. The devil whom she had excluded from her theology came back in this insidious form. And, like his prototype in the Middle Ages, he is not content with his more serious employments, but delights in acts of petty annoyance. He gives his enemies toothache and indigestion, plays Old Harry with the printers, freezes the water-pipes, and makes the domestic boilers leak. Each of Mrs. Eddy's dethroned favourites has in turn been accused, nay, is still accused, of practising these vile arts. The chapter on "Demonology" in the 1881 edition of *Science and Health*[1] contains an almost incredible attack on Richard Kennedy. "His power to heal," she writes, "failed because of his sin. His mental malpractice has made him a moral leper." He spreads ruin and death around ; he has perverted wholesome human affection, alienated wives from their husbands, broken up happy homes, has caused many to be affected with disease and ultimately brought them to death.

In January, 1878, Daniel Spofford, who had managed the sale of Mrs. Eddy's book and for some years been one of her prime favourites, was expelled from the Association of Christian Scientists for "immorality."[2] A few months later he was brought before the law-court at Salem on the charge that he was a Mesmerist and that he had "at divers times and places and with intent to injure the plaintiff [a disciple of Mrs. Eddy's] caused the plaintiff by means of the said power or art great suffering of body and mind and severe facial pains and neuralgia." In Salem two hundred years ago the denunciations of one hysterical girl were sufficient to procure the condemnation of many to death. But times are changed. Mrs. Eddy made her appearance in court supported by a crowd of twenty witnesses to denounce this practitioner of the New Witchcraft. But all in vain. *Solvuntur risu tabulæ.*

The sequel to this amazing prosecution was more amazing still. If Mrs. Eddy was afraid, genuinely afraid, of Spofford and his devilish arts, Spofford was quite as much afraid of

[1] This chapter has for some years ceased to appear in the successive editions of *Science and Health*. The chapter on Animal Magnetism in the most recent editions is shorn of all personal references.

[2] "Immorality" is used by Mrs. Eddy in an esoteric sense, as meaning disloyalty to the principles of Christian Science. Any Christian Scientist at the present day who is found disloyal is liable to the same accusation of "immorality." Compare Mrs. Eddy's definition of an adulteress as one who has adulterated truth !

Mrs. Eddy. In the course of the same year (1878) there came to him a mysterious stranger, who represented that he had been suborned by the Christian Scientists to make away with the enemy of their faith. Spofford fled into safe hiding. Arens, who had succeeded Spofford as prime minister, and Eddy, the blameless consort, were arrested for conspiracy to murder. Preliminary evidence was taken. But the original informant was a bad lot, too well known to the police, and the other witnesses for the prosecution, with two exceptions, were not much better. The two exceptions, however, were detectives, and it is not easy to explain their evidence. On the other hand, Asa Gilbert Eddy, the blameless consort, was obviously not of the stuff of which midnight murderers are made. The defendants were admitted to bail of three thousand dollars each. In the event the State Attorney, after considering the evidence, refused to proceed. Spofford's honesty can hardly be questioned; the whole incident remains inexplicable. But it affords, at any rate, an illustration of the real terror inspired by Mrs. Eddy's extraordinary vindictiveness.[1]

A year or two later Arens himself, who had presented the petition against the New Witchcraft in the court of Salem, fell from his high estate and was numbered amongst the malpractitioners. In June, 1882, Eddy died; the *post-mortem* examination showed that the cause of death was heart disease. But Mrs. Eddy persisted in her belief that the death was due to " arsenic," mentally administered by means of Malicious Mesmerism, and told a Boston reporter so.[2] Incredible as it may seem, Mrs. Eddy's terror appears to have been perfectly genuine; she is said to have been half-paralysed with fear after Eddy's death at this palpable proof

---

[1] Another woman founder of a new religion, Mdme. Blavatsky, seems to have had the power of inspiring equal terror in those who had incurred her displeasure. The present writer is acquainted with two instances in which Mdme. Blavatsky was able to avert exposure by this means.

[2] See article in the *Boston Post* for June 5, 1882, quoted in *McLure's Magazine*.

of the power of her enemies. A secret circle was forthwith organised amongst her most devoted followers, which met daily for "adverse treatment." But the devil seems to have had the best of it. Richard Kennedy and the other male-factors were not a penny the worse for all the retributive evil invoked upon their heads.

In October, 1881, to continue the history, there was a serious secession from the Christian Science Association. Many of the older and most influential members left. In a circular letter explaining their reason for this step they stated that, while still acknowledging the truth of Mrs. Eddy's teaching, they deplored "her frequent ebullitions of temper, love of money, and appearance of hypocrisy."

Mrs. Eddy's famous Metaphysical College, of which she was the president and the sole professor, had been founded in the early part of the same year. She now thought it time to remove the College and herself from Lynn, and in 1882 she came to Boston. There her fame and influence grew rapidly. In April, 1883, the *Journal of Christian Science*—a monthly periodical—was started. In 1886 was founded the National Christian Science Association, and in 1887 there were one hundred and eleven professional Christian Science healers and twenty-one academies for the teaching of the new gospel. Two years later, however, fresh dissensions arose and Mrs. Eddy's supremacy was seriously endangered. Ultimately the dissentients were forced to secede. But Mrs. Eddy from this time initiated a remark-able change of policy. In 1889 she retired from Boston to the small provincial town of Concord and there shut herself up in a hermit-like seclusion. She expressly forbade her students henceforward to consult her, "verbally or through letters," on personal or business affairs. She resigned the editorship of the *Journal*, she disbanded—if that is the correct term—the Massachusetts Metaphysical College,[1] and, finally, she dissolved her Church organisation. The *Journal*

---

[1] Of late years the Massachusetts Metaphysical College has been reconstituted. The Sessions last for "not over one week" in the year (*Church Manual*, art. xxx.).

explains the reason for this last action as follows: "The bonds of the Church were thrown away so that its members might assemble themselves together to provoke one another to good works in the bond only of love."

Three or four years later the Church organisation was restored. But it was not the same organisation. The old Church had both money and power. The present Church has neither. Both are invested exclusively in Mrs. Eddy. Prior to the enforced dissolution the Church members had contributed nearly £1,200 to the purchase of a site valued at £2,000, the balance being held on mortgage. "Guided by divine love," and assisted by a lawyer who has since been disbarred, Mrs. Eddy got the mortgage into her own hands, foreclosed, and acquired the whole site. She then made over the property to a Board of Trustees chosen by herself and responsible to her, with the proviso that, on any breach of the trust the whole property—on which now stands a church which has cost over two million dollars to build—should revert to "Mary Baker G. Eddy, her heirs and assigns for ever." But Mrs. Eddy's personal property is now very large. Her lecture classes—the fees for the whole series of four courses amounting to no less than eight hundred dollars (£160)—were crowded in these later years. Her writings are sold at preposterous prices and have brought her in very large sums. Of *Science and Health* upwards of half a million copies have been sold. In its cheapest form the book costs three dollars (in England 12s. 6d.). Many editions of this book have appeared, and the zealous disciple is expected to purchase the most recent.[1]

So far back as 1895 Mrs. Eddy's royalties on the sale of

---

[1] In the trust deed of 1892, by which the land was conveyed for the Mother Church, reference is made to the 71st edition. There are now between 400 and 500 editions. Most of these so-called editions are no doubt what the ordinary publisher would call a new *impression—i.e.*, simply a fresh batch printed from the stereo plates. But there have been very many—possibly some scores—of new editions in the accepted sense. Mrs. Eddy is constantly making slight verbal changes, and on several occasions the book has been completely revised and the order of the chapters changed.

T

her publications *for one year* amounted to 18,481 dollars— say £3,700; and the sales have, no doubt, very largely increased since that date.[1]   In 1887 Mrs. Eddy bought a house in the best part of Boston for £8,000.   On her return to Boston twenty years later she spent £20,000 on a house and as much again, it is said, in preparing it for her reception.   A recent lawsuit disclosed that her personal property amounted in 1893 to at least 100,000 dollars, and in 1907 to about a million.[2]

But in her later years, at any rate, it is not money which Mrs. Eddy seeks, but power.   And she has power—power absolute and unlimited—over the organisation which she has built up.   The government of the Mother Church is vested in a Board of Directors, President, Clerk, and Treasurer. Mrs. Eddy nominated the original members of the Board of Directors, and all vacancies are filled subject to her approval. The President, the Clerk, and the Treasurer are elected by

[1] Mrs. Eddy's other books are priced at proportionately high rates. *Retrospection and Introspection*, a booklet of scarce 20,000 words, costs a dollar—and 30,000 copies had been sold in 1906.   At 6d. the book would have yielded a good profit.   And there are other sources of income.   Mrs. Eddy's photograph, in its cheapest form, sells for one dollar.   In announcing in the *Journal* its issue Mrs. Eddy adds, " I simply ask that those who love me purchase this portrait."   Then there is the " Mother spoon"—a silver spoon bearing a portrait of Mrs. Eddy, a picture of Pleasant View, and a motto.   In pushing the sale of this article Mrs. Eddy writes over her own signature, " Mother expects that each Scientist shall purchase at least one spoon, and those who can afford it, one dozen spoons."   The price is 5 dollars (see *McLure's Magazine*, May, 1908).

[2] From the same source it appeared that Mrs. Eddy, for purposes of taxation, returned her property in 1901 as only 19,000 dollars, and her Secretary, Calvin Frye, had year after year repeated the statement.

The suit in question was brought by Mrs. Eddy's son, Mr. G. W. Glover, and others as " next friends," against Calvin Frye and the officers of the Mother Church, praying the court to determine that Mrs. Eddy was incompetent, through failing powers, to manage her property.   Mrs. Eddy, as a counterstroke, appointed responsible trustees for the management of her estate, and transferred to them property amounting to 913,000 dollars (report of the " Masters" interview with Mrs. Eddy on August 14, 1907, in *Boston Herald*, quoted by Powell, *op. cit.*, p. 224).   Mr. Glover's action was withdrawn.

the Board of Directors, again subject to Mrs. Eddy's approval. Any officer of the Church can be dismissed at her pleasure.[1] The original constitution included the Executive, or First, Members, and in their case the initiative was taken by Mrs. Eddy, the procedure being apparently modelled on that of an older Church. Mrs. Eddy would write to the Directors requesting them to elect certain persons to the Executive, and "they shall be elected," the rule continued, "by the unanimous vote of the Board of Directors."[2] If in issuing a *congé d'élire* in this fashion Mrs. Eddy would seem to have borrowed a royal prerogative, by another bye-law she assumes a power which not the most despotic of Western monarchs would venture to claim. Mrs. Eddy is empowered to summon any Christian Scientist from his ordinary duties, and call upon him to live in her house and serve her in any capacity she may choose. His salary in such event is to be fixed at £200 a year and expenses. If Mrs. Eddy wants a housemaid or a cook, the Board of Directors "shall immediately appoint a proper member of this Church therefor, and the appointee shall go immediately in obedience to the call. 'He that loveth father and mother more than me is not worthy of me.'"[3]

But Mrs. Eddy aspires to control the lives and, so far as possible, the very thoughts of her followers. No Christian Scientist may belong to any club or society of any kind— with the exception of the Freemasons and one or two other organisations. His membership of the Christian Science Church is held sufficient for all social and intellectual needs.[4] None of the disciples is allowed to read any book dealing with religion or metaphysics except the Bible and Mrs. Eddy's own works. In the meetings for personal testimony

[1] See *Church Manual* (1908), article xi. sections 7 and 9, and article i. section 5.

[2] The bye-laws relating to executive members were repealed in July, 1908 (*Church Manual*, 1908, p. 18).

[3] *Church Manual* (1908), p. 69. Mrs. Eddy is personally responsible for the wording of the bye-laws and the selection of the scriptural quotation.

[4] *Church Manual*, article viii. section 16.

one may again and again hear the convert relate that he has shut up all other books, rejected all profane philosophies, and gladly acquiesced in drawing his mental nourishment from *Science and Health* alone. If his library happened to include any books on Animal Magnetism, he would sometimes go further, and burn them.

Originally the Christian Science Churches had pastors, who, as in other religious bodies, preached or lectured to the congregation. But Mrs. Eddy scented danger, and in 1895 she issued a ukase that there should be no more preaching.[1] There has been none since that date. In every Christian Science meeting—and the branches are now numbered by hundreds—the service is the same. It consists exclusively of the reading of certain selected passages from the Bible, and of passages, purporting to be elucidatory, from *Science and Health*, interspersed with the singing of hymns. The only prayer used is the Lord's Prayer, followed, line after line, by Mrs. Eddy's paraphrase.

The followers of Mrs. Eddy, then, are privileged to hear no sermons. They also hear few lectures. No Christian Scientist, except those appointed for the purpose, may lecture upon Christian Science; and a copy of each lecture must be sent, before delivery, to the clerk in Boston. No Christian Scientist, again, may engage in a public debate on Christian Science without the consent of the Board of Directors. There are special officers appointed to answer all attacks in the Press or furnish information to the public. The ordinary Christian Scientist publishes any defence of his faith under peril of discipline. The result is that Christian Science has no literature. There is *Science and Health*; there are Mrs. Eddy's other writings; there are the *Journal* and the *Sentinel*, both periodicals inspired by Mrs. Eddy; and there are a few magazine articles. Literally, that is all. Herself, presumably, understanding no foreign language, Mrs. Eddy

---

[1] " In 1895," she writes, referring to this ukase, " I ordained the Bible and *Science and Health with Key to the Scriptures*, as the Pastor, on this planet, of all the Churches of the Christian Science Denomination."

will not even allow *Science and Health* to be translated, lest heresy should creep in undetected.

Notwithstanding the severity of the discipline, and the incredible meagreness of the intellectual fare offered, the members of the Mother Church in Boston in June, 1907, numbered 43,876, and the total membership was probably between 50,000 and 60,000.[1]   There are now upwards of 1,100 branch Churches[2] and Societies, and over 4,000 authorised healers.[3] The great majority of the Christian Scientists are, of course, residents of the United States; and in many of the New England towns large and costly churches have been built by the contributions of the faithful.[4]   But the movement has obtained some hold in this country, and is still spreading.[5]

Such is Mrs. Eddy's kingdom—and it is all her own. *L'état, c'est lui.*   And in these latter days she has assumed more than royal state.   On her journey from Concord to Boston two years ago a special train conveyed her and her party, preceded by a pilot engine, and followed at some distance by a third engine to guard the rear.   No Christian Scientist may approach the Pastor Emeritus uninvited; none may haunt the streets in the hope of seeing her.[6]   For some years, when otherwise invisible to her faithful followers, the Pastor Emeritus has once a year allowed a pilgrimage to her house at Concord, and has shown herself for a few moments on the balcony.   Those who cannot take part in this annual pilgrimage can still visit the empty shrine—the " Mother's

---

[1] No more exact figures are available. The *Church Manual,* article viii. section 28, now prohibits " numbering the people."

[2] *I.e.,* Societies, not buildings.

[3] These figures are taken from the *Christian Science Journal* for November, 1908.

[4] Some of them are fine examples of classical architecture (see the illustrations accompanying articles in the *Arena,* U.S.A., for January and May, 1907).   The structure in Sloane Terrace, it should be added, is by no means a favourable example of Christian Science architecture.

[5] According to the *Journal* for November, 1908, there are 37 " Churches" and Societies and 161 Christian Science practitioners in these islands.

[6] *Church Manual,* article viii. section 27.

room " in the Mother Church at Boston—and marvel at the gold-plated water-taps on the washstand and at the stained-glass window which represents Mrs. Eddy seated in the attic room at Lynn reading the Bible, whilst the rays of a star fall through the uncurtained skylight on her bowed head.

CHAPTER XVI

CHRISTIAN SCIENCE

Christian Science brings healing, comfort, and the hope of a new life
—Various testimonies quoted—The substance of the new philosophy
and religion : mainly derived from Quimby, but Mrs. Eddy a disciple,
not a plagiarist—Characteristic defects of her style and thought, less
conspicuous in *Science and Health*—The nature of her " inspiration "—
Characteristic tenets held in common with earlier prophets : symbolic
interpretation of Bible : Malicious Animal Magnetism : condemnation
of friendship and marriage : parthenogenesis : decrease of human
mortality : our Father-Mother God—Her claim to be the divinely
appointed author of a new gospel.

THE secret of Mrs. Eddy's extraordinary influence
over her followers can be told in a word. She has
brought them healing and comfort. There are, of
course, no statistics available of Christian Science cures. The
man who has failed to achieve a cure by faith has nothing of
interest to tell; and in telling it he writes himself down either
an infidel or a fool. Nor are the cures claimed to have been
effected by Mrs. Eddy's disciples recorded in a manner
acceptable to science. We look in vain here for the attestations of qualified physicians. We can rarely extract even
a plain, straightforward account of the case. " Christian
Science," says Dr. Goddard, " has unwillingly yielded its
facts and philosophy to our work."[1] The general attitude
of the believer is further emphasised by H. W. Dresser.
" Actual facts," he writes, " are almost never procurable from
a Christian Scientist. There was ' nothing ' troubling the

[1] "The Effect of Mind on Body," *American Journal of Psychology*,
vol. x. (1899), p. 444.

patient in the first place; he was cured of 'nothing,' so there is 'nothing' to relate."[1]

But though evidence is rarely forthcoming such as would enable a physician to determine what was the nature of the disease, and what the significance of the cure, the testimony of thousands of persons who for years had believed themselves seriously ill, and now believe themselves free from disease and from pain, is entitled to some weight. Weekly meetings for "testimony" are held in the Christian Science Churches, at which, one after another, men, women, and children, rise to give thanks to God and Mrs. Eddy for their relief from ailments covering the whole range of human suffering, from chapped hands to cancer. The diagnoses may be untrustworthy, but it is impossible to doubt the honesty of the witnesses. They did unquestionably feel ill, and they now feel well. The sceptic may say, and in many cases not unreasonably, that the "feeling" was all there was of the disease. But they did feel pain, and now they feel no pain. On that point, at any rate, the testimony of an honest witness cannot be gainsaid. Some of the cures have been published. In the 1907 edition of *Science and Health* there is a chapter entitled "Fruitage," which contains nearly one hundred testimonies from grateful patients, selected, as the editor tells us, out of some thousands.[2] In reading through these cases it is impossible not to be struck with the general resemblance to the evidence cited in Chapter I. from Deslon's patients. There are, of course, minor differences; the part played 120 years ago by the spleen is now taken by the liver or the kidneys. A great majority of the Christian Science patients, moreover, appear to be women;[3] whereas in Deslon's book the men were in the majority. Moreover, the later testimonies proceed exclusively from the patients themselves; they have not been inspired or edited by a

<hr />

[1] *Methods and Problems of Spiritual Healing*, p. 37.

[2] Other testimonies are quoted in the *Miscellaneous Writings* (1900), pp. 401–471, and scattered through the pages of the *Journal*.

[3] "Appear to be," for the sex is not, in most cases, expressly stated, and the testimonies are signed with initials only.

physician. But the ailments described are of the same general character as in the earlier book. In some cases the nature of the illness is not described at all, or the description is perfectly indefinite. Here are a few descriptions taken at random : Malignant cancer—chronic constipation, nervous headache, astigmatism and hernia—chronic invalid (bowel trouble, bronchitis, and a number of other troubles)—fibroid tumour of sixteen years' standing—epilepsy of twelve years' standing—broken arm—sore eyes of many years' standing—valvular heart disease, lifelong—seventeen years' indigestion and gastritis—internal cancer and consumption, many years—numerous complaints, hereditary and chronic (the only description given of any particular complaint is "eyes in a dreadful condition ")—spots on skin from liver, of twelve years' standing—twenty years not a day without pain—congenital deafness, dropsy, and consumption—semi-invalid for many years—catarrh of stomach for five years—so-called incurable spinal disease for ten years—illness of frequent occurrence—so ill that life was a burden to me : stomach trouble, inward weakness, and bilious attacks.

Like Deslon's patients, these later witnesses claim, for the most part, to have suffered for many years, and from a complication of ailments. But in one most important respect the later records are the more valuable. They have frequently been written some years after the cure. Whatever the nature of the disease, then, the cure in these cases has been lasting. These people did for years feel sick and miserable ; they have now, for years, been feeling strong and healthy. Life before coming across *Science and Health* was a burden ; it is now a joy. Testimony of this kind is proof against criticism.

So much, then, Mrs. Eddy has done for her followers. But, as all who have any personal acquaintances in the ranks of Christian Scientists know, she has done more. The speakers at testimony meetings rarely forget to testify that bodily health is the least of the benefits which they owe to God and Mrs. Eddy. They tell us of a changed outlook on life, of happiness instead of suffering, perpetual peace in place of worry and anxiety, love and goodwill where there had been quarrels and contentions. The lives of many Christian Scientists do, in fact, form the best advertisement of their creed. In the written accounts less stress is laid upon the moral benefits. The witnesses are for the most part too preoccupied with their release from physical suffering. But there are some significant testimonies. One speaks of " a nobler aim and purpose in life "; others of peace and harmony restored, of spiritual uplifting and regeneration, of release from a sense of fear. Says one :—

"I ran up the street, saw people passing to and fro, and said to myself, ' My God ! is this thing in the world and you don't know it ? ' It was then I realised that I did not have to have human will. I had found my God, knew He was always beside me, and I had only to declare Him. Smoking, the habit of a lifetime, left me in a night. Veil after veil has been torn aside, illusion after illusion has blown away. I am now a healthy, prosperous, and happy man. . . . Mrs. Eddy's wonderful book has unlocked for me the great saying spoken by Jesus, ' Ye shall know the truth, and the truth shall make you free !' "[1]

In short, Mrs. Eddy has given her disciples a religion. But the manifestations of this new religion are in some respects curiously unlike what we have been accustomed to connect with the word. The religion of Christian Science oils the wheels of the domestic machinery, smooths out business troubles, releases from fear, promotes happiness. But it is entirely egoistic in expression. Nothing that promotes the happiness and well-being of an individual can, of course, be without effect on the happiness and well-being of those around him. But for Christian Scientists there is no recognised service to their fellows, beyond the force of their example. Poverty and sin, like sickness, are illusions, errors of " mortal mind," and cannot be alleviated by material methods.[2] If a man is sick he does not need drugs ; if poor,

---

[1] *Science and Health* (1907), p. 662. See also testimonies to like effect in *Miscellaneous Writings* (1900), pp. 401, *sqq.*

[2] There are no charities or institutions of any kind for social service in connection with the Christian Science Churches. Those who can

he has no need of money ; if suffering, of material help or even sympathy. For the cure in all cases must be sought within.

The New Religion, then, is without the enthusiasm of Humanity. It is, in fact, without enthusiasm of any kind. We shall look in vain here for spiritual rapture, for ecstatic contemplation of the divine. There is no place here for any of the passions which are associated with Christianity, nor, indeed, for any exalted emotion. There can be no remorse where there is no sin ; compassion, when the suffering is unreal, can only be mischievous ; friendship, as we shall see later, is a snare, and the love of man and woman a hindrance to true spirituality. There is no mystery about this final revelation, and there is no room, therefore, for wonder and awe. Here are no "long-drawn aisles and fretted vault"; the Scientist's outlook on the spiritual world is as plain and bare as the walls of his temple, shining white under the abundant radiance of the electric lamps. And it boasts as full an illumination, for Mrs. Eddy's gospel reached its four hundred and fortieth edition two years ago.

The central tenet of the philosophy taught by Mrs. Eddy is the non-reality of disease, sin, matter ; these all are illusions of "mortal mind," itself having no real existence.

The fundamental propositions of "divine Metaphysics" are as follows :—

" 1. God is All in All.
" 2. God is Good. Good is Mind.
" 3. God, Spirit, being all, nothing is matter.
" 4. Life, God, Omnipotent good, deny death, evil, sin, disease."

---

afford to pay the fees may attend Christian Science classes. A Sunday School for the benefit of children and young persons is held on Sunday mornings, and there are reading-rooms in which all Mrs. Eddy's writings, the *Journal of Christian Science*, the *Christian Science Sentinel*, and the few pamphlets written by the few authorised exponents of the doctrine can be read. For these educational facilities, it should be added, no charge is made.

These propositions can, it is claimed, be proved mathematically. Like an equation, they remain true if the terms are inverted, thus :—

"All in All is God, Mind is Good, Good is God, and so on." [1]

Two or three passages may be quoted as illustrating the practical application of the doctrine.

"You say," she writes, "'I have burned my finger.' This is an exact statement, more exact than you suppose ; for mortal mind, and not matter, burns it." [2]

Again, "You say a boil is painful ; but that is impossible, for matter without mind is not painful. The boil simply manifests, through inflammation and swelling, a belief in pain.; and this belief is called a boil." [3]

Drugs are stupid substitutes for Divine Mind ; they have no power in themselves ; they operate by "the law of a general belief." [4] A disease, in the terminology of the sect, is a "belief," or a "claim," and the proper treatment is to "deny" it, or to "demonstrate" over it.

Of course there are difficulties in the practical application of this theory of the non-reality of matter, and Mrs. Eddy's interpretation of Genesis makes the head swim. In one place she states that "the animals created by God are not carnivorous," [5] from which we must infer that God created a vegetarian lion, and man supplied the teeth, claws, and stomach. The existence of pain, cruelty, and disease is not explained by denying it. You cannot solve the insoluble problem by calling evil "an awful unreality"; and if it is true that "God is ignorant of the existence of mortal mentality," [6] it would seem to follow that His knowledge and therefore His power are by so much diminished. But if Mrs. Eddy has failed to guess the riddle of the Sphinx, she is, of course, in no worse case than her predecessors. In this respect, at any rate,

---

[1] *Science and Health* (1907), p. 113.   [2] *Ibid.*, p. 161.
[3] *Ibid.*, p. 153.   [4] *Ibid.*, pp. 155, 158, 160.
[5] *Ibid.*, p. 514.   [6] *Ibid.*, p. 512.

she may claim to be classed with Democritus and Plato, with Spinoza, Descartes, and Kant.

So far Mrs. Eddy's philosophy would seem to be simply a restatement of Quimby's. It is obvious, indeed, that she owes much to Quimby. We know from her own words that for some years she regarded him as her master. We know from other sources that during those years she carried about with her a manuscript of Quimby's, and taught from it. And apart from the similarity of the doctrine, the numerous coincidences in the terminology would be sufficient to prove the debt. The very phrase " Christian Science " is Quimby's. So is the curious use of " Science " to connote all that other religions signify by " faith." To both, again, " God is Principle." The classing of " Mind " (Quimby), " Mortal Mind " (Mrs. Eddy) amongst the things that don't count is peculiar to the two writers. Characteristic also, though not peculiar—since, as Mr. Wiggin informs us, it is an old Gnostic heresy—is the distinction between " Jesus " and " Christ." [1]

But to admit that Mrs. Eddy is a pupil of Quimby is not to deny her right to be heard on her own account. Recent critics have perhaps over-emphasised the relationship to meet Mrs. Eddy's reiterated denials.[2] We are all the pupils of all those

[1] " Christ was not crucified, that doom was Jesus' part " (*Christ and Christmas*, by Mrs. Eddy).

[2] Mrs. Eddy has for many years persistently denied her indebtedness to Quimby, and asserted that the latter was only a Mesmerist, or that he healed by electricity. She has even claimed that, so far from being indebted for her ideas to his writings, it was she who corrected his random scribblings and put them into intelligible shape. When Julius Dresser published some of the letters and articles in which Mrs. Eddy had lavished praise upon Quimby as her Healer and Teacher she invoked her serviceable fiend, Malicious Animal Magnetism. She wrote to the *Boston Post* (March 7, 1883) as follows : " Did I write those articles purporting to be 'mine ? I might have written them twenty or thirty years ago, for I was under the mesmeric treatment of Dr. Quimby from 1862 until his death. . . . My head was so turned by Animal Magnetism and will-power, under treatment, that I might have written something as hopelessly incorrect as the articles now published in the Dresser pamphlet." For her own recent account of the matter see *Miscellaneous Writings*, " Inklings Historic," p. :378 ; and *Retrospection*

who have worked and thought before us. However large the share of the inheritance which we may seem to derive from this or that predecessor, the debt is in all cases a collective one. Our inheritance is swollen by legacies from many sources. And each of us adds something—little enough perhaps—of his own. Mrs. Eddy, no doubt, proceeds from Quimby, but as the topmost branch of a tree proceeds and draws nourishment from the branch below. Both are outgrowths of the Tree of Life. Mrs. Eddy has, in fact, realised Quimby's philosophy. She has made it part of her very self by pondering over it, but, above all, by living it in her own person. The work was begun, as we have seen, with the fall on the ice in 1866. No doubt in the next ten years there was occasion for much "demonstration" over false belief in pain and sickness. There was also probably much hard intellectual work, for Mrs. Eddy had to learn her trade as a writer, and with all her efforts has learnt it but imperfectly even now. However deeply in her youth she may have studied Greek and Latin, Logic and the Moral Sciences, the writings of her maturer years betray as little taint of literary culture as of capacity for ordinary human reasoning. She has had obviously a very imperfect literary training ; she has little sense of the value of words, and is incompetent to express a train of thought in an orderly sequence of sentences. Her miscellaneous writings—to

and Introspection, p. 38. Christian Scientists rely upon the judgment in the Arens case as settling the question of Mrs. Eddy's originality. But that judgment has little bearing upon the real question at issue. Arens, in 1881, after he had become a Malicious Mesmerist, published a pamphlet in which he quoted freely from *Science and Health.* Mrs. Eddy brought a writ for infringement of copyright and won. Arens's defence was that *Science and Health* was based upon Quimby's MSS. But even if Arens had been able to produce the Quimby MSS. in court I doubt if he would have won his case. It is probable that the actual composition of *Science and Health* was Mrs. Eddy's own ; indeed, as will be shown later, there are ideas in it which she could not have borrowed from Quimby. But to admit so much does not affect the question of her intellectual debt to Quimby. That question has never been brought before the courts, and never can be. "Divine philosophy" is not a personal chattel.

leave *Science and Health* on one side for the moment—are characterised by extraordinary vagueness and incoherence. The sentences hang about the meaning like ready-made clothes. The metaphor is a useful one. Her writings, in fact, seem to consist mainly of the piecing together of approved ready-made phrases, and when a purple patch comes to hand she works it in, regardless of the pattern. A good example of her method will be found in Hymn No. 161 of the Christian Science Hymnal, "Shepherd, show me how to go."[1] The writing of hymns, for one who is content to piece together borrowed phrases of conventional piety, is perhaps the humblest of literary exercises ; but Mrs. Eddy cannot even arrange her borrowed material in intelligible sequence. Another specimen of her unaided English, which is incidentally valuable for the light thrown upon her character, may be quoted at length.

It had come to Mrs. Eddy's knowledge that some students, instead of buying *Science and Health* for themselves, had copied extracts from the book, and read them aloud at public meetings. Mrs. Eddy poured out her indignation against the practice in five pages of circumlocutory rhetoric. In the following passage she touches the real gravamen of the offence :—

" To the question of my true-hearted students, 'Is it right to copy your works and read them for our public Services ?' I answer : It is not right to copy my book and read it publicly *without my consent.* My reasons are as follows :—

First : This method is an unseen form of injustice standing in a holy place.

Second : It breaks the Golden Rule—a Divine rule for human conduct.

Third : All error tends to harden the heart, blind the eyes, stop the ears of understanding, and inflate self ; counter to the commands of our hillside Priest, to whom Isaiah alluded thus: 'I have trodden the winepress alone ; and of the people there was none with Me.' Behind the scenes lurks an evil which you can prevent ; it is a purpose to kill the reformation begun and increasing through the instruction of

---

[1] Also reprinted in *Miscellaneous Writings,* p. 397, and in *Pulpit and Press,* p. 25.

Science and Health with Key to the Scriptures; it encourages infringement of my copyright, and seeks again to ' cast lots for His vesture '—while the perverter preserves in his own consciousness and teaching the name without the spirit, the skeleton without the heart, the form without the comeliness, and the sense without the Science, of Christ's healing."[1]

All this magnificence of outraged morality—five pages of it !—because Mrs. Eddy stood in danger of losing a few dollars in royalties. From the literary standpoint, however, more noteworthy even than the general looseness of thought and expression is the method—a method thoroughly characteristic of Mrs. Eddy—in which the Scripture texts are employed. They do not, it will be seen, illustrate or in any way connect with their surroundings. They appear, in fact, simply as expletives, safety-valves for passion grown incoherent. Mrs. Eddy cannot relieve her feelings by saying "Confound your impudence!" so she quotes Isaiah instead.[2]

But the style of *Science and Health* differs materially from the style of Mrs. Eddy's Autobiography, her hymns, and other unedited writings. The book as it appears in the latest editions is, no doubt, the work of many pens. The whole work was thoroughly revised in 1885 by Mrs. Eddy's then literary adviser, the Rev. J. H. Wiggin,[3] and has been revised, it is said, by others since. It is now, whatever else we may think of it, a sound piece of literary work, correct in grammar and construction, and fairly coherent in

[1] *Miscellaneous Writings* (39th edition, 1900), pp. 301, 302.
[2] It is not necessary here to illustrate further the defects in Mrs. Eddy's writings ; her hopeless entanglement of metaphors—*e.g.*, the passage quoted by Mark Twain, "What plague spot or bacilli was gnawing at the heart of this metropolis and bringing it on bended knee " ; her confusion and misuse of words—" gnostic " and "agnostic," " adulteration " and "adultery," "antipode " as the singular of "antipodes," &c., &c. Even as I write this note I come across the following, " Permit me to say that your editorial is *par excellence"* (*Miscellaneous Writings*, p. 313). Mrs. Eddy no doubt meant to say that it was an excellent editorial. The reader who wishes to pursue the subject is recommended to read Mark Twain's *Christian Science.*
[3] Powell (*op. cit.*, p. 226) tells us that he has seen the actual copies of *Science and Health* used by Wiggin in his revision.

thought. The earliest editions, though in purely literary qualities inferior to the editions subsequent to 1885, are far better than the style of Mrs. Eddy's other writings would lead us to expect. But the superiority, so far as the present writer has had the opportunity of observing, lies not so much in the grammar and construction of the sentences, which are still very faulty, as in the consecutiveness of thought. From the first, in writing *Science and Health*, Mrs. Eddy seems to have had something to say and to have succeeded in saying it. She had, it may be conjectured, through years of suffering and hardship won her way to a belief which she felt entitled to call her own. And what she felt deeply she was able to express with more or less clearness.[1]

Mrs. Eddy, of course, claims that the book was written under divine inspiration.

"The works I have written on Christian Science contain absolute Truth. . . . I was a scribe under orders, and who can refrain from transcribing what God indites?"[2]

Again :—

"I should blush to write of *Science and Health with Key to the Scriptures* as I have, were it of human origin, and I, apart from God, its

---

[1] Mark Twain (*op. cit.*, 1907, p. 292) finds the earliest editions of *Science and Health* so far superior in their literary qualities to Mrs. Eddy's writings, that he inclines to the opinion that Mrs. Eddy did not write the book at all. I am reluctant to set my opinion against that of so distinguished a critic, especially as my own opportunities for comparison have been scanty—the earliest edition I have been able to consult is the third (1881). Of course, Mrs. Eddy received some literary assistance at the outset, as we know from the action brought by G. W. Barry ; and very likely there were others who helped her. But only an exhaustive literary analysis, such as has not yet been attempted, could justify the conclusion that the first edition of *Science and Health* was not, in the main, Mrs. Eddy's own composition. For if she stole her gospel ready-made, as Mark Twain suggests, how can we account for her career ? That she believes in her divine mission it is hard to doubt. Her belief in her Devil affords some measure of the intensity of her belief in her God, and her Devil, at any rate, is all, or nearly all, her own.

[2] *Miscellaneous Writings*, p. 311.

U

author ; but as I was only a scribe echoing the harmonies of Heaven in divine metaphysics, I cannot be super-modest of the Christian Science text-book." [1]

We may admit inspiration, of the same kind as has been already claimed for Mrs. Eddy's predecessors, the Spiritualist prophets. All literary composition seems to involve some degree of detachment from ordinary mental impressions, and all degrees of this detachment may be found up to the extreme forms of psychic dissociation in trance or ecstasy. We do not know whether Mrs. Eddy actually passed into a trance ; probably not. But there seems no sufficient reason to doubt her explicit statement that she was "inspired." It is only the source of the inspiration which we presume to question. It seemed to her, as she tells us, a power not her own which impelled the pen. But the power for all that came from within ; it was her own mind drawing upon its concealed stores which thought and wrote wiser than she knew.

If we analyse her gospel, and especially the parts which she did not owe to Quimby, we shall find clear proof that Mrs. Eddy belongs by right to that mystical brotherhood of whom T. L. Harris was the most conspicuous example in the last generation.

In style and in emotional qualities, indeed, the two prophets have little affinity. The note of the true prophet is passion. Even the anæmic Davis finds his blood run warmer when he contemplates the harmony of the heavens, or turns to look below on the sufferings of mankind, entangled in the web of iniquity. The secret of Madame Blavatsky's influence lay partly in her disinterested enthusiasm for the finer elements in the life around her. Harris's pages still glow, as we have seen, with pity and generous wrath. But Mrs. Eddy's accents are cold, inhuman, passionless—with one exception. Her emotions are aroused only by a more intimate appeal ; her rhetoric is poured out only on those who threaten her person, her property, or her dignity : on Richard Kennedy and the

[1] *Christian Science Journal*, January, 1901.

Malicious Mesmerists; on disciples who copy extracts from her book instead of buying it; on the daring heretics who claim rival inspiration.[1] Save for these vivid outbreaks of personal feeling there are no threads of scarlet to relieve the grey tissue of her writings. There is no indignation against the wrong-doer who has done no wrong to her. There is no pity for the sufferings of those around her ; the long tragedy of human history leaves her unmoved. Can we call this thing a gospel, an inspiration,

> "Whose life, to its cold circle charmed,
> The earth's whole summers have not warmed " ?

But Mrs. Eddy, for all that, belongs in some sort to the fellowship of the prophets. Consider her " Science "—is it not another name for Faith, and Faith of the thoroughgoing old-fashioned sort, expressed by the mediæval scholar in his *Credo quia impossibile ?*[2] It is faith of an heroic kind which the New Gospel exacts from its devotees. Further, Mrs. Eddy is imbued with many of the peculiar mystical doctrines. Her whole gospel is based on the Science of Correspondences.[3] She gives symbolic interpretations to the Scriptural writings, as Davis and Harris did, as, in a word, every mystic has done since the days of Swedenborg. Her interpretation differs, no doubt, from those of her predecessors, but the principle is the same. Like those who have travelled the same road before her, Mrs. Eddy makes words mean what she wants them to mean. *Dan*, according to Mrs. Eddy, means Animal Magnetism ; so do the *Devil*, the *Red*

---

[1] See the denunciation of Mrs. Woodbury quoted in *McLure's Magazine* for April, 1908, p. 712. The passage is made up almost entirely of fragments of biblical phrases, but the whole is pieced together with skill, and forms a really magnificent piece of rhetoric.

[2] Aptly translated by a modern schoolboy as " Faith is believing what you know ain't so."

[3] The phrase is Swedenborg's, but the idea of a universal symbolism is common to mystics. It appears, *e.g.*, in the Paracelsian doctrine of *Signatures.*

Dragon, and the *Serpent* [1] *; Elias* means Christian Science; *Gad, Euphrates, Hiddekel*, the *Holy Ghost*, the *New Jerusalem* mean Divine Science, which is the same thing; *Mother* means God ; *Sheep*, "those who follow their leader " ; *Adam* means a whole page—amongst other things red sandstone! [2]

Of her belief in witchcraft enough has been said in the previous chapter. Whatever good Mrs. Eddy may have done in her day—and there can be no question that she has brought healing and comfort to many — there is a heavy claim to set on the other side of the account. She has inspired her followers with her own dread of Animal Magnetism ; she has done what she could to revive in our generation the panic fear which oppressed all Europe for centuries, which seems, indeed, to have oppressed the human race from its cradle. Daniel Spofford's terror of material vengeance was not, perhaps, altogether unreasonable. The temper of those who believe in Malicious Animal Magnetism is the temper of those who tortured and put to the flame thousands of friendless old women, and even feeble girls and children, in the name of religion and humanity.[3]

[1] *Cf.* Davis's interpretation of the Serpent as corresponding to "an unfavourable and unhappy mental development."

[2] See the Glossary included in the later editions of *Science and Health.* " Red Sandstone" seems absurdly misplaced in a system of symbolism, which deals with abstract or non-material conceptions. It is possible that it may be an unconscious reminiscence of Davis's *Divine Revelations*, in which the Old Red Sandstone plays an important part. Davis seems to have drawn his inspiration in this particular from Hugh Miller, the Scotch mason geologist.

[3] For some years the *Journal of Christian Science* devoted a column to the subject of Malicious Animal Magnetism, heading it with the text, " Also they have dominion over our bodies and over our cattle at their pleasure, and we are in great distress." An illustration of the effect of this teaching is afforded by the tragic story of the death of little Edward —— quoted in *McLure's Magazine* for October, 1907. The unhappy mother who allowed her child to die in her arms, believing that the mental malpractice which was killing it could be met only by mental resistance, was a loyal disciple of Mrs. Eddy's. She was, no doubt, familiar with her teacher's statement, " Our Christian students have seen children thrown into fits by the hidden influence of mental malpractice, covered with virulent humours from the same cause . . . and until they destroyed the effects of this mesmerism the children

Most significant of her mystical affinities is Mrs. Eddy's doctrine of celibacy and spiritual generation. Like other prophets, she dislikes all merely human ties as tending to divert devotion from spiritual things and from the Teacher of spiritual things. It is this feeling, no doubt, which is partly responsible for her extraordinary attempt to monopolise, as far as that is humanly possible, the title of "Mother."[1]

could not be cured. But for the skill of Christian Scientists the slaughter of innocents at this period and by the aforesaid means would gain more hideous proportions than it has already done" (*Science and Health*, 1881, p. 20). See also the extraordinary passage on p. 38 of the same volume on "the Nero of to-day regaling himself through a mental method with the torture of Christians." The chapter on Demonology, from which these extracts are taken, has been withdrawn from the later editions of the book. But Mrs. Eddy remains of the same opinion still, though her utterances grow more guarded in these later years. See *Miscellaneous Writings* (1900), p. 48. A recent "declaration as to the animus of Animal Magnetism and the possible purpose to which it can be devoted has, we trust, been made in season to open the eyes of the people to the hidden nature of some tragic events and sudden deaths at this period." In the later editions of *Science and Health* she speaks in more general terms, but not less plainly. "The mild forms of Animal Magnetism are disappearing, and its aggressive features are coming to the front. The looms of crime, hidden in the dark recesses of mortal thought, are every hour weaving webs more complicated and more subtle . . ." (*Science and Health*, 1907, p. 102). And again : "The march of mind and of honest investigation will bring the hour when the people will chain, with fetters of some sort, the growing occultism of this period. The present apathy as to the tendency of certain active yet unseen mental agencies will finally be shocked into another extreme mortal mood—into human indignation" (*Id.*, p. 570).

[1] Article xxii. section 1 of the bye-laws originally ran as follows : "*The Title of Mother.* In the year 1895 loyal Christian Scientists had given to the author of their text-book, the Founder of Christian Science, the individual and endearing term of Mother. Therefore, if a student of Christian Science shall apply the title, either to herself or to others, except as the term for kinship according to the flesh, it shall be regarded by the Church as an indication of disrespect for their Pastor Emeritus, and unfitness to be a member of the Mother Church." In more recent editions of the *Church Manual* Christian Scientists are instructed that it is their duty to drop the word "Mother" and to substitute "Leader." This is only one of many instances in which bye-laws which had been unfavourably commented on by Mark Twain and others have been dropped or modified, notwithstanding the original inspiration claimed for them.

Even friendship is a serious snare; she calls it "the great and only danger in the path that winds upwards."[1] But of all forms of human relationship marriage is the most dangerous to the prophetic supremacy. Mrs. Eddy had, no doubt, been familiar from her childhood with the idea of religious celibacy. The Shakers had several Settlements in New England, one only a few miles from Tilton, where much of Mary Baker's youth was passed. Other celibate sects had emigrated from the Continent of Europe during the eighteenth and early nineteenth centuries, and settled in various parts of the United States. As Mrs. Patterson, Mrs. Eddy had taken part in the early Spiritualist movement, in which the question of the relation of the sexes was freely canvassed, and many strange solutions proposed. It is, however, to Thomas Lake Harris that we must turn for the nearest counterpart to her special teaching on the relation of the sexes. Like Harris, Mrs. Eddy does not forbid her disciples to marry, but she regards celibacy as preferable.[2] In the chapter on "Marriage" in *Science and Health* she deals with it primarily in its bearings upon the welfare of the husband and wife, as a more intimate form of friendship, having as its object "to happify existence." In the article on "Wedlock" in the *Miscellaneous Writings*—an authentic and unedited utterance on the subject—she remembers the children only to suggest that they would be better unborn: "Human nature has bestowed on a wife the right to become a mother; but if the wife esteems not the privilege, by mutual consent, exalted and increased affections, *she may win a higher.*"[3]

In short, Mrs. Eddy, like the Seer of Brocton, regards marriage after the flesh only as a concession to unregenerate human nature. "Until the spiritual creation is discerned and the union of male and female apprehended in its soul sense,

---

[1] *Miscellaneous Writings*, p. 9.
[2] "Is marriage more right than celibacy? Human knowledge indicates that it is, while Science indicates that it *is not*" (*Miscellaneous Writings*, p. 288).
[3] *Miscellaneous Writings*, p. 289.

this rite [marriage] should continue."[1] But even now marriage is not necessary for the continuation of the species. " To abolish marriage at this period, and maintain morality and generation, would put ingenuity to ludicrous shifts, yet it is possible in *Science*, although it is to-day problematic."[2]

Is Mrs. Eddy, then, an advocate of Free Love? By no means. She merely wishes to indicate that reproduction is essentially asexual. "Until it is learned that generation rests on no sexual basis, let marriage continue."[3] In another passage she indicates her meaning yet more plainly.

"The propagation of their species by butterfly, bee, and moth, without the customary presence of male companions, is a discovery corroborative of the Science of Mind, because these discoveries show that the origin and continuance of certain insects rests on a principle apart from sexual conditions. The supposition that life germinates in eggs . . . is shown by divine metaphysics to be a mistake."[4]

It should be added that one at least of Mrs. Eddy's disciples believed that she meant what she said. In June, 1890, Mrs. Woodbury gave birth to a son, whom she proclaimed, Mr. Woodbury not dissenting, to have been conceived by mental generation in accordance with the doctrine of Christian Science.[5]

[1] *Science and Health*, vol. ii. p. 152 (1881). The passage has been materially modified in later editions.

[2] *Miscellaneous Writings*, p. 286.

[3] *Science and Health*, p. 274 (1897). In the 1907 edition (p. 64) the passage runs, " Until it is learnt that God is the Father of all, marriage will continue."

[4] *Science and Health* (1891), p. 529. According to Powell (*op. cit.*, p. 251), this reference to butterfly and bee appears in all editions up to and including that of 1906. It does not appear in the 1907 edition, which contains instead a statement by Mrs. Eddy that she does not believe in agamogenesis, and that the only person of her acquaintance who ever did believe in it was insane (p. 68). But what then is the meaning of the four passages quoted in the text ? *Litera scripta manet.* Even in the 1907 edition Mrs. Eddy harps upon this same idea of asexual generation amongst the lower animals (see pp. 548–554).

[5] For an account of this immaculate conception and the " war in Heaven " which resulted between Mrs. Woodbury and Mrs. Eddy, see *McLure's Magazine* for April, 1908.

Like disease, Death itself is only a delusion, and can be overcome by " Science." Doctors, by the poison of their belief, have, it is true, succeeded in seriously shortening the span of human existence, as we can see by the lives of the antediluvians, who had no doctors.[1] But there is hope.

" In 1867 I taught the first student in Christian Science. Since that date I have known of but fourteen deaths in the ranks of my about five thousand students. *The census since* 1875 (the date of the first publication of my work, *Science and Health with Key to the Scriptures*) *shows that longevity has increased.*" [2]

We are reminded of the boast of Thomas Lake Harris, that amongst his disciples " two things decrease—the propagation of the species and physical death." On Mrs. Eddy herself, we may conjecture, the " belief " in death is losing its hold. Already she is proof against poison.[3] But she has not yet openly claimed, like her predecessor, to have put on her resurrection body.

The idea of God as both masculine and feminine is found generally amongst the latter-day mystics. But in Mrs. Eddy it reaches its supreme expression. God, according to Christian Science, is more feminine than masculine.[4] As we have already seen, the Glossary defines *Mother* as meaning " God." In Mrs. Eddy's latest revision of the Lord's Prayer, for " Our Father which art in Heaven " we are bidden to say " Our Father-Mother God, All-harmonious." [5] And, finally, we have a new version of the Trinity : " This rule clearly interprets God as Divine Principle—as Life, represented by the Father ; as Truth, represented by the Son ; as Love, represented by the Mother." [6] With Thomas Lake Harris the ascription of a feminine

[1] *Science and Health* (1907), p. 8.   [2] *Miscellaneous Writings*, p. 29.
[3] *Christian Science Journal*, April, 1885, quoted in *McLure's Magazine*, October, 1907.
[4] *Science and Health*, p. 517.   [5] *Id.*, p. 16.
[6] *Id.*, p. 569. The word " rule " affords another illustration of Mrs. Eddy's loose and inconsequent writing. The previous paragraph ends " Self-abnegation . . . is a rule in Christian Science." But the present writer has not succeeded in tracing any connection between this and the passage quoted in the text.

nature to God was the outcome of genuine chivalry. What is the inspiring motive in the case of the later prophetess the reader may discover for himself. Woman, Mrs. Eddy reminds us, was the first to confess her fault in eating the apple. "This enabled woman to be first to interpret the Scriptures in their true sense."[1] In the interpretation of the Apocalypse the exaltation of woman is carried a little further. "And I saw another mighty angel come down from Heaven . . . and he had in his hand a little book open."[2] "Did this same book," asks Mrs. Eddy, "contain the revelation of Divine Science?"[3]

On the next page another text is quoted, "And there appeared a great wonder in heaven ; a woman clothed with the sun, and the moon under her feet, and upon her head a crown of twelve stars."[4] Mrs. Eddy does not identify the woman with anybody in particular; she quotes the text, points out that "in the opening of the sixth seal, typical of six thousand years since Adam, the distinctive feature has reference to the present age," and leaves the rest to her followers. The language of *Science and Health* on such personal topics is generally guarded ; but when Mrs. Eddy has no editor to hold her in check she lets herself go. Consider these two passages from her recent Autobiography : " No one else can drain the cup which I have drunk to the dregs as the discoverer and teacher of Christian Science."

.   .   .   .   .

" No person can take the individual place of the Virgin Mary. No person can compass or fulfil the individual mission of Jesus of Nazareth. No person can take the place of the author of *Science and Health*, the discoverer and founder of Christian Science. Each individual must fill his own niche in time and eternity.

" The second appearance of Jesus is unquestionably the spiritual advent of the advancing idea of God as in Christian Science."[5]

[1] *Science and Health*, pp. 533, 534.   [2] Revelation x. 1, 2.
[3] *Science and Health*, p. 559.   [4] Revelation xii. 1.
[5] *Retrospection and Introspection*, pp. 47 and 96.

In *Christ and Christmas* occurs the stanza—

> "As in blest Palestina's hour,
>   So in our age,
> 'Tis the same hand unfolds His power,
>   And writes the page."

On the opposite page is a picture of Christ seated, holding by the hand a woman whose features bear an unmistakable resemblance to those of Mrs. Eddy. This woman holds out a scroll inscribed " Christian Science." [1]

Loyal Scientists have not been slow to act on the hints supplied to them by Mrs. Eddy. Let one extract suffice. A lady who had been on one of the pilgrimages to Concord, and had been privileged to have a momentary view of the Pastor Emeritus, writes thus of her feelings :—

" I will not attempt to describe the Leader, nor can I say what this brief glimpse was and is to me. I can only say I wept, and the tears start every time I think of it. Why do I weep? I think it is because I want to be like her, and they are tears of repentance. I realise better now what it was that made Mary Magdalene weep when she came into the presence of the Nazarene." [2]

The comparison which is here hinted has been deliberately

---

[1] *Christ and Christmas*, an illustrated poem by Mary Baker G. Eddy. The poem first appeared in 1893, but Mrs. Eddy was forced by the public outcry to realise that she had gone too far, and the book was withdrawn after it had gone into a second edition. See her explanation for the reason of the withdrawal (*Miscellaneous Writings*, p. 307). The poem is now republished, but it is still apparently regarded as too strong meat for babes. It is not placed with Mrs. Eddy's other writings on the table of the Reading Room at Sloane Terrace, but is kept under lock and key. The neophyte may admire the outer cover in a glass case, or may spend 12s. 6d. in buying it.

In the *Miscellaneous Writings* (p. 3) Mrs. Eddy writes : " We " (royal or editorial plural) " shall claim no especial gift from our divine origin." This ought to mean that the writer regards herself as of divine origin, but it is possibly only another illustration of her inability to write English.

[2] *Christian Science Journal* for June, 1899, quoted in *McLure's Magazine*, May, 1908.

emphasised by more outspoken disciples.[1] Forty years ago Mrs. Eddy is reported to have said to Richard Kennedy that she should yet live to hear the church bells ring out her birthday. That prophecy has been fulfilled, and the Church was of her own foundation. How many years shall pass away before the same church bells shall summon loyal Christian Scientists all the world over to the worship of a new Saint—or a new Deity?

[1] See the quotations on the subject from the *Christian Science Journal* given in *McLure's Magazine*, February, 1908, pp. 388, 389.

INDEX

x

𝕿𝖍𝖊 𝕲𝖗𝖊𝖘𝖍𝖆𝖒 𝕻𝖗𝖊𝖘𝖘,

UNWIN BROTHERS, LIMITED,

WOKING AND LONDON

For EU product safety concerns, contact us at Calle de José Abascal, 56–1°,
28003 Madrid, Spain or eugpsr@cambridge.org.

www.ingramcontent.com/pod-product-compliance
Ingram Content Group UK Ltd.
Pitfield, Milton Keynes, MK11 3LW, UK
UKHW040617240426
470322UK00010B/177